RUNNING THE SMOKE

26 FIRST-HAND ACCOUNTS OF TACKLING THE LONDON MARATHON

MICHAEL McEWAN

First published in Great Britain in 2016 by
ARENA SPORT
An imprint of Birlinn Limited
West Newington House
10 Newington Road
Edinburgh
EH9 1QS

www.arenasportbooks.co.uk

ISBN: 9781909715387
eBook ISBN: 9780857903327

Every effort has been made to trace copyright holders and obtain their
permission for the use of copyright material. The publisher apologises for any
errors or omissions and would be grateful if notified of any corrections that
should be incorporated in future reprints or editions of this book.

British Library Cataloguing-in-Publication Data
A catalogue record for this book is available on request from the
British Library.

Designed and typeset by Polaris Publishing, Edinburgh
www.polarispublishing.com

Printed in Great Britain by CPI Group (UK) Ltd, Croydon CR0 4YY

CONTENTS

'The greater the obstacle,
the more glory in overcoming it.'
Molière

'When a man is tired of London, he is tired of life;
for there is in London all that life can afford.'
Samuel Johnson

For Juliet,
and the three little ones who'll
never run a marathon but are with
us every step of the way.

PREFACE

EVERYTHING HURTS.

The soles of my feet, my shins, my calves, my knees, my thighs, my hamstrings, my hips, my chest, my shoulders, my forearms, my head.

Everything.

I might be imagining it but I think I can feel each individual hair pulsing in the crown of my skull in time to my heartbeat and, just for good measure, I've even managed to get sunburnt.

Suddenly, a realisation hits me: I'm crying. At least I think I am. I sweep the back of my hand across my cheek to make sure. At first, the friction of dry skin on dry skin feels as though I'm dragging sandpaper across my face but then I feel them. Tears. Warm, humiliating, inexplicable tears. Great.

I'm exhausted. I'm dehydrated. My shorts and T-shirt are rinsed in sweat.

I'm a mess.

There's not much I can do about any of that right now, though, so I hobble forward to collect my medal. A volunteer in her fifties picks it up, opens the lanyard and is ready to pass it over my head and down around my neck when she hesitates. Right then, I realise I'm not just shedding a few tears. I'm sobbing almost uncontrollably, like a scolded child.

Somehow, I manage an embarrassed laugh. 'I'm really sorry,' I say. 'It's just that I've been waiting for this moment for most of my life.' A trifle melodramatic but not entirely untrue, either.

The woman smiles, continues and, as she adjusts the way the ribbon sits on my neck, she pats me on the shoulder and says: 'Well, you've earned it.'

I force a grateful nod of acknowledgement and shuffle along, studying my medal as I go. As I gaze at it, I feel almost hypnotised and, in that instant, every pain evaporates at once. Right at this moment, I feel only one thing: pride. Immense, immeasurable, irresistible pride.

It has taken me years to get to this point and, for good measure, a further four hours, forty-one minutes and fifty-nine seconds to complete the punishing but magnificent course. But it has all been worth it.

It's Sunday, 13 April 2014 and I have just run the London Marathon.

*

I THINK I'm quite like most other runners in that I don't run for pleasure.

It is not, in my opinion, a particularly enjoyable activity. Putting one foot in front of the other as fast as you can – what's to enjoy?

Instead, I run for fulfilment. I do it for the rush, the buzz, the sense of accomplishment as you cross the finishing line. Nothing compares to that feeling. Your veins pop, crackle and fizz. Your senses jingle, your nerves jangle. You feel ten feet tall and entirely invincible. It's unique. It's brilliant. It's addictive.

I first encountered it at school. I ran throughout my time there, although not to any great standard. Whilst most of my classmates dreaded the annual December cross country race, I looked forward to it. I never won it. Never even came close. But I always got what I wanted out of it: that *feeling*.

I entered my first timed race at the age of twenty-two – the Great Scottish Run in Glasgow – and subsequently took part in numerous 10k events.

My first marathon was Loch Ness in September 2011. I followed that up with the Berlin Marathon exactly twelve months later. But I wanted more. I wanted London.

As a little boy, I used to watch it on television every year sitting in the living room of our family home. I loved it from the moment I first saw it. It leapt off the screen. The elite runners left me dumbstruck. The fancy dress worn by the fun runners made me smile. The anthem at the beginning of the BBC coverage made my heart swell. More than anything, I loved its tangible camaraderie and warmth. The London Marathon is so much more than a sporting event. It is entirely transcendent.

It was, therefore, inevitable I would run it one day. It was just a question of when. For me, that 'when' was that sunny Sunday in April 2014. Did it live up to my expectations? More than. Did it hurt? Oh God, yeah. Do I want to do it all over again? Like you wouldn't believe.

Standing on the start line that morning, I took a moment to look around at all of the other runners. More than 36,000 people took part that day and, like me, all were there for a reason. Mine was to complete a lifetime ambition.

For others, it was to run in memory of a loved one, to celebrate overcoming an illness, to raise money for a charity, to lose weight, and so on and so forth.

That's where the idea for this book first crystallised. I decided I wanted to find twenty-six inspirational people who have completed the London Marathon and find out more about their motivations for getting to the start line as much as their experiences between there and the finish.

In my research, I have spoken to some truly wonderful people who have, truthfully, left a profound and lasting impression on me. It is so easy to get cocooned within the minutiae of our own lives, isn't it? The only way to maintain an anchor-point on reality and understand the true context of our 'troubles' is to talk to others. It's an underrated medium in this era of 'text-speak' and digital communication.

Some of the stories that follow are funny. Others are remarkable. More still are illuminating. And some, I'm afraid to say, are impossibly sad. Each and every one has been my immense privilege to hear at their source and share herein with you.

Whether you have run the London Marathon before, dream of running it in the future, or simply just enjoy reading about ordinary people doing extraordinary things, I hope you will draw inspiration from what follows. I know I have.

Enjoy the book.

Michael McEwan
April 2016

A BRIEF HISTORY
OF THE LONDON MARATHON

EVERY race starts somewhere.

Incongruous as it may seem, the London Marathon can trace its own beginnings to a pub in south-west London. It was in the Dysart Arms, adjacent to Richmond Park, that plans for what would become one of the world's most iconic running events were hatched in 1979.

The bar was the home of the historic Ranelagh Harriers Running Club. Its members would meet there after their Wednesday evening training sessions to recall, as the club's own website puts it, 'how fast they ran when in the full flush of youth and dream of new challenges to conquer'.

Dating back to 1881, the Ranelagh Harriers Running Club is one of the oldest athletic clubs in the UK. Indeed, it was one of the founder members of the English Cross Country Union in 1883. Originally based out of the Green Man bar on Putney Heath in south-west London, the club moved into an old pavilion at the back of the Dysart Arms in the 1930s, where it has been based ever since.

Because of the size and popularity of the club, members of the Ranelagh Harriers have, over the years, become regulars in some of the most famous races in the world, never mind the UK. One of its most industrious and enterprising members in the 1970s was Steve Rowland, the manager of a small running shoe shop in Teddington called 'Sweatshop'. The shop was co-owned by Chris Brasher, the winner of the men's steeplechase gold medal in the 1956 Olympic Games, and John Disley, a bronze medallist in the steeplechase four years earlier in Helsinki.

Described as a 'crazy runner who was always up for a new challenge', Rowland's competitive instincts were piqued in 1978 when he read an article about the success of the 1977 New York Marathon. The piece told how almost 4,000 people completed a 26.2-mile circuit through all five of the Big Apple's boroughs – Manhattan, Brooklyn, Queens, the Bronx and Staten Island – cheered on by tens of thousands of well-wishers who lined the route.

The story captured Rowland's imagination to such an extent that he decided to enter the race for himself in 1978. He even went so far as to place a small advert in *The Observer* and *Athletics Weekly*, the pre-eminent running publication of the day, for other runners to join him. Around forty people took him up on the invitation, including half a dozen of his fellow Ranelagh Harriers.

Neither Rowland nor any of his companions troubled the prize board. The famous American long-distance runner Bill Rodgers won the men's race, the third of four consecutive victories for the man they called 'Boston Billy', whilst the late Grete Waitz from Norway became the first non-American to win the women's race, clocking a new course record in the process. However, the British contingent returned home with the next best thing: a raft of memories to last a lifetime.

Unwinding in the Dysart Arms after their Wednesday training sessions, their conversations would regularly turn to their shared experiences in New York. It was the infectious enthusiasm of four of the New York runners that reportedly aroused the interest of Brasher.

By now retired from competitive athletics, Brasher had made a name for himself as a successful journalist and broadcaster. Hearing the tales of the New York Marathon, and sensing a story, he entered the race in 1979. He convinced *The Observer*, for whom he had previously served as sports editor, to pay for his trip and persuaded Disley to join him, too.

Just like their club mates a year earlier, the pair found the whole experience utterly captivating and, seven days later, Brasher recalled the race in articulate, lucid detail in his newspaper column.

He wrote: 'Last Sunday, in one of the most violent, trouble-stricken cities in the world, 11,532 men, women and children from forty countries of the world, assisted by 2.5m black, white and yellow people, Protestants and Catholics, Jews and Muslims, Buddhists and Confucians, laughed, cheered and suffered during the greatest folk festival the world has seen.'

He concluded: 'I wonder whether London could stage such a festival? We have the course . . . but do we have the heart and hospitality to welcome the world?'

Just 517 days later, on 29 March 1981, he got his answer.

*

IT was not as though London didn't already have a marathon. It had, in fact, a successful and well-established one in the form of the Polytechnic Marathon.

The 'Poly' was introduced when the 1908 Olympic Games were relocated to London in the wake of the eruption of Mount Vesuvius in 1906. It was a disaster that killed more than 100 people and required funds intended for the Rome Olympics to be used instead for the reconstruction of Naples.

The race was organised by the Polytechnic Harriers, the athletics club of the Polytechnic at Regent Street in London, which is now the University of Westminster.

At that time, there was no set distance for a marathon. It was simply a long race in the region of 40km. The Polytechnic Harriers mapped out a course that started in front of the Royal Apartments at Windsor Castle and ended on the track at White City Stadium – the since-demolished home of the 1908 Games – in front of the Royal Box. All in, the course measured 26 miles plus an extra 385 yards. They didn't know it at the time but the Polytechnic Harriers had just created a new uniform standard distance for a marathon.

That first event really captured the imagination of the public, not least because of its dramatic finish. Dorando Pietri of Italy took the lead with just two kilometres to go but, as he entered the stadium for the final 400 metres, he took a wrong turn and was redirected by umpires. Suddenly, he fell to his knees in front of a watching crowd of some 75,000. The umpires helped him to his feet but he fell again. And again. And again. And again. Each time, he was helped to his feet and, somehow, he managed to cross the line in first place. Of the two hours, fifty-four minutes and forty-six seconds he spent running that day, he used up ten minutes to complete that final lap.

Pietri finished ahead of American runner Johnny Hayes but, when the US team lodged an official complaint over the assistance the Italian runner received from the umpires, Pietri was disqualified, handing the gold medal to Hayes.

The Italian's fate became headline news. As compensation, Queen Alexandra gifted him a gilded silver cup, whilst the great novelist Sir Arthur Conan Doyle, commissioned by the *Daily Mail* to produce a special report on the race, wrote: 'The Italian's great performance can never be effaced from our record of sport, be the decision of the judges what it may.'

Acknowledging the interest generated by Pietri, Hayes and the Olympic marathon, the *Sporting Life* newspaper commissioned a spectacular trophy – made at a cost of £500, roughly £50,000 in today's money – to be contested in an annual international marathon that would be second in importance only to the Olympics. The Polytechnic Harriers were asked to organise the event and so it came to pass that, on 8 April 1909, the first Polytechnic Marathon was staged.

It continued to use a course spanning 26 miles and 385 yards, which, in 1924, became adopted as the international standard for all marathons.

For a long time, the Poly went from strength to strength. It even survived, in 1961, the loss of the support of the *Sporting Life*.

What it couldn't survive, however, was evolution. The Windsor-to-Chiswick route that it had used since 1938 fell victim to the London traffic, restricting the race to the Windsor area from 1973. The world record-setting performances that had been so common in the 1950s and 1960s tailed off, too, as mass marathons and big-money events – such as the New York Marathon – took off.

By the time that Chris Brasher's new London Marathon took place for the first time on 29 March 1981, the Poly was in terminal decline. It survived under the auspices of various different bodies until 1996 when it was staged for the last time.

The Poly's diminished status was in stark contrast to the immediate popularity of the London Marathon. Having secured the support of top shaving brand Gillette, which pledged to back the fledgling race to the tune of £75,000 per year for the first three years, Brasher established charitable status for his event. He also set out six goals in an attempt to emulate the success of the New York Marathon and others like it. Those goals were:

- To improve the overall standard and status of British marathon running by providing a fast course and strong international competition;
- To show mankind that, on occasions, they can be united;
- To raise money for sporting and recreational facilities in London;
- To help boost London's tourism;
- To prove that 'Britain is best' when it comes to organising major events; and
- To have fun, and provide some happiness and sense of achievement in a troubled world.

Over 20,000 people applied to run in that first race. Of those, 7,747 were accepted in line with restrictions placed upon the race by the police. The vast majority crossed the finishing line on Constitution Hill between Green Park and Buckingham Palace. Competitors ranged in age from fifteen to seventy-eight and, at 9 a.m. on a wet Sunday morning in Greenwich Park, in the south-east of London, they were sent on their way by the boom of a twenty-five pound cannon.

Two hours, eleven minutes and forty-eight seconds later, the tape stretching across the finishing line was burst in scenes almost as dramatic as the conclusion to the Olympic Marathon seventy-three years earlier.

American Dick Beardsley and Inge Simonsen of Norway had been separated by little more than a few paces the entire race. Passing the *Cutty Sark*, crossing Tower Bridge, leaving St Paul's Cathedral in their wake – they were side by side almost the entire way. As they closed in on the finishing line, they passed Buckingham Palace and turned onto Constitution Hill where, picking up the pace for one final burst, they spontaneously joined hands and burst through the tape in unison.

The incident passed immediately into sporting folklore as the 'Hand of Friendship'. Two men, two competitors, living and training over 3,000 miles apart, joining forces to complete a remarkable feat of sporting endurance in the most sportsmanlike of ways – it was precisely the launch pad the London Marathon needed. Completing a near-perfect first edition was the sight of Joyce Smith, a forty-three-year-old mother of two, breaking the British marathon record to win the women's race. Smith's time of 2:29:57 was also the third fastest marathon time ever recorded by a woman.

These scenes and many more like them were beamed directly into homes across the United Kingdom by the BBC, with stories of Beardsley and Simonsen's iconic win, in particular, relayed by news outlets around the world.

The following year, over 90,000 people applied to take part in the race. The entry restrictions were relaxed to allow 18,059 to do so.

Since then, the popularity of the London Marathon has grown almost year on year. In 2006, it was one of the five founding members of the World Marathon Majors series along with New York, Chicago, Boston and Berlin. As of 2016, more than one million runners have completed the race.

A host of categories have also been introduced to cater for the variety of runners that the race attracts. Indeed, in 1981, fewer than five per cent of all participants were women, while there were no wheelchair athletes, no Mini London Marathon race for children, and certainly no runners in fancy dress.

Today, it's a different story altogether. The proportion of female competitors has grown markedly to the extent that women accounted for almost thirty-seven per cent of all those who ran in 2015. There are also separate men's and women's wheelchair races. The men race in two separate classifications as outlined by the International Paralympic Committee: T53/54, for athletes with normal arm and hand function and either no or limited trunk function or leg function, as well as T51/52, for athletes with activity limitations in both lower and upper limbs. At present, the women's wheelchair race is contested only by athletes in the T53/54 class.

There are also races for athletes with other lumbar impairments that meet with the T42, T44, T45 and T46 IPC classifications, as well as athletes with visual impairments, so defined by the T11, T12 and T13 classifications.

A junior race, the Mini London Marathon, was introduced in 1986. It spans the last three miles of the official London Marathon course – taking in the route from Old Billingsgate to The Mall – and is open to those aged between eleven and seventeen. There are also four junior wheelchair races along the same course, open to children under seventeen years of age.

However, arguably the most celebrated and iconic aspect of the London Marathon is the philanthropy of its so-called 'fun runners'. It is reckoned that as many as three-quarters of all of those who take part in the race do so to raise money for charity, with more than £50 million raised for good causes every single year. The event itself holds a Guinness World Record for one-day charity fundraising, a record it has broken each year for the most part of the last decade.

In total, over £770 million has been raised for charity by those running in the London Marathon, whilst in the thirty-five years since it was founded, The London Marathon Charitable Trust has used profits from the race and other London Marathon events to make grants exceeding £57 million to more than 1,000 organisations.

The BBC continues to broadcast the event annually, although it is now syndicated into homes in almost 200 countries. Roughly three-quarters of a million people, meanwhile, line the streets of the route to cheer the runners on.

From singlets, to fancy dress, to full deep-sea diving suits, the widest imaginable spectrum of fashion has been worn in the London Marathon since its inception. It is a colourful, dramatic, inspirational and awe-inspiring sight to see.

Equally, it is an unforgettable, emotional, invigorating and often life-affirming event to participate in. As you will discover reading this book, running the London Marathon is both a deeply personal decision and a community-forming experience. It unites people in a way that few other sporting events can, whilst bringing out the very best in society, whether that's those pounding the streets of the capital in the race itself or the crowds willing them on from the sidelines.

It is, in the simplest of terms, a race that is truly good and decent from both the top down and the bottom up.

Not bad going for an event that was discovered at the bottom of a pint glass.

CHAPTER ONE

DICK BEARDSLEY

Together with Inge Simonsen of Norway, Dick Beardsley was the joint winner of the inaugural London Marathon. The Minneapolis-born runner, who had celebrated his twenty-fifth birthday just eight days before the race, completed the course in a time of 2:11:48.

EVEN now, decades later, I still get emotional when I think back to that wet, breezy day in London.

I didn't know it at the time but 29 March 1981 would transform my career forever. I woke that morning as a full-time long-distance runner of a pretty good standard and later went to bed as the winner of a marathon. It was one of the most important, significant days of my life.

My London Marathon story, however, begins 4,000 miles away and many years earlier near Minneapolis. I was quite a shy kid at school but, like every other young guy, I wanted to be popular with girls. They, in turn, seemed to want to talk pretty much exclusively to the guys who wore the high school letterman jackets, the jackets which separated the kids that were good at sports from those that, well, weren't.

I set my sights on becoming one of those guys, so I tried out for the school's American football team. There was just one problem: I weighed only 130 pounds. That's too light by half. I lasted one practice.

Instead, I switched my focus to running. It came quite naturally to me, although I was far from the top dog on the school's cross country team. I think

I got by on my enthusiasm as much as anything else and my coach seemed to like that about me. He let me run in enough race meets to qualify for one of the jackets I so desperately craved. I was absolutely elated!

By the time I left high school, running had become a big part of my life, so I joined my college team. I continued to combine competing with my studies but, even then, I had no intention of pursuing running as a career. In fact, when I graduated with an Associates Degree in Agriculture, I actually became a dairy farmer for a while. Running was a hobby, a passion, but nothing more.

It wasn't until August 1977 that I entered my first marathon, the Paavo Nurmi Marathon in Hurley, Wisconsin. It had been on the calendar for eight years by that point and was pretty popular. More to the point, it was just four hours' drive away from where I lived, so it was nice and convenient.

I ran it in 2:47:14. Not bad for a first-timer but not that great either. I figured I could run faster – and I was right. In subsequent marathons, I got steadily quicker: 2:33:22, 2:33:06, 2:31:50.

Before I knew it, I was becoming a really good runner and, in 1980, I noticed that the qualification time for the US Olympic Trials Marathon was 2:21:56. 'Wow,' I thought, 'that's just ten minutes faster than my best time.' I entered the Manitoba Marathon in Canada and met the qualification standard with only two seconds to spare.

I ran the trial in 2:16:01, continuing a streak of new personal records that ultimately spanned forty-six months and thirteen marathons. It wasn't enough, though. I finished in sixteenth place and had to watch the 1980 Olympic Games in Moscow from my home in Minnesota.

It was disappointing to miss out. Of course it was. But I was encouraged by my performance. I had seen enough to give me the belief that I could get better. Much better. What I needed was to dedicate myself to running full-time. If I did that, I told myself, there was no reason why I couldn't qualify for the 1984 Olympic Games. Besides, they were taking place in Los Angeles. Running in the Olympics on home soil in front of a partisan crowd – it became more than a dream; it became my goal.

There was just one problem. Professional running wasn't a particularly lucrative industry. I still had to find a way to keep a roof over my head, pay bills and so on. Without support, that's something I'd never have been able to afford.

As it turned out, I couldn't have picked a better time to try to make it as a pro. America was in the midst of a real running 'boom' in the late seventies and early eighties. The sport was massively increasing in popularity and I was fortunate enough to secure some backing from New Balance, one of the leading running shoe manufacturers. I've been told they were on the lookout for the next Bill Rodgers, one of America's top distance runners and a winner of four Boston Marathons, including three in a row from 1978 to 1980. Luckily, New Balance saw something in me that they seemed to like and, with their sponsorship and support, I was able to become a full-time runner. I could train and prepare for races without having to fit it all around a job. It was an incredible opportunity.

It also opened up a lot of doors, London being one such example. You see, as well as being the organiser of the first London Marathon, Chris Brasher was also a European distributor for New Balance shoes. It was early in 1981 when he called the New Balance global headquarters in Boston, Massachusetts, to ask if they had any athletes that they would be interested in sending over to compete in his new race. They got in touch with me and said 'Hey, Dick. How would you like a free trip to London?'

It was an easy 'yes'. It was just too good an opportunity to turn down. For one thing, I'd never been to London before and it was somewhere I'd always wanted to visit. I mean, come on! It's one of the greatest cities in the world! Equally, though, I was excited at the prospect of taking part in the first-ever London Marathon. Obviously, I didn't have a sense at the time of just how big an event it would go on to become – nobody did – but something told me that it would be a special, memorable occasion.

From a 'form' point of view, I was confident about my prospects. In January 1981, I finished runner-up in the Houston Marathon with a new personal best time of 2:12:48. Less than a month later, I raced in Beppu, Japan, where I was third, crossing the line in 2:12:11. I was feeling good and feeling sharp. I was also young, so I recovered quickly, which was just as well given that London came only a month after Beppu.

I arrived in England about a week or so before the race. I was keen to acclimatise properly but I also wanted to make the most of the opportunity to see the city. I did all the typical things a tourist would do, went to all of the popular sights and landmarks, that kind of thing. I remember being a little overwhelmed by it all at first. It was so big and fast-moving, whereas I was just a kid from a quiet little town in Minnesota. It was a dramatic change of pace. However, what struck me most were the people, particularly the younger people in their late teens or early twenties. They wore these incredible, outlandish clothes and many had bright colours in their hair. I had never seen anything like them in my life. It's funny what you remember. To this day, I can still see some of their faces. They were all so friendly, though. Not just the flamboyant kids; all the people. Everyone was nice, welcoming, accommodating. I was thousands of miles from where I grew up but, strangely, I felt right at home almost immediately.

I had a lot of fun that week but, equally, I made sure not to do too much. I have always found the week before a race quite difficult. The main bulk of your training, which has been so much a part of your life for the weeks and months immediately prior, is over and you have drastically reduced your mileage to ensure you arrive at the start line in peak condition. Fit, healthy, ready to go, not over-prepared. It's a delicate balance and, more often than not, I felt like a caged tiger for much of the forty-eight to seventy-two hours before a race. London was no different. I just wanted to get started.

As excited as I was to take part, however, there were others who were very sceptical about the London Marathon. In fact, in the days leading up to it, I remember reading a newspaper, which seemed to be of the belief that the race wouldn't be a success. There was a bit of negativity towards Chris Brasher and the other race organisers, which I thought was both very unfortunate and unfair. On top of that, the forecast was for cold, wet conditions. 'Nobody will come out to cheer the runners on,' the editorial insisted. How misinformed a piece it would prove to be.

I was put up in a small hotel close to the middle of the city. Things were a lot different then to the way they are now. These days, the top runners are all exceptionally well looked after. As well as some of the best hotel rooms in London for them and their entourage, they are also given large appearance fees to take part. In 1981, there were no such incentives for those of us who were expected to contend for the win. Don't get me wrong, my hotel was nice enough but, well, here's the deal: I'm a tall guy; my bed was small. I had to sleep in the foetal position just to stay on the mattress! But it was no big deal. I was just delighted to be there and tickled pink that somebody clearly wanted me there enough that they picked up my air fares and covered the cost of my accommodation. They even gave me enough money for a few hamburgers a day, which I remember being quite excited about!

Hamburgers, though, are really not the best things to be eating in the days leading up to a marathon, so I instead remember that I went out for dinner by myself the night before the race for some spaghetti and meatballs. Again, it's probably not the ideal prep food but it had plenty of carbohydrates, so it suited me just fine.

The morning of the race dawned and I was picked up and taken by a courtesy car from my hotel to the start line in Greenwich Park. There was real excitement in the air. Unfortunately, there was also some rain. It wasn't torrential by any means but it was drizzly enough that you got wet through pretty quickly, particularly as there was nowhere to go to stay out of it. I managed to spot a sponsors' tent, though, and hung out in there until it was time to set off.

There were a lot of spectators around the start line. I guess they were there out of curiosity as much as anything else. They wanted to catch a glimpse of this new event, to see what it was all about. As we gathered for position ahead of the gun going off, I took a look around at the competition. England had some fabulous runners at that time and I remember thinking that we were in for quite a race.

The start back then was slightly different to what it is now. For one thing, we had to exit the park out of a gate just to get onto the first part of the route! Not only that, we took a lot of twists and turns and corners. Way more than you would usually have and, certainly, far more than the race has these days.

Now, let me give you an insight into my race day tactics. I never raced a marathon over the first half of the course. To me, that was always about finding my rhythm, getting a good flow going and trying to ensure that I stayed at the front of the pack or as close to it as possible. If you get that bit right, the second half of the race is where marathons are either won or lost.

Halfway in London is just after that famous moment where you cross Tower Bridge. It was shortly after that, as we were making our way towards the Isle of Dogs, when I decided to make my first move. There must have been around eight of us in the leading pack at that point and I can remember thinking to myself, 'There are too many people here. I'm going to need to break this up a bit.' So, I made a burst. Only Inge Simonsen responded and came with me.

It was actually a good thing that he did. That next part of the race went through what was, at that point, an old, industrial part of the city. It's different now, of course. It's actually one of the most beautiful parts of the race these days, in my opinion. But back then, it was quite old, run down and didn't really have many spectators out there cheering you on. That was big for me. I have always been someone who has responded well to people cheering me on and willing me to do well, push harder, run faster, that sort of thing. I guess you could say that I enjoy other people's company, so when Inge came with me on that break, it turned out to be for the best. It kept me focused and gave me somebody to bounce off when there was really nobody else out there.

We stayed on each other's shoulders for the next eight miles or so and it was around the twenty-one-mile mark, as we went past Tower Bridge again, towards Big Ben and the Houses of Parliament, that we really started to race – and I mean race. When I made a move, Inge responded. When he made a counter-move, I kept pace. It went on like that for the next few miles. What complicated matters, though, was the condition of the road. Back then, that area was all old cobblestone paving, which obviously isn't the ideal surface for runners. It's so uneven that it really requires you to pay close attention not just to where your feet are landing but where you strike off from, too. However, when you add in a lot of rain, it becomes truly treacherous. The slabs just get so slippery that all you want is to try to find an even area where you can move freely and without putting too much strain on yourself.

Plus, at that stage of a marathon, the very last thing you want to have to worry about is wet cobblestone paving. It really wasn't ideal! Still, we continued to press. We both badly wanted to win, so we pushed and we pushed and we pushed.

With about two or three miles to go, the crowd suddenly got really big and everyone started going crazy. I had never heard noise like it before. It was deafening. I can still feel the adrenaline surging through me as I soaked it in. It gave me a fresh burst of energy to kick on and press for the finish line. Clearly, it had the same effect on Inge. I couldn't shake him and he couldn't shake me. There was nothing between us, nor had there been for most of the way.

Then something really strange happened. It occurred to me that, you know what? We both deserve to win this race. It was clear at that point that either one of us was going to as we were so far ahead of the chasing pack. But having run so well together for almost twenty-six miles, the thought flashed through my mind that it would be sad if one of us was to lose.

I turned to Inge and said, 'So, what do you think? Are we going to duke this out until the end or do you want to go together?'

He said something back to me but, in all honesty, I couldn't make it out. He might have said, 'Sure, let's race,' or 'Okay, let's do this together,' but, in that moment, with the noise of the crowd ringing in my ears, I couldn't work it out so I figured it was best to just work on the assumption that he wanted to race all the way in.

With a few hundred yards to go, I kicked hard for the line and, again, Inge came back at me. We were giving it absolutely everything. Then, all of a sudden, with just twenty metres to go, he reached over to me, grabbed my arm and lifted both his arms and mine into the air. It was instinctive. It was wonderful. And it was right. We burst through that tape at exactly the same time as one another.

It was the first marathon I'd ever won and I was overjoyed but even more so because of the way it happened. It truly was one of the great thrills of my career to share it with Inge.

I didn't actually know him before that day. I mean, sure, we'd raced in the same events a couple of times but that was the extent of our relationship. He was in Norway; I was in Minnesota – when would our paths ever cross outside of a race? However, since that day, we have become great friends. I even ended up going to Oslo to race against him in a half-marathon not long after our battle in London. That's how much our duel captured the imagination of the public.

I think that was partly down to the fact that, the day after the race, pictures of us crossing the finishing line together appeared in newspapers all around the world. People acclaimed it as a great example of sportsmanship, which I guess it was. It wasn't some premeditated, deliberate thing. It was just the product of an unspoken but mutual respect between two athletes who appreciated what each other had just gone through for the last twenty-six miles or so. It was real. It was genuine. It was authentic. I suppose people liked that about it. Heck, even I like that about it! I've since watched the footage back on several occasions and I get goose bumps every time. I also wonder how I could ever have run that fast but that's a different story!

After the race, we had various media commitments to fulfil before attending a banquet hosted by the organisers and attended by sponsors, guests and so on. I got the feeling that night that everybody there knew they were on to something truly special with the race. It was as if they all realised simultaneously that it had the potential to become one of the biggest and most influential marathons in the world. There was a real sense of accomplishment and pride in that room and rightly so.

When I finally got back to my hotel, I wanted to phone home and share my good news with my parents. Remember, this was in the days before mobile phones and the internet, so people had to rely on other means to share news, means that would probably be considered incredibly primitive these days! However, there was just one problem: I didn't have enough money on me to pay for the call! I had to try to reverse the charges and hope they would pick up. Luckily, they did.

It was my mum who answered and I can vividly remember saying, 'Mum, mum – I did it! I won! I won the London Marathon!' Well, she just screamed. She screamed and screamed and screamed down the handset. She was so pleased she burst into tears. She passed the phone to my dad and his reaction was just the same. It's an incredible feeling when you make your parents proud of you. There are few things in life that compare to it.

When I flew back to the States, the reception that greeted me as I landed was incredible. I arrived at Minneapolis airport shortly before midnight and there must have been a couple of hundred people waiting for me at the gate. They were all cheering and waving and holding up banners. They had even brought along the kids from the orchestra section of the local high school to play some songs, including the theme from *Chariots of Fire*. It was a buzz that I can't even begin to find the words to describe. Whatever ones I'd choose wouldn't do it justice, believe me!

People often ask me how my prize money for winning that race compares with the prize money on offer for the winners today. That's easy because I didn't get any. In fact, there wasn't any prize! Inge and I were given a bottle of Champagne to share and were later sent these really beautiful gold-plated medals. But, no, there was no money, new TV set or anything like that. I honestly didn't care, though. I still don't. I was fortunate enough to be invited to one of the world's great cities to compete in – and win – the first edition of what has become one of the world's most important running events. No amount of money, nor anything else for that matter, can compare with that. I've run faster times, I've set course records and I've won other races outright, but the 1981 London Marathon has always held a very special place in my heart and it always will.

I went back to the London Marathon in 2015, but as a spectator rather than a competitor. My wife Jill and son Christopher were taking part, so I went to cheer them on. It was interesting to see it both through the eyes of and in the company of the spectators. I was able to appreciate the race on an entirely different level. You can't help but be struck dumb by the kindness of the people who stand there for hours and hours on end, cheering on every single runner who comes through. Whether it's one of the elite competitors or somebody struggling wilfully to complete the race in less than eight hours, they are roared on with the same vigour and intensity. It's so genuine, too. They might be total strangers, from completely opposite backgrounds and may never cross paths ever again but, for that brief moment in time, they are united. They become a team. Runner and supporter. Supporter and runner. Working together to achieve something extraordinary, something that less than two per cent of the world's total population has ever achieved: completing a marathon. It's a humbling, inspiring thing to see, hear and be surrounded by. It's awesome. Truly, it is.

Today, running is still a massive part of my life. I may have two artificial knees – not the result of a lifetime of racing, I hasten to add – but I go to bed at night and can hardly wait to get up in the morning to go for a run. I still love it just as much as I ever did.

When I retired, so many people said to me, 'I bet you'll never run again.' Truth is, I could never do that. I still class myself as a runner, a competitor. That fire still burns and I truly believe that it's in every single one of us. You just have to fan the flames every so often.

It doesn't matter if you've never run before. You're never too old to start. I know that sounds like a cliché but the only reason you hear it so much is because it's true. I've had people come up to me who have sat on the couch most of their lives and, suddenly, they hit fifty or sixty and decide to run a marathon. And, at first, that's all you need – desire. Sure, you've got to train, watch what you eat and be prepared to make some temporary sacrifices but you can't even get to that point without desire. It's what separates marathon runners from would-be marathon runners. It is, in simple terms, the difference.

If you're thinking about running the London Marathon, my advice is simple – stop thinking and start doing. It's an incredible race, in a beautiful city, well organised, with generally good weather conditions and perhaps the greatest support you will ever experience putting one foot in front of the other. If your motivation is the entitlement to say, 'I ran a marathon', there's no better event.

I hear its name, I see its pictures, I watch its footage and every hair on the back of my neck stands to attention.

It changed my life. It will change yours, too.

CHAPTER TWO

LLOYD SCOTT

Former professional footballer and firefighter Lloyd Scott was given less than a ten per cent chance of survival when he was diagnosed with leukaemia in 1987. Incredibly, he pulled through and, in 1990, ran the London Marathon to prove there is life after the illness. Subsequently, he has become one of the UK's most prolific charity campaigners, raising more than £5 million for worthy causes through a variety of endurance-based challenges. The most memorable of these? The time he completed the London Marathon in a deep-sea diving suit.

YOU know the guy who ran the London Marathon in a deep-sea diving suit? That was me. And the guy who ran it dressed as Indiana Jones, dragging a large boulder behind him like the famous scene from *Raiders of the Lost Ark*? Also me. Or the guy who ran it wearing a suit of armour, or as the 'Iron Giant', or as 'Brian the Snail' from *The Magic Roundabout*? Me again.

Yeah, it goes without saying that I love a challenge. In addition to my various London Marathon experiences, I have also completed the Marathon des Sables, a 150-mile ultramarathon through the Sahara Desert; undertaken expeditions to both the North and South Poles; run the world's first-ever underwater marathon in Loch Ness in 2003; walked from Land's End to John o'Groats; and climbed Mount Kilimanjaro. And that's just for starters.

Each and every thing I've done has been demanding and difficult in its own way, but nothing compared to the very first big challenge I ever faced: beating leukaemia.

I was diagnosed with the condition in November 1987. At the time, I was a firefighter and part-time footballer. I'd played in goal for the likes of Blackpool, Watford and Leyton Orient. Anyway, one evening, I was called out to help tackle a house fire in Dagenham in east London. Two young boys were trapped inside and I went in to rescue them. During that operation, I inhaled toxic smoke and was taken to hospital for what I thought would be some routine tests. One of them was a blood test, the results of which showed that something wasn't quite right. Further follow-up tests revealed that I was suffering from chronic myeloid leukaemia. It's scary to think that if I hadn't inhaled the smoke that night, it may have gone undetected for many more weeks or months and, of course, with any type of cancer, early diagnosis is crucial.

Even so, my initial prognosis wasn't good. I needed a bone marrow transplant but immediately hit a stumbling block when neither my brother nor my sister proved to be a match for me. They would be a perfect match for one another, ironically, but not me so I needed to find an 'unrelated' match, which, at the time, was both very difficult and very rare. My odds of beating the disease at that point were less than ten per cent. I felt like I was staring down both barrels.

I can remember thinking, 'Jeez, this is it. This is how I'm going to die.' However, I gave myself a shake and tried as much as possible to focus on the possibility that I could be cured, no matter how unlikely it seemed at the time. Don't get me wrong, I had my moments. I can remember one time getting in the car in the middle of the night and driving to London to see the Fire Brigade welfare officer – who was an absolute angel – because I found it hard to share my concerns with my family. As much as possible, though, I tried to just carry on as normal. I continued going to work, kept playing football and so on.

Fortunately, a suitable unrelated donor was found for me to have a transplant at some point in the future. The eighteen-month wait that followed was extremely difficult. It was a real battle just to stay positive. It was around that time that I read the story of a woman who had been undergoing treatment for leukaemia and whose family had decided to bring Christmas forward so she could celebrate with them; you know, in the event that she didn't pull through. As somebody who was going through something similar, I found that quite unnerving, not to mention upsetting.

It made me want to do something to redress the balance a little bit. Something positive. Lots of people are diagnosed with leukaemia every year. In the UK alone, it's currently around 8,600. However, the majority of the stories you hear are negative and pessimistic. I decided I wanted to tell a happier story and show everybody that receiving such a diagnosis doesn't have to be the beginning of the end.

That's why I signed up to run the London Marathon in 1989. A date had, by then, been arranged for me to enter Hammersmith Hospital for my bone marrow transplant and taking part in the marathon was just my way of showing other sufferers that, despite having a life-threatening illness, you can still make the most of any situation. I wanted to offer some hope, some encouragement, even some inspiration for other people who had been diagnosed. Why? Because I needed it just as much as they did.

I needed to know that my diagnosis wasn't a pink slip, that it wasn't the end, and that things like cancer and leukaemia can be beaten. I needed something to cling on to.

From a personal point of view, I also wanted to be in good physical condition for having the procedure. It was important for me to feel strong to help me cope with the treatment I was about to receive. I wanted to have the transplant when I was fit and well, not wait until the disease had eaten away at me and have the transplant be some kind of last-ditch effort to cure me.

The training was really tough. I'd agreed to be part of a clinical trial which involved injecting myself every day with a drug called Interferon and the side effects of it were really quite unpleasant. It was a bit like injecting yourself with the flu. I had headaches, tiredness, nausea, an upset stomach – all kinds of horrible things. It was only when they took me off it, about six weeks before the transplant, that I started to feel better.

The morning of the 1989 marathon finally dawned and I don't mind admitting I was pretty nervous about it all. I had run it a couple of times before. The first of those was in 1985, when I completed it in around three-and-a-half hours. I then did it again the following year, wearing my full firefighter gear, which I suppose was the first hint at what was to come for me in the future!

Still, 1989 was different. As well as I'd trained and as fit as I felt, I knew I was ill and on the brink of the fight of my life – a fight *for* my life. I'm not sure how but I managed to get around in just over three-and-a-half hours. It actually would have been even quicker than that but the BBC was filming me for a documentary and so I kept having to stop to be interviewed and say hello to various people along the way. It's an unusual excuse for clocking a slower time than I'd anticipated but I think it's a valid one!

It was a great day, though, and was just what I needed to buoy me up ahead of the transplant. It also immediately became my ambition to be around to do it again the following year. It became my focus for survival.

The transplant was enormously difficult. I thought I was going to die several times throughout the process. I also had just about every side effect it's possible to have. I contracted shingles, pneumonia and a condition called Graft-versus-host disease, whereby the donor cells start attacking your own body. So, life wasn't exactly a bowl of cherries for a while there.

I got through it, though, and was finally discharged after ten weeks in hospital. Three days later, there was a fun run at the Crystal Palace Sports Centre for a leukaemia charity. I thought to myself, 'I've got to do that.' Obviously, I wasn't in great shape. My legs were pencil thin and I was very wobbly on my feet but I felt this urge to take part, which I did. Completing it was an amazing feeling. I felt as though I had been handed this second chance at life and I was determined to make the most of it.

I started running regularly again, but under the cover of night at first because I looked quite a sight. I started slowly, jogging from one lamppost to the next. Gradually, my strength returned, and less than eleven months after my transplant, I ran the London Marathon again. I can't even tell you how that felt. I set out to prove that there was life after leukaemia and that day – Sunday, 22 April 1990 – I did.

Around a year or so after my transplant, I returned to 'front-line duty' in the fire brigade. It wasn't just as simple as joining the team again. I had to retrain before I was allowed back out there but, on my very first night back, I had an accident which led to me being medically retired. It felt as though somebody was trying to tell me something.

At the time, I was volunteering for the Anthony Nolan Trust – the charity that found my bone marrow donor – and, when they heard what had happened, they offered me a position. I accepted almost immediately. It seemed like a good way to combine a desk job with continuing to do some fundraising challenges.

After doing a number of challenges, I set about thinking, 'What's the worst costume I could wear for the marathon?' I wanted to do something truly difficult. If it was easy, I wasn't interested.

It was on the eve of the 2001 marathon that it hit me. I went to Greenwich to meet some runners and wish them all the best for the race, that kind of thing. It was that night, as everyone was getting ready to tackle the marathon the next day, that I had my 'Eureka!' moment: I could run it in a deep-sea diving suit.

I've no idea where the idea came from. It just popped in there. It excited me straight away and so I shared it with a few of our runners at the start line the following morning. I didn't get much of a reaction from them, though, which I can understand. Let's be honest: they had more important things on their minds! Still, I felt strongly within myself that it was a good idea and so I started formulating a plan for seeing it through.

The first thing I needed to do, obviously, was get my hands on a deep-sea diving suit – but where do you even start with that? It's not like there's a 'Deep-Sea Diving Suits R Us' that you can just stroll into. So, as a first port of call, I contacted the Historical Diving Society and they gave me a list of people to get in touch with. The first one I rang was a guy called Tony Pardoe, who lived in Exmouth. I liked Tony straight away. When I explained to him what I wanted to do, he wasn't fazed by it at all. He was really enthusiastic. His attitude was very much one of 'bring it on'.

I paid him a visit and he said he thought he'd be able to sort me out with some genuine diving gear that wouldn't be too heavy. 'Fantastic,' I thought. 'That'll make everything so much easier.' Well, what did I know! I picked up the diving helmet that he found me and had to really heave to lift it. I remember thinking if this was light, I didn't want to know what heavy was! It was the same with the boots. They were very cumbersome and, at that point, I genuinely doubted if it could be done or not. Even so, I knew I had to at least try. You only ever regret the things that you don't do, never the things you do – right? So, we pressed ahead. Tony removed the glass from the helmet so that I could breathe but added in some bars to give it a fully authentic look.

Once the suit was sorted, the next thing was getting the support of the London Marathon organisers. This was going to be quite an unusual marathon attempt in so much as I wouldn't be able to complete it in one day. Realistically, it was going to take me the best part of a week to get to the finish line, so I needed to know that they were okay with that. Fortunately, they were. They just asked that I start from the back so that I didn't get in anybody's way.

Training was good, if a little unique. In addition to work-outs on a cross-trainer wearing a weighted vest, I also used to put on the boots and go out for walks around the neighbourhood, again usually under the cover of darkness so that nobody would think I was crazy!

It quickly became clear that the key to success was getting comfortable with bearing that kind of weight on my shoulders and feet for a long period of time. All in, the helmet probably weighed about seventy pounds, so we had to find a way to try and protect my shoulders from as much of that load as possible. We considered foam padding but there was none thick enough or dense enough to make much of a difference. As an alternative, I came up with the idea of putting a gel cover for a bicycle saddle on each shoulder, a bit like a large pair of epaulettes. That worked pretty well.

As for the boots, a normal pair of running shoes are designed to be light so that they move with your feet. The diving boots being as heavy as they were meant that they needed to be heaved along. However, much of that forward motion came from the bottom of my shin, which wore away at my skin. The solution? Another two gel covers! We strapped them to the bottom of each shin and, in addition, installed five insoles of varying thicknesses in the base of each boot. I also wore three or four pairs of socks – a thin pair and a couple of thicker pairs – to fill out the boots and to compact my feet. I needed them to be static to rule out the risk of things like blisters, which obviously could have scuppered the whole thing.

So, I felt quite prepared when I finally arrived at the start line. I drove to Greenwich the night before in a campervan that was to become my home for the week. I also had a support team of five or six people who very kindly gave up their time to help me.

The next morning, the starting cannon went off, followed by around 36,000 excited runners. There, right at the very back of the queue, as instructed, was me. It took the best part of an hour to get from my position to the official start line, by which time everyone had gone. The only people left were the guys taking down the gantries and collecting up all the rubbish. It was a bit odd.

I managed to cover around five miles that first day and stopped at the East Greenwich Fire Station, where I slept in my motorhome. The following morning, my team and I moved on towards the *Cutty Sark*, where we were met by a photographer from the *Daily Mail*. A picture appeared in the newspaper the next day and, off the back of that, interest in what I was doing suddenly started to intensify.

It was on the Tuesday that Dave Bedford from the London Marathon approached us. He told us that the marathon's head office had fielded so many press enquiries about what I was doing that they wanted to take over the handling of that side of things. That was great news. We were too small a team to manage all of that on our own, so we were delighted to have their support.

On Wednesday morning, I appeared on national breakfast television and everything just snowballed from there. People drove from all over London to donate. Others threw money out of bus windows and office buildings. One guy even contributed £1,000 to the charity in return for us eating in his restaurant one night. Honestly, the generosity and kindness shown to me by the public was almost overwhelming at times.

As a result of the extra attention we got as the week went on, I needed to recruit more people to join my support team, so I roped in as many friends and people from the charity as I could. The Royal Green Jackets Association was an incredible help, too.

One of the people who mucked in was a friend of mine called Barry. He was a painter and decorator and joined up with us on the Wednesday. He was basically a 'bucket shaker'. Any time traffic stopped at the lights or people passed us in the streets, it was his job to try and get them to donate. Anyway, at the end of the day, he came up to me and said, 'Lloyd, I've had such a brilliant day, I want to see this through with you.' The only problem was that he had a job on for an elderly woman and he'd promised her that it would be finished that week. He was determined not to miss out, though, so said he'd explain the situation to her and that he'd see us the next morning as early as he could get there.

Sure enough, he turned up the next morning with a big grin on his face. I asked him what was so funny. He explained that he'd told the lady that he was helping out a friend who was running the London Marathon in a deep-sea diving suit, that he was raising money for a children's cancer charity and that he'd come back first thing on the Monday to finish the job. The lady replied, 'That's fine. Your friend's doing it in a diving suit, is he? That's funny. There was another bloke on the TV this morning and he's doing the exact same thing!' We had a right good laugh about that one!

By the end, I was ready for it all to be over. Everything had gone to plan, apart from us unexpectedly having to send for a replacement pair of boots on the Wednesday because I'd worn through the soles; they're absolutely not meant to be worn on dry land, right enough! Anyway, we were in position for our planned Friday finish.

I remember being pretty tired on the Thursday night. I think, by that point, all of the aches and strains had started to take their toll. Almost throughout the challenge, there was something that hurt. If it wasn't my shoulders, it was my lower back. If it wasn't my lower back, it was the front of my legs. It was tough going – definitely not your average stroll through the streets of London!

I picked up on Friday morning where I'd left off the night before at Lower Thames Street. I was quite surprised to discover that I had acquired a group of followers, a bit like Forrest Gump. The marathon organisers also put up a special finishing line for me, which was a really nice touch.

During the week, my mum – who is quite patriotic – asked me to carry the flag of St George as I crossed the line. (*I should point out that I carried a Saltire across the line when I completed the Edinburgh Marathon a few years later, just in case anybody thinks I'm too partisan!*) Well, you've always got to do what your mum says, don't you? So, I got one specially made and had somebody on hand to pass it to me with around fifty yards to go.

Crossing the line had to be carefully coordinated because it was being broadcast live on TV, so I was given a fairly detailed list of instructions outlining what I needed to do.

I asked what I should do with the flag when I crossed the line and was told just to hand it to somebody wearing one of the organisers' yellow jackets. That was all fine.

The finish went pretty smoothly and more or less as planned. There were lots of people there and a piper piping as I crossed the line. Next thing I knew, there were Champagne corks being popped and I got dragged away to do a live television interview. As I went, I caught a glimpse of a yellow-jacket-wearer standing next to me and so I said, 'Excuse me, would you mind keeping a hold of this flag for me?' The person took it from me and off I went to do the piece to camera.

About ten minutes later, somebody said to me, 'Oh, Lloyd, you need to get your medal.' With everything that was going on, I'd forgotten all about it. I said, 'Sure, what would you like me to do?' They told me, 'Paula Radcliffe is actually coming down to present you with it.' She had won the women's race in the marathon that year – the first of her three victories – and so had been invited along to do the honours. 'That's fantastic,' I said. 'Where is she?' The person pointed over my right shoulder and said, 'She's right there.' I turned around to see her, you guessed it, holding my flag – I was mortified!

The next couple of days were crazy. I appeared on *Breakfast with Frost*, where the then Prime Minister, Tony Blair, invited me to Downing Street. I was also asked to appear on stage with Joan Rivers during her one-woman show at the Theatre Royal Haymarket in London. That was brilliant fun and Joan was a wonderful lady. I told her that I was planning to do the New York Marathon in a diving suit later the same year and she said she'd help out in terms of getting some coverage for me. True to her word, she did just that.

It really was just an incredible experience. When I first had the idea, I never envisaged that it would capture people's imagination. I'm just so grateful that it did. It also led to further London Marathon challenges, like running dressed in a suit of armour and pulling a 200lb dragon in 2006. That took me six days. The following year was my 'Indiana Jones' challenge, where I dressed like Harrison Ford's character from the movies and dragged a 350lb 'boulder' behind me. In 2008, I dressed as the 'Iron Giant' in a nine-foot tall robot suit that weighed 70lbs, which, again, took me six days. The next year was my 'Beatles' theme, where I dressed like one of the characters from the *Sgt Pepper's Lonely Hearts Club Band* album cover, complete with yellow submarine.

My most recent London Marathon challenge was the so-called 'Magic Marathon', where I dressed like 'Brian the Snail' from *The Magic Roundabout* and crawled on my hands and knees the whole way around the course. That took me twenty-seven days, averaging about a mile per day.

I'd like to think that I've still got one more big challenge left in me but I don't know what it will be. I definitely feel that, after all I've been through and the big part that the London Marathon has played in my life, I need to go out on a high. We'll see what happens, I guess!

If I never do anything else, though, I can put my feet up happy in the knowledge that I achieved what I set out to do – I proved that there's life after leukaemia.

There really is, you know. That's why you should never give up, never give in, never accept 'the inevitable'.

Remember: I was given just a one in ten chance of survival. I've subsequently had a life that's one in a million. You can't ask for more than that.

CHAPTER THREE

SIR STEVE REDGRAVE

Arguably Great Britain's greatest-ever sportsman, Sir Steve Redgrave won five gold medals at five consecutive Olympic Games – the only athlete ever to accomplish that feat. He retired from rowing in 2000 and, the following year, ran the London Marathon for the first-ever time.

IT was the day after the 'Scullers Head' rowing competition on the River Thames. A few friends and I were sitting in a bar having a few drinks when a man came in holding a bunch of running numbers. He said that there was a new race taking place the next morning and he wondered if we'd be interested in taking part. If we were, he said he could get us in.

The date was 28 March 1981, and the 'new running event' he was referring to was the first-ever London Marathon.

At the time, my friends and I were only around nineteen or twenty years old and being young, fit and probably a little bit cocky, we thought running a marathon at a day's notice was a great idea. We took the race numbers from the man and I'm pretty sure we fully intended to see it through. We hadn't really heard a huge amount about the marathon beforehand and I think we thought it would be pretty easy. Fortunately, we never made it to the start line. Instead, we had a few more drinks and forgot all about it.

It's funny looking back on that day. I really could never have known how big a part of my life the London Marathon would become.

It wasn't until 2001 that I took part in it for the first time. It was never really something I thought much about during my rowing career. Even if it had been, I couldn't have done it. If you want to be successful at anything, you have to be prepared to devote your time to it and give it your full attention. Rowing is no different. For almost thirty years, I dedicated myself to being the very best rower that I could be and I'm immensely proud to have achieved as much as I did, particularly winning gold medals at five consecutive Olympic Games.

However, that didn't leave a huge amount of time for anything else and so I had never even contemplated running a marathon until I retired after the 2000 Olympics in Sydney.

It was my coach, Jürgen Gröbler, who insisted that I complete what he called a 'wind-down programme' after I hung up the oars. He had a point. Nobody had ever rowed at the top level for as long as I had, nor had they come close to achieving the same intensity. I really did give it my all, so to suddenly give up and allow my training to grind to a complete halt would have been a real shock to the system, and Jürgen – a proud and focused German – was not about to let that happen.

The thing is, I'm six foot four and weigh the best part of eighteen stone. I'm not what you would call a natural runner. In fact, if I'm being totally honest, you wouldn't call me a runner, natural or otherwise. I was a decent enough sprinter in my youth but the furthest I had ever run by the time I retired was a half-marathon, when I completed the Great North Run in 1997.

The other problem with me is that I need motivation. I have to be working towards something, otherwise I have no interest in going through the process. Maybe it's an 'Olympic' thing. For four years at a time, everything builds towards one moment, one event. You complete it, learn from it, reset and go again. It's a constant cycle. So I needed a goal, a reason to want to keep working into my sporting retirement. That's why, in 2001, I established my own charitable trust – The Steve Redgrave Fund – and set myself the ambitious target of raising £5 million in five years for a variety of worthy causes. I announced these plans at the same time as I confirmed my retirement from rowing. My first real fundraising event for the Fund? The 2001 London Marathon. For good measure, my wife, Ann – an Olympic rower in her own right – decided that she would join me. It seemed like the perfect time and place to begin this new venture and chapter in my life.

Now, I'm not going to lie; we didn't exactly train as well as we should have. I remember the two of us going to the Pride of Britain Awards a few months before the race and bumping into Tanni Grey-Thompson. Tanni is a wonderful athlete, a true icon of the Paralympic movement and a dear friend of many, many years. She was also well aware that Ann and I were planning to run the London Marathon.

'How did your eighteen-mile training run go today?' she asked.

'We didn't do it,' I replied. 'To be totally honest, the furthest we've run at this point is a half-marathon, just over thirteen miles.'

Now, like I say, Tanni and I go way back. This, however, was the first time that I had ever seen anything close to fear on her face. I knew immediately that we'd underestimated the enormity of the challenge we had committed to.

Tanni recovered quickly, forced a smile and said, 'Oh well, I'm sure you'll be okay.' Deep down, I knew she was worried about what we'd let ourselves in for. I turned to Ann and said, 'What have we done?'

Anyway, the morning of the race dawned. We made our way to the start line where I had been given the honour of being the official race starter that year. Well, I say that. The truth is that Dave Bedford, the former race director of the London Marathon, really started the race. Dave is a wonderful, lovely man and played a key role in establishing the London Marathon as the iconic event that it is today. However, he was also incredibly paranoid about anything going wrong with the start of the race! It should have been a simple job, really. Wait for the signal and push down on the large, mushroom-shaped button. That, in turn, would trigger a loud, klaxon-like noise that would be the cue to get going. However, from what I gather, that button had a tendency to misbehave and so, when I was standing up on the podium at the start line, with my hand over the button, Dave was crouched underneath with an air horn! It might have looked like I started the race but, in reality, it was all Dave!

Still, it was an honour to be asked to start it, whether ceremonially or otherwise, and even more so to be given the '1' race number. That was the first time that the defending champion – who, in 2001, was the Portuguese marathon runner António Pinto – hadn't been given the number. I remember being so proud to get that opportunity, although I'll bet it has never gone back down through the pack as quickly in the history of the race. I might have been wearing '1' but I finished goodness knows where! Somewhere in the 'thousands', probably.

After 'starting' the race, Ann and I jumped into the crowd and started to run. It was amazing. You've trained for weeks and months on end more or less by yourself and then, suddenly, you're surrounded by hundreds of people on either side of you. It was just an incredible feeling and a wonderful, warm atmosphere.

Still, Ann and I are competitors at heart. It wasn't enough to think we could get through the race; we had to have a plan for it, so we decided to try to draw on some of our rowing experiences.

Rowing and long-distance running have some similarities. They're both feats of endurance, for one thing, and being mentally strong is almost as important as being physically strong.

We knew that we'd be tempted to be swept along by the atmosphere and adrenaline in those first few miles and end up going off too fast. And, remember, in 2001, pacing watches were still probably around a year or two away from really taking off, so the only two frames of reference you had were your watch and the mile markers.

As it happened, we passed the first mile marker roughly one minute quicker than planned, so we had to adjust our pace accordingly. In the end, we managed to cross the finish line in a time of 4:55:36. That was a little disappointing, as we had wanted to complete the course in under four hours. However, we did succeed in another of our goals – to not get overtaken by somebody dressed in a rhino outfit! Three or four Lottery balls overtook us, which was a little annoying, and coming down the Embankment, fifteen guys tied together like a centipede went past us. I remember noticing them and thinking that I recognised one of them. As it turned out, he was an old rowing opponent! I actually saw him again the second time that I ran – in 2005 – but he wasn't overtaking me then. He was really struggling, actually. I guess the other fourteen guys in that 'centipede' must have been particularly strong runners!

But back to 2001. One of my enduring memories of the race, and I know this is true for the vast majority of people who run the London Marathon, is the sheer warmth of the crowds. They cheer and support every single person who goes past them. It's an overused word these days but it's a truly unique atmosphere.

I could really feel everyone willing me on and I'll always be grateful for that. I wondered at the time how so many people could recognise me in the blur of faces that went past them. I figured it was partly because I was wearing the '1' race number. However, that night, when we got back to our hotel, Ann and I watched back some of the footage from the race. The cameras showed us at the *Cutty Sark*, around six miles into the race, and we were both struck by how much we stood out. I mean, as I've already pointed out, I'm a tall guy. Ann, too, is quite tall, measuring around six foot. However, we seemed to stand out head, shoulders and torso above most of the people around us on the BBC footage! That would have made us pretty easy to spot, I suppose.

That leads me to a funny story that happened around seventeen miles into the race. It's a tough part of the route where you can feel yourself starting to flag. Fatigue is setting in and nine more miles to go feels like ninety. On top of that, you are running on some cobbled, narrow roads, through tall buildings back down towards Tower Bridge. It's a challenging stretch, for sure.

Anyway, we had tucked in behind a group of people for a few miles, one of whom was a guy just a few paces ahead. On the back of his shirt – and presumably the front – was his name, printed in big, block capitals: 'STEVE'. He had been struggling along like the rest of us through that gruelling part of the course. His head had been down, his body was hunched over a little and he was shuffling more than running.

As we approached Tower Bridge and the crowds on the sides of the streets started to get bigger and bigger, the noise they made rattled around the buildings.

'Come on, Steve!'

'You can do it, Steve!'

'Not far to go now, Steve!'

With each cheer, you could see this chap feeding off their energy. He transformed in front of our eyes. The spine straightened, the head popped up, the chest puffed out. The crowds were cheering his name and he was responding, even waving back to them, until another runner drew alongside him, tapped him on the shoulder and pointed his thumb backwards as if to say, 'Look behind you.'

The poor guy glanced round, caught my eye and his shoulders sank as if somebody had stuck a pin in him and let out all the air. I felt so bad for him but I like to think that, even if the crowd were cheering me on, they were rooting for the other 'Steve', too.

It was a wonderful day, though, and the support I received from everybody – roadside well-wishers and fellow runners alike – is something I'll never forget. I regard the 2001 London Marathon as the biggest lap of honour of my career. The next day, my arms were arguably more tired than my legs, what with all the waving and hand-shaking that I did. People wanted to come up and speak to me, get a picture and all that sort of thing. It was incredibly humbling.

Speaking of the next-day pain, yes, I was pretty immobile but here's something that you can all take heart from. Ann and I were staying in the same hotel as the 'elite' runners. The next morning, we got up and wearily, slowly made our way down to breakfast. The guy who won, Abdelkader El Mouaziz, was hobbling around every bit as much as we were. Granted, he ran the race almost three hours quicker than we did, but still, it was reassuring to see that even the best in the world feel the effects of running twenty-six miles!

That, to me, is one of sport's most redeeming qualities: it's a great leveller. Events like the London Marathon are particularly good in that respect. Think about it for a second. What other major sporting event can you compete in where the top athletes in that particular field are also taking part? Okay, so you're not going to run it alongside them or keep pace with them – and if you do, you'll probably not do it for long – but they're there taking part on the same day, the same course and under the same conditions as you. That's quite something.

People don't always believe me when I tell them this but one of the proudest moments of my sporting career happened in the 2003 London Marathon. I didn't actually run that year. I was meant to but, unfortunately, I picked up an injury that kept me out. Instead, I had the enormous privilege of holding one side of the tape when Paula Radcliffe crossed the finish line in first place in the women's race. It was her second victory – her second consecutive victory, for that matter – and she achieved it in 2:15:25, a world record that stands to this day. It was a phenomenal run by a phenomenal athlete and I remember showing family and friends the pictures in the newspapers the next day. 'Look,' I said, 'that's my hand!' To witness such a fantastic performance by a British athlete at such close quarters was a genuine honour.

I ran again in 2005 and 2006. It was during the latter that we smashed through the £5 million target for the Steve Redgrave Fund. That year, I decided to make full use of my contacts in the corporate world and get them to sponsor me by the mile. In return, I wore a T-shirt with their logo on it for the duration of that mile.

It seemed like a great idea at the time. I figured all I would have to do would be to get T-shirts printed, roll them up tight and put them in a rucksack. That's fine in theory. However, twenty-six T-shirts, even rolled up tight, take up a lot of room. Never mind one rucksack, we needed three! I roped in a couple of trustees from the Fund to wait at designated spots beside each mile marker where I'd meet them and change into the next shirt. On the one hand, it worked out great. I got to take twenty-six breaks! On the other, it had to be planned and executed with military precision, which, fortunately, it was.

I got twenty-six different companies to sponsor me and I subsequently sent them the T-shirt – washed and signed – and with a copy of my finisher's certificate for them to either keep or auction off for charity.

For the final few hundred yards, I wore a T-shirt with all of their logos on it. I kept that one. I've still got it, too. I've also kept all three of my London Marathon finisher's medals. That might sound strange given some of the other medals that I own but those London Marathon ones are special in their own right. We're not an especially 'showy' family. There's actually nothing in our house that shows off any of what either Ann or I have accomplished in our sporting lives and all of the Olympic medals and so on are safely stored well away elsewhere under lock and key. However, my London Marathon medals are in a drawer in my office and every so often I see them and smile. How couldn't I?

Sometimes I find myself driving from our home in Marlow into the centre of London and I think about those three races I completed, as it's roughly twenty-six miles. Every time I do that drive, it seems crazy to me that people, myself included, can and have run that distance.

Then I think back to how blasé I was about it all before I first ran it. People told me that I would be knocked sideways at the sense of accomplishment I'd feel afterwards. 'Really?' I thought. 'What I've done, what I've achieved, am I really going to feel anything about finishing a marathon?' And like that my mind goes straight to The Mall, coming up those last few hundred yards, total strangers cheering you all the way to the finish, and the pride, the satisfaction, the sheer unadulterated joy of it washes over me again as if for the first time. Like I said earlier, it's unique.

No other word does it justice.

CHAPTER FOUR

SADIE PHILLIPS

London-born Sadie Phillips has twice defeated cervical cancer: in October 2012 and August 2014. Shortly after getting the all-clear the second time, she and her boyfriend Jon received places to run the 2015 London Marathon on behalf of Cancer Research UK.

THE only thing worse than being told you've got cancer is being told it twice.

I grew up in Newquay in Cornwall, on the south-west coast of England, and, for the first twenty-eight years of my life, I'd been quite a healthy person. I'd never really been in hospital, hadn't ever broken a bone or anything like that. Everything, as far as I knew, was fine. The first sign that it wasn't came early in 2012 when, between periods, I had started to notice a bit of bleeding or 'spotting' as they call it. I went to my doctor, more as a precaution than anything. I was up to date with my smear tests, so I wasn't especially concerned.

Almost straight away, the doctor told me she could see a small lump but that it just looked like a polyp, which she said was quite common. She referred me to a specialist at my local hospital, who agreed with that diagnosis. He didn't think it looked particularly threatening. Instead, he figured that not only would it be fairly straightforward to remove but I would be able to have it done within a couple of weeks, too.

So, I went back in, had it removed and, shortly afterwards, got a phone call from my gynaecology consultant surgeon asking me to come in to see him. To be completely honest with you, the thought didn't cross my mind that it could possibly be cancer. Like I said, I was twenty-eight, fit and healthy. Cancer was something that happened to older people, other people, not me. Because I didn't think I was getting any news of any particular significance, I went to the appointment on my own – naively, as it turned out. As soon as I walked into the room, I saw a Macmillan nurse sitting there next to the doctor. She was wearing her uniform so there was no mistaking who she was.

The doctor didn't beat about the bush. He sat me down and explained that it wasn't good news. 'We've tested the lump that we removed from you,' he said, 'and I'm sorry to say that it's cancer.'

In that instant, my life changed. Initially, I was in total shock. I couldn't believe what I was being told. I only recall the finer details of what happened next because the doctor gave me a photocopy of the sheet that he and the nurse talked through. The whole thing just felt completely surreal. I remember driving home thinking to myself, 'How on earth am I going to break this news to my parents?' It was awful. Even now, it's a difficult moment to re-live.

The only good thing, I suppose, was that the whole thing moved along at a reasonably quick pace thereafter. Subsequent follow-up tests showed that the residual cancer that was left was quite small and manageable, so they booked me in for a cone biopsy, a procedure that removes abnormal tissue high up in the cervical canal. They assured me it was a straightforward operation that would only take about a week to recover from.

So, that was fine. I had the cone biopsy on 17 August 2012, and was sent home to rest whilst they checked the tissue they removed. Just under two weeks later, I got word that the procedure hadn't been entirely successful. My margins still weren't clear and the cancer was still there.

There were a couple of options available to me at that point but the one with the least risk was a radical hysterectomy. For anyone who doesn't know what that is, it is a procedure whereby your entire uterus is removed. In other words, having it meant sacrificing my chance to have children.

That was a dreadful realisation. I wasn't married, I wasn't trying for a baby, nor did I have any plans to do so any time particularly soon. I guess I just took it for granted that, when the time came, it wouldn't be a problem. So, to have that taken away from me was devastating. Still, what choice did I have? It was either be cured of cancer or not. It was that clear cut and so, on 11 September 2012, one week before my twenty-ninth birthday, I went in for the procedure.

Luckily, they were able to do it with keyhole surgery and, again, I went home to recover and wait for the results.

Around a month later, on 14 October, I was contacted to say that the operation had been a success and that my cancer was gone. That was amazing. From the moment you hear those dreaded words – 'You have cancer' – you are just waiting to hear it's gone.

Even so, the weeks and months that followed were quite strange. Everything had happened so quickly – from being diagnosed in the July to being told that my cancer was gone less than three months later – that I was left wondering, 'Did that really happen?' When you're in the midst of something like that, you're just dealing with it and getting on with things as best you possibly can. You're living from appointment to appointment and, although you're not aware of it at the time, it's as though you're on a treadmill that just keeps going and going and going. Then, suddenly, almost without warning, it stops and you're standing still. That comes as a shock and it was only when it happened that I was able to start to recover emotionally. I was able to properly come to terms with the terrible realisation that I'd had cancer and, similarly, absorb my altered reality, specifically the fact that I was now never going to be able to have children. I can't describe it any other way than to say I went through a bit of a grieving process. I grieved for the children I'd never be able to carry and the loss of that part of my future. I never really felt anger about it; just heartbreak.

Luckily, I had a lot of wonderful people around me to help get me through it. At no point did I ever feel alone and, looking back, that was so important, particularly as I still had to go for regular, monthly check-ups at the hospital to make sure the cancer wasn't returning. That, in itself, was very traumatic. I had a couple of weeks of fear building up to each appointment, followed by the appointment itself, then a week or so of waiting for the results, getting good news, having a bit of momentary relief that everything was okay, before the whole horrible process started again with the fear of the next check-up. It was a very unpleasant time, fraught with anxiety. My mind was never totally at ease.

Still, I couldn't just sit around and let the stress of those few months burden me forever. If nothing else, my experiences showed me that you have to make the most of your life because it can so quickly and drastically change or, worse still, be taken from you. It's a cliché but you've got to make the most of it. For me, that meant retraining as a teacher. I had worked in PR and marketing for most of my adult life but had always harboured dreams of going into teaching. It had been something I'd thought about before I fell ill but I always just dismissed it as something I'd get round to. Now, though, I wasn't prepared to wait any longer and, in September 2013, I started a Postgraduate Certificate in Education (PGCE).

It was barely four months into the course, on 6 January 2014, that one of my monthly check-ups revealed abnormalities. Three days after that, I was back in the hospital having a colposcopy where biopsies were taken to assess those abnormalities for cancer. On 21 January, I got the news that I had been dreading since getting the all-clear in October 2012 – it was back.

Just as it had been first time around, the news was absolutely gutting, not least because I knew that I would have to put my PGCE on the back-burner for a while. I kept going with it for as long as I could – my previous experiences had shown me that one of my most successful coping mechanisms was to keep busy – so I continued to do it throughout all of the initial tests and so on. However, when it became clear I was going to undergo chemotherapy and radiotherapy, I had no option but to put my studies on hold.

Neither chemo nor radiotherapy had been planned to begin with. Initially, the intention had been to operate and remove the tumour that way. I even made it as far as the operating theatre. However, when I awoke from my sedation, I immediately knew that the procedure hadn't happened. I groggily put my hand towards the bottom of my tummy and felt no padding or bandaging. I asked what had happened and was told by my surgeon that, just as they were preparing to operate, they spotted some more abnormalities and were forced to cancel the procedure. In other words, my cancer had spread and operating was no longer an option.

Nothing can prepare you for news like that. To be honest, it was the first time I thought I might die young. The disease was spreading quickly and, at that point, the odds of survival weren't great. I had a genuine fear that I wouldn't live to old age.

I was referred to an oncologist on 19 February 2014, and told that the next stage would be to try and treat me with five consecutive weeks of chemotherapy and radiotherapy. That started on 3 March. I had both chemotherapy and radiotherapy on Mondays, followed by radiotherapy on Tuesdays, Wednesdays, Thursdays and Fridays. I was in hospital more often than not.

Having chemotherapy particularly worried me but I was lucky that the type of chemo that I had didn't make my hair fall out, nor did it make me especially ill. That was a huge relief.

It was an intense five weeks but I was comforted by knowing that something was being done to try and cure me. When you're waiting for a surgery date to come around, even if it's only a couple of weeks, it's easy to feel frustrated because it feels like nothing's happening. It seems as though all you're doing is twiddling your thumbs. However, with the treatment I received, as full-on as it was, I felt like progress was being made.

I was also fortunate that my mum came to every appointment with me and stayed with me on each of those long, tough days in hospital. It was great to have her company. We'd play cards, watch movies on my iPad, read magazines, chat – basically just do everything we could to fill the hours and make the best of a bad situation.

At the end of those five weeks, I went for a specialist treatment called brachytherapy. It involves placing radioactive 'seeds' near the tumour, which gives a direct and high radiation dose to the tumour whilst, at the same time, reducing the amount of radiation the surrounding healthy tissue is exposed to. It's basically radiotherapy from the inside out and lasts for about six to eight hours. It was my final day of treatment. I then had to wait three months for the results. With radiotherapy, it continues to work after your treatment, so you have to give it time to fully do its thing. It was at the end of the August that I got the all-clear, which, again, was just amazing. Against the odds, I had beaten cancer not once but twice.

Back in the midst of my treatment, a very good friend of mine ran the London Marathon. I can remember watching Suzie on the TV and tracking her progress online. I got so into it and swept up by the excitement of it all that I decided to apply to run in the 2015 race. I figured I'd put my name down and see what happened. Unfortunately, the deadline for the ballot had already passed by the time I got around to it, so I decided to try to get in through a charity. I wrote to Cancer Research UK to apply for one of their golden bond places and I didn't really think any more of it until, in the same week that I got the all-clear from the doctors, they got back to me to say that, out of the thousands who applied for one of their 500 places, I was getting not one, but two: one for me and one for my boyfriend, Jon. It was absolutely brilliant. I started crying on the phone when they called and the lady on the opposite end of the line got quite emotional, too. From worrying about the results of my treatment, to getting the all-clear, to getting a place in the London Marathon, all within the space of a few days – it was simply incredible.

The thing about running the London Marathon is that it's such a huge thing to do and was something that had been on my 'bucket list' for a while. Being diagnosed with cancer just made me more proactive about doing some of the things on it so, when Cancer Research UK phoned me to offer Jon and I places, we accepted straight away.

When I told my doctors and nurses what I was doing, they were amazed. I think they possibly thought I was a bit mad as well! At the same time, it was important that I did something physical. The chemotherapy and radiotherapy had stopped my ovaries from working, so I had started to go through the menopause before I'd even turned thirty. I knew that developing osteoporosis was one of the risks of early menopause, as a result of my body no longer producing oestrogen, so I had asked my medical team what I could do to stave this off. They said that weight-bearing exercise was one of the best solutions.

I had been quite sporty at school but, after leaving university and starting full-time work, I struggled to find time to keep fit. I did a bit of yoga during treatment, mainly to help keep my limbs supple and strong for the radiotherapy and also for the calming benefits of it. That, though, was about as much as I'd done, so I was really starting from scratch.

However, I was incredibly motivated to do it, particularly because it was for Cancer Research UK. To have twice had the all-clear from cancer and to be able to give something back to everything that its research had done for me was an incredible opportunity, so raising money through sponsorships became my new number one goal. All I wanted was to make it to the end of the race and to raise funds for an incredible cause, and the more that people sponsored me, the more determined I became. I think there were quite a lot of people who felt quite helpless when I'd been ill, so the response we received for the fundraising was overwhelming.

One of the perks of being picked for the Cancer Research team was being invited up to London for a photo call. It was the lead charity for the 2015 race – they choose a different cause to back each year – and so Jon and I were invited to go along to their event where I met Sir Richard Branson. As a coincidence, it was my birthday on that particular day and so Sir Richard even presented me with a bottle of Champagne, which was a lovely surprise and something I would never have experienced had I not made the conscious decision to take this awful negative and turn it into something positive.

That's not to say it wasn't difficult. The training was especially hard work. Coming off the back of so much treatment, I had to be very careful. I'd had a lot of radiotherapy to my pelvis and, because all my lymph nodes had been removed, I was prone to swelling in my legs, so taking it slow was vital.

Still, as difficult as it was, the training was also good for me and not just in terms of the obvious physical benefits of it. Psychologically, it was hugely beneficial. If I was having a bad day training, for example, I'd just think about all of those weeks that I was in hospital and didn't have the luxury of being able to go out for a run whenever it suited me. That really spurred me on.

The day before the race, we came up to London to stay with my friend, Fiona, who lives close to the start line and, before we knew it, it was the next morning and time to get going.

It was as you get to the point near the start line where the non-runners can't go any further that I got quite emotional just saying goodbye to my friends. The enormity of everything that had happened to me in the past two years hit me right at that moment along with the realisation that, after today, I might be able to move on and close the chapter on that part of my life.

Anyway, Jon and I made our way to the start. We even bumped into somebody else from Newquay on our way, my older sister's best friend, and I remember thinking that was a good omen. I was struck by how friendly and cheerful everybody was. People were offering one another words of encouragement or bits of advice. It was such a humbling thing to be part of. I'd never run in a race that big or that long before, so to be doing it somewhere as iconic as London was just amazing. Jon and I went with the attitude of just going there to finish it, to enjoy it and to soak it all up, and I think we certainly did that.

Cancer Research had loads of cheering points set up all along the route, which was fantastic. Getting so much support from them, our friends and family – and everyone else lining the way, for that matter – helped to keep us moving. It was around about twenty miles in, when you just want it all to be over, that I saw one of their cheering stations up ahead. You knew that they were there because you could see all of their balloons in the distance and

I remember getting really emotional that they were cheering for us. You're innately aware that these total strangers have given up their day to come along and support you for no other reason than out of the goodness of their hearts. That kindness, that thoughtfulness – it was almost overwhelming.

The whole day was filled with unforgettable moments. One that particularly stands out was on the Embankment as we approached Big Ben with only a couple of miles to go. We were struggling on as best we could when we heard the crowd around us suddenly start to go crazy. Out of nowhere, they got really loud. We looked around to try to identify the cause of it and we saw these three guys. One was dressed as Mario from the Super Mario Brothers video game, and he had a cardboard cut-out 'Mario Kart' attached to the braces on his costume; another was dressed as Luigi, again with a kart attached to him; and the third guy was, hilariously, dressed as the Princess from the game, complete with a wig and pink princess car.

Now, obviously, because the race was on, there was no traffic allowed on the road, but the traffic lights were still activated. As these three guys reached a red light, they came to a stop. They stood there bobbing around waiting for the light to turn green and, when it did, they sprinted as hard as they could. That sent the crowd wild and, when they reached the next set of red lights, they stopped and did it all again. They repeated it all along the Embankment and it was just such good banter; great fun at a time in the race when you really need some comic relief. It was such a nice little moment to be part of.

Getting to the finish line? It was brilliant. It was everything I'd imagined it would be and more. It was also the year that the London Marathon organisers were promoting a 'hand in hand' initiative for finishers, so that's how Jon and I crossed the line: holding hands. He'd been by my side through it all – the diagnosis, the treatment, the training – and he'd always been there to hold my hand whenever I needed it most. It just felt like such a huge accomplishment. After getting the all-clear from cancer, it was the best feeling I've ever had.

So, how are things these days? I'm doing well. I still have check-ups but now I have them every six months rather than monthly, which is great. I think that having had a recurrence of cancer I'll always have a bit of fear every time I go for a check-up but it's definitely getting easier.

On top of that, I've started a new career as a teacher and moved to London with Jon – it's a really exciting time in my life. I'm happy, content and looking to the future.

The journey I've been on has taught me two things above all others. Firstly, go and see your doctor as soon as you can if you notice changes in your body. Whatever your symptoms are, get them checked. That's what your doctors are there for and, for women specifically, make sure you keep up to date with your smear tests. Early diagnosis is crucial to surviving cervical cancer. I was lucky. We caught mine fairly early on, otherwise, well, it doesn't bear thinking about.

Secondly – and this is just as important – you only live once, so you have to make the most of it. Anything less is just wasting time, and that's something I'm not prepared to do.

CHAPTER FIVE

CLAUDE UMUHIRE

After surviving the Rwandan genocide as a child, Claude Umuhire came to London with his mother. Years later, after finding himself homeless on the streets of the capital, he was introduced to running by an organisation called The Running Charity. That helped to transform his life and, in 2015, brought him to the start line of the London Marathon.

A KNOCK on the door changed my life forever. It was the summer of 1994. I was four years old and lived in my home in Rwanda with my mum, my dad, my six-year-old sister and my baby brother. We were quite a normal family and, for the most part, those first four years of my life had been really happy and innocent. A typical childhood, really.

Then came that knock. My father opened the door to Hutu militia, who rounded us all up and marched us to what turned out to be a killing field. It was the height of the Rwandan civil war and the genocide that claimed the lives of around one million people, most of whom were Tutsis, like my family. Tutsis were targeted in the aftermath of the assassination of President Habyarimana, a Hutu who was killed when his plane was shot down as it approached Kigali airport in Rwanda in April 1994. Paul Kagame, who would become the president of the country further down the line, was blamed for the attack. At the time, he was the leader of a Tutsi rebel group, which opposed the Hutu-led regime. This prompted a spilling over of years of ethnic tension between the two tribes, which resulted in a swift and coordinated attempt by Hutu extremists to effectively exterminate the country's entire Tutsi community.

That's what brought them to our door that day. We were easy to identify. For one thing, everybody had to carry ID cards, on which, in big bold writing, it said whether you were Hutu or Tutsi. On top of that, everybody knew everybody. Your neighbours knew which tribe you were and so they directed the militants towards you.

Trying to escape was pointless. They had put up roadblocks everywhere, so there was nowhere to run. There was nothing you could do but go where you were taken. We were escorted to a large open area, probably about the size of Regent's Park, where we were put together with other people who had been captured. The militants then encircled us all, took out their machetes and started to kill people, working from the outside in.

People were crying, praying, begging for their lives. I could hear them being slaughtered all around me. Sometimes, in my head, I still can.

My father and I had ended up separated from my mum and my siblings because of all of the commotion that was going on. As the militants approached us, he lay on top of me to try and protect me. I owe my life to him for that. He was killed as he lay there. I'm not sure exactly when it happened because I tried to play dead hoping that nobody would hurt us. I just lay there and waited.

It was dark when I heard my mum calling my name. She called for me, my sister and my baby brother. I was the only one who answered. The others were dead. I could tell from her shouts that she was quite some distance away, so I followed the sound of her voice to get to her, walking over countless dead bodies beneath me. When I finally reached her, we just lay on the ground. There was nowhere we could go and, in any case, mum was bleeding heavily from injuries she had sustained. We just lay together all night, trying to be as still as we possibly could in case they came back.

The next morning, we awoke to heavy gunfire, when the Rwandan army intervened. Everything after that is a bit of a blur but I do remember my mum being taken to hospital where she had emergency surgery that, ultimately, saved her life.

When she was discharged, we went to stay with some relatives but mum wanted out of Rwanda altogether. She decided she wanted to come to the UK, which she did, via Tanzania, in 1996. She left me with my aunties and uncles whilst she got herself established and it wasn't until January 2001 that, at the age of ten, I finally went to join her.

That was the start of my life in the UK and it was a very strange time. When I arrived, mum was in a new relationship with another guy and was pregnant with my little sister, which was quite surreal. It was strange just to see her again. Whilst I recognised her as my mum, it felt as though she was a different person with a whole new life that I wasn't really a part of. Simple things like hearing her speak a whole different language really unsettled me. It took me a long time to get used to being around her again.

For the first year, I didn't really feel as though I fitted in. I was in a strange city, in a strange country, where everything looked different, where everyone spoke differently, where the weather was unlike anything I'd ever experienced before, and where my mum had this whole new life. It was a tough time. I felt as though I just didn't belong.

Still, I got on with it. I picked up English pretty quickly and went through the school system. I did pretty well, too, and managed to get a place on a sports science course at the University of Derby.

That's when the problems started. I quit my course after a year. I hated being at uni. It really wasn't for me and, besides anything else, I didn't like being so far away from my mum. So, I dropped out and went home. Ironically, that really upset her. She has always really believed in the importance of education. She thinks it is the cure for everything, so she was not happy that I had decided to give up on it. Consequently, things between us quickly became strained. We argued pretty much every day to the point that our relationship almost completely broke down. I couldn't see any way that we could resolve our issues, so I decided to leave.

I tried to sofa-surf for a while but the trouble with that is that you run out of friends pretty quickly. People are happy to put you up for a little while but, before long, they just want their own space back, which is perfectly fair. It was when I ran out of sofas that I ended up on the streets. I slept on Warren Street, near Euston Station, as well as in a park in the University College of London and pretty much any bus that I could get on.

It was a scary experience. People talk about 'sleeping rough'. I don't know about them but I didn't do a whole lot of sleeping because I was so worried about being attacked. Other homeless people I spoke to told me about being beaten up and that definitely made me quite worried, so I actively sought out the most secluded areas I could find. Behind bushes, behind buildings and so on.

Oddly enough, there was one time when I was sleeping not all that far from my mum's flat in Camden but I never thought about turning to her. I was too proud, too stupid. I felt like going back would make me a failure and, even though I had nowhere to go, I didn't have it in me to make contact with her. Looking back, I can see how silly that was but I wasn't thinking clearly at that time. To be honest, I wasn't looking any further ahead than tomorrow.

It was after about a month on the streets that I went to the council to look for help. Unfortunately, they said there was nothing they could do for me. They said that, because I was nineteen, male and in reasonably good health, I didn't qualify for their support. Instead, they gave me two leaflets. One was for a place in Euston called 'New Horizon'. I wasn't staying too far from it at the time so I decided to check it out.

New Horizon is a day centre for homeless people between the ages of sixteen and twenty-two and, as well as giving you food, they also try to help your housing situation. Doing that for me proved to be pretty tricky. I had refugee status in the UK but had lost all of my travel documents, so they couldn't really help me. As a result, I basically bounced from shelter to shelter before I found 'Shelter from the Storm', a fantastic night shelter. You go there, get a hot meal and then, when the sun comes up, you get up and go about your day. I ended up being there for about eight months and it was a pretty frustrating time. I didn't want to be homeless. I didn't want any of that. What I wanted most was to improve my circumstances. To do that, I needed an ID. To get one, I needed papers confirming my identity but they were all with mum. Without an ID, I couldn't get a job. Without a job, I couldn't make money. Without money, I couldn't get a place to stay. Without a place to stay, I had to keep using the shelters. It was the most vicious of vicious circles. I felt completely stuck and, to be honest, it made me very depressed. I figured that this was how things were going to be for the rest of my life.

Basically, I was at rock bottom. Of course, from there, there's only one way you can go and that's up. Sure enough, that's how it turned out.

On Wednesday evenings, the New Horizon centre hosted a men's event. One particular Wednesday, Alex, an officer at the centre, told me there was a guy coming in to talk to us about the possibility of running the London Marathon. I remember thinking to myself, 'Yeah, right. No chance could I ever do that.' Anyway, the guy's name was James Gilley. He was the co-founder of an organisation called The Running Charity. He told us his story of running the London Marathon in memory of his friend who had died from a heroin overdose whilst he was living on the streets. Running had helped him to come to terms with what happened, so he set up a charity to try and help homeless people like his friend – homeless people like me – use running as a means to work through their issues. It was an eye-opening event. The whole thing just made me think.

A few months later, I enrolled in The Running Charity's programme and started working out. I hadn't exercised since leaving university almost a year earlier, so I wasn't in the best of shape, either physically or mentally. I was depressed, quiet, introverted, I didn't really like speaking to people. I also wasn't eating especially well and was barely sleeping. So, it was tough at first but it really helped me. When I was working out, I forgot all about being homeless. That was particularly true anytime I went for a run. Throughout that whole time, I wasn't a guy with a load of problems; I was a guy trying to run the best he could for as long as he could.

Early on in the programme, I was asked by the guys at New Horizon if I fancied enrolling in a Park Run. It's a free-to-enter, five-kilometre race that takes place on Hampstead Heath and, figuring I had nothing to lose, I went along.

Well, it was awful. I really, really struggled. It was cold, I was tired and I must have walked about eighty per cent of the way because I was so unfit. Still, as soon as I finished, I knew I wanted to do it again to see if I could better my time. I sat down with James and Alex, told them how I felt and they, in turn, told me about goal-setting. They said that was the quickest and best way to improve. They told me to come to training every day, to make sure I showed up at the shelter for all of my meals so that I would be well fed, and other things like that. I took their advice on board, stuck to it and, at the next race, I improved my time by ten whole minutes. As anyone who has ever completed a race knows, that's an amazing feeling and, before I knew it, running became a huge part of my life. I ran everywhere I could, as often as I could.

It occurred to me how much goal-setting had played a part in all of this and so I wondered if I could maybe use it to improve my personal circumstances. Part of the problem was that everything had muddled together to create this one big mess that felt too overwhelming to tackle. However, if I just broke it down and took each issue on one at a time, I might be able to fix them.

I also realised that I wouldn't be able to do it all on my own. James and Alex's advice had made me a better runner than I would have been if I had just kept plugging away on my own, so I knew that if I swallowed my pride and asked for some help, I stood a much better chance of resolving all of my other issues.

The first thing I had to do was get an ID. By that point, I had been moved to another shelter where I'd met a guy with a lot of experience working with refugees, so he helped me with that. After that, I decided I needed to plan how to get a job, so, again, I set myself some small goals. Things like, 'I need to get this many CVs made up on Monday,' and 'I need to hand them out to this many places on Tuesday,' and so on. By doing that, I managed to get myself a job and, within a few months, I had enough money to rent a room of my own. All in, it took about three years from becoming homeless to starting work and getting myself somewhere of my own to live, but I could never have done that without James coming in and talking to us about the London Marathon that first Wednesday evening. Meeting him, hearing his story, falling in love with running and learning more about goal-setting completely transformed my life.

Things were going well, so much so that Alex asked me if I'd like to mentor a new batch of young people at New Horizon. I quite liked the sound of that, so I booked some time off work and got involved. As much as anything, I wanted to give them a bit of hope that they, too, could turn their lives around. I also filled in for the trainers any time that they were unable to make a session by leading the group.

Through doing that, I was asked by Alex if I wanted to come and work for the charity. It was an amazing opportunity. The job I had was just a standard 'nine to five' office job, which I didn't really like, so I leapt at the chance.

Around the same time, Alex said that the charity had a spare London Marathon place and that it was mine if I wanted it. It was around seven months away from race day and, whilst I was a little bit sceptical as to whether or not I could actually do it, I told him I'd give it a go.

I trained every chance I got and was surprised at just how much I enjoyed that part of the process. I remember one time doing a twenty-mile run without realising how far I'd gone. I looked at my phone, which was tracking my distance, and was totally stunned. That's when I really started to believe I could do it.

It was also the point at which my relationship with my mum began to improve. We had been in touch a little bit before then but hadn't properly reconciled. Things were still quite strained between us, but when I phoned her up and told her I was going to run the London Marathon, she was so proud. It was a big turning point in our relationship and really helped to bring us closer together. She even booked time off work to come and watch me run, which was really nice.

I also stayed at her house the night before the race. That was the first time we'd stayed under the same roof since I'd left home but it felt great to be there. She made me a big bowl of pasta to fill me with carbs; she got me up at six in the morning to prepare; she even helped me pin my race number to my running top. It was fantastic.

The journey to the start line was amazing. The Tube was full of runners and there was this exciting, highly charged atmosphere. Some people were talking and telling stories about why they were running the marathon. Others were quieter and more visibly nervous. I just soaked it all up.

Before I took my place in my starting wave, I met up with James and Alex who tried to lighten the mood with a bit of banter. I appreciated them trying to keep me relaxed and it was great to share that moment with two people who were so responsible for me being there. I chatted at the start to a German couple who had flown in just to take part, which was nice, and then we were off.

The first half flew by. I reached the midway point feeling fantastic and on course for a three-and-a-half-hour time. It was between mile fifteen and sixteen, however, that I got horrible cramps in my hamstrings. No matter what I did, I couldn't get rid of them and so I stopped at a medical check-point to see if somebody there could help me. They gave me a quick massage and asked me if I wanted to stop but there was no way I was going to do that. Giving up just wasn't an option, so I forced myself to keep going.

When I reached mile seventeen, that's where my mum said she was going to wait for me. She ran right through the barriers into the middle of the road to give me a hug, which, looking back, was amazing. At the time, though, I was too tired to appreciate it. Plus, just a little bit further on, I could see some showers where you could cool off, so I pushed her away and made a beeline straight for them. It was a couple of miles later that I realised that I'd just had that moment with her and I had to fight back the tears. It was quite emotional, particularly after all we had been through.

By mile twenty, I was out on my feet. My hamstrings were screaming at me and I was utterly exhausted. That's when I saw Alex, James and all of the young people from The Running Charity whom I'd been mentoring. They were all shouting and cheering my name, which was exactly the boost I needed at exactly the time I needed it. I could feel this massive surge of energy coursing through me as the adrenaline kicked in and so I blocked out the pain and kicked hard towards The Mall.

Suddenly, the finish line was there in front of me. Right then, I thought back to the marathon Expo where I'd gone to register twenty-four hours earlier. There, I'd spoken to some seasoned runners who told me that, no matter how many times they'd completed a marathon, they had always cried when they crossed the finishing line. At the time, I thought to myself, 'That'll never happen to me, I'm not that kind of person.' But, sure enough, I bawled my eyes out as I hit the mat. There's nothing that compares to that feeling of achievement. You kind of relive the entire experience in almost a split second. I thought about the amazing support I'd had the whole way round, like the woman who had seen me struggling and had offered me some of her Gummi Bears. And, of course, I thought about that hug with my mum. Nothing, not even the pain in my hamstrings, could taint that moment. I was genuinely, truly happy for the first time since I was a little kid playing with my friends in Rwanda.

It was shortly after I finished that a thought struck me. I used to sleep on the streets where I had just run. It was a real clash of memories. On the one hand, there were the old memories of being alone, cold, isolated and desperate, just trying to survive. Then, there were these new, fresh memories of running through those same streets, past some of the most important landmarks in the country and being cheered every step of the way by thousands and thousands of people. I didn't win the race but I felt totally triumphant as I made my way home. Home to my mum's house.

These days, our relationship is probably better than it has ever been. We're really close and I see her at least once a week. It's wonderful having her back in my life and I'm so grateful for that.

I have to admit, it does make me emotional sometimes when I think how far I've come. I was a happy kid, whose life was turned upside down because of unspeakable, unthinkable evil. I lost my father, my siblings, my home and, for a long time, I lost my mum. To be honest, I lost my place and my way in life. Through one chance encounter, though, I heard about the London Marathon and that was the beginning of the rest of my life. It's not that long ago I was ashamed of my pride. It had taken me to the lowest place a person can be. These days, I'm still proud but in a whole different way. I'm proud of what I've done and how I've changed my circumstances. I owe so much of that to the London Marathon. Without it, I'm not sure I would be here now. I am, though, and that's all that matters.

CHAPTER SIX

STEVE WAY

A self-proclaimed 'fat kid' in his youth, Steve Way decided to run the 2008 London Marathon in a bid to get healthy after weighing close to seventeen stone in September 2007. That proved to be his catalyst for a new life in running, which resulted in Steve representing England in the 2014 Commonwealth Games in Glasgow.

SITTING opposite Gary Lineker in a BBC studio in Glasgow, where I'm discussing my Commonwealth Games marathon debut earlier in the day, I can't help but laugh at how far I've come. Only a few years earlier, I was the heaviest I'd ever been, tipping the scales at almost seventeen stone. My diet consisted of takeaways, sugary snacks, beer and cigarettes, whilst my idea of exercise was nipping to the shops to get all of the above.

And now? I'm sitting being interviewed on national television about how much I enjoyed representing my country in one of the world's biggest international sporting events. The whole thing is just so inexplicably weird.

I discovered I had a talent for marathon running by chance and somewhat belatedly. I grew up in Poole, a large coastal town in Dorset on England's south-west coast. I wasn't a particularly sporty kid. I was actually quite clumsy and had what I guess you'd call 'weight issues'. It yo-yoed all through my teens and into my twenties. That was a problem because I was never very good with food. I've got a sweet tooth and I'm quite gluttonous so, left to my own devices, it didn't take long for me to put on weight. Equally, though, if I had something that I wanted to look good for, I could drop it quite quickly. If you were to look at my wedding photos, for example, I look pretty slim there.

On top of that, I was around sixteen or seventeen when I started smoking and drinking. I'd go down the pub with my schoolmates, all of us wearing our fancy shirts and pretending to be eighteen. I wasn't a heavy drinker. You'd never have found me in the middle of the week consuming shedloads of alcohol. Instead, I was basically in a routine where my weekend's entertainment involved going out and getting pissed. That lasted until my mid-twenties, by which time I was a little bit older and couldn't be arsed going out and getting hammered anymore. So, as well as being a binger on sweets, I was also a weekend drinker and full-time smoker. It was quite a combination.

The only thing that stopped me smoking forty cigarettes a day was having to go to work. But at the weekend? I could get through two packs a day quite easily.

As for sport, the only games I was interested in playing were video games. You know those guys who queue up outside shops at midnight for the launch of the latest PlayStation or Xbox? Yeah, that was me.

I suppose I was a bit of a slob but I got away with it all through my twenties. I never really felt particularly unhealthy, even though I obviously was. I just thought of myself as an average bloke: a bit overweight, loved his computer games, enjoyed eating fast food, smoking and getting drunk at the weekend. I think a lot of blokes in their twenties would recognise either themselves or their mates in that description.

That's not to say I was happy with the way I looked. I was no different to any other guy in that I wanted to look my best for going out on the pull. So, any time I found myself putting on weight, I always did the same thing: I cut down my calorie intake and went out for the occasional jog. It was pretty straightforward but, if I did that for a week or so, I could lose a stone pretty easily.

Running for me was never about enjoyment. It was a means to an end. Nothing more, nothing less. Even so, there were signs that there was a good runner in me just dying to get out. For example, even when I was at my unhealthiest, I could still go out and run for an hour quite comfortably. I wasn't going particularly fast but so what? An hour's an hour. A lot of people train for weeks, if not months, to get to that point.

I started to enter some races. Half-marathons and so on. I'd rock up at the start line, having done next to no training, and just go. It was about losing weight, not racing the clock. That was my motivation and that's how it was the first time I ran the London Marathon. I entered the ballot for the 2006 race and, to my surprise, I got a place.

Now, most people would do, what, sixteen to twenty weeks' worth of training? I did four. That's how seriously I took it. I remember it got to March and a thought occurred to me: 'Shit, it's a month away, I'd better do something.' I went out for a few runs but there was no real structure to it. I hadn't researched how to train for a marathon or anything.

Anyway, I turned up at the start line in Greenwich that morning – and proceeded to run it in 3:07:08. Of course, I had no idea of the significance of that at the time. I mean, sure, I knew it was good in so far as there were thousands of people behind me but I didn't know any runners and, therefore, I had no running friends to compare notes with. So, I went home and put the trainers back in the wardrobe. That was April 2006.

Over the next eighteen months, my weight ballooned to the point where I was the heaviest I'd ever been. I was also smoking the most I'd ever smoked. I guess there's no other way of describing it other than to say I relapsed. I'd gone all the way back to square one – and then kept going backwards.

It was when I saw the scales teetering on the brink of seventeen stone on the morning of 28 September 2007 that everything changed. I wasn't obese but I certainly wasn't slim either. That was the turning point. It dawned on me that I couldn't go on the way I was going. I neither looked healthy nor felt healthy. I'd had enough. I was fed up seeing my man-boobs getting bigger in the mirror every morning and I resented having to buy jeans in a bigger waist size.

Then there was my smoking. It was slowly killing me. I was having sleepless nights through coughing so much – I had developed a full-on smoker's cough – and I was becoming more and more prone to colds and other bugs. It was a combination of those two things that made me realise I needed to exercise better and more often. I couldn't just run as and when I felt a bit crap or a bit low on self-esteem. I had to commit to a healthier lifestyle.

And so I did. On 28 September 2007, I started running properly. And I haven't stopped since.

My way of taking it seriously was to enter the London Marathon again, except this time I promised to do it right and train properly. To that effect, I bought a book called *Advanced Marathon Running*. Why that particular one? Simple: I liked that it had the word 'advanced' in the title. It wasn't any old running; it was 'advanced' running.

As it happened, I couldn't have picked a better training manual if I'd tried. Some of the world's top runners swear by it and it had a six-month plan, which I followed to the letter. I don't think I missed a single run. Again, though, I didn't realise this at the time but I was able to do things that a lot of other people wouldn't have been able to. The plan, for example, built up to seventy miles a week, which is a hell of a lot, but it came quite naturally to me.

My target for that second London Marathon was to do it in under three hours. I'd managed three hours and seven without any proper training just two years earlier, so with better application, I figured I could chop seven minutes off. As the weeks went on, I was running faster and faster and getting fitter all the time.

I first realised that I might be better than I thought I was when I ran the Bath Half-Marathon in the lead-up to London. I crossed the line in seventy-two minutes alongside the leading Kenyan lady. Of the 10,000 or so people who entered that particular race, I finished thirty-seventh.

I subsequently went to London and completed it in 2:35, finishing in exactly 100th place overall. I could have done it quicker, too. I was wearing a sports watch which, as well as tracking my time and distance, also measured my heart rate. When I looked at it afterwards, it was quite clear that I was running well within myself and that, had I pushed myself, I could have got pretty close to two-and-a-half hours that day.

It was in the build-up to that particular race that I got head-hunted by Bournemouth AC, my local club. The club captain had seen me, this unattached runner that nobody had ever heard of, popping up in a few local races and he invited me to join. The week after London, I did just that.

By the time the 2008 London Marathon came around, I'd caught the running bug in a big way and, for the first time in my life, I was enjoying sport. Whereas it had previously been something that I did to take my mind off smoking, drinking and eating crap, running was now something that I did for the competitive element of it. I don't think there was ever any chance of me putting the trainers away again like I did after the marathon in 2006 but, to make sure that I didn't, joining a club seemed like a sensible thing to do. It also opened my eyes to a whole world of new challenges, like taking part in track races and cross country competitions and all these other things I had never previously heard of.

As well as getting better results out of my body, I was also putting better things in it for the first time in a long time. I cut back on beer and fast food. I also went cold turkey on cigarettes. Believe me, that was harder than any run. It still is, actually. If somebody was to tell me I could never again drink another pint of lager, I'd be okay with that but cigarettes are a whole other matter. I still class myself as a smoker, even though I no longer smoke. The closest I come is a cigar as a special treat whenever anything particularly good happens in my career. I can't say I particularly enjoy cigars but they're my way of smoking without having a cigarette. I know that if I was to have even a few draws on a ciggy today, I'd be back on them full-time tomorrow.

It's funny, though, the reason I stopped smoking is not because it will kill me but because it will make me run slower. More than anything else, I guess that alone demonstrates my commitment to running.

It's a commitment that I think some of my friends found quite hard to take seriously at first. They'd seen me run occasionally before and I think they just thought, 'Here goes Steve trying to pretend he's a runner again for a few weeks.' Even after the 2008 London Marathon and me finishing in the top 100, I think they still pretty much expected me to give up eventually but, as the years have gone on, they've come round and decided to embrace this 'new me'. That's just as well because he's not going anywhere any time soon!

The one thing that has gone is my day job. For a number of years, I worked in IT for Barclays as a Unix Infrastructure Technician. That sounds awfully fancy but the reality is that I built big servers for banks, so nothing very glamorous. I did that for about sixteen or seventeen years until I got paid off, which rather nicely coincided with my running career starting to blossom. Working forty hours a week and, at the same time, trying to squeeze in around 140 miles' worth of training just isn't feasible, so getting laid off was by no means a tragedy. Since it happened, I've been pretty much a part-time house husband, looking after my wife and I's three dogs whilst earning some bits and bobs through running-related activities. I'm very fortunate that I have an extremely understanding other half who has a very well-paid job. We have an agreement that she pays the bills and, in return, doesn't have to do anything around the house or relating to the dogs. I send her off to work in the morning with a packed lunch and have dinner waiting on the table for her coming home at night. It works pretty well. She really likes her job, whereas I hated mine. It was just about the money for me. I never particularly enjoyed what I did. But running? That's something I do like. In fact, it's something I love. It's given me so much in such a short space of time, including, of course, that chance to run for England in the 2014 Commonwealth Games in Glasgow.

I've got to be honest, it wasn't something that was on my radar. I knew that there were places up for grabs at the London Marathon that year but, whilst I was entered in the race, it wasn't with a view to running in Glasgow. Instead, I was using it as one of the last big training runs for my target race, the UK 100-Kilometre Championship, which was taking place three weeks later.

The original plan for London was for me to pace one of my good friends and club mates to his first sub two-and-a-half-hour marathon. I was going to do 2:29:50 with him, which would be well within my limits for my training for the 100km event.

However, with a week to go, I noticed some trends in my training which suggested I was actually in marathon 'personal best' shape. On top of that, I knew I had the endurance capabilities for it because I had been doing some crazy-long training runs for the 100km. Just fourteen days before the 2014 London Marathon, for example, I had done a 50-mile trail run, so that wasn't an issue.

All of this got me thinking and I ended up running a poll on my blog asking my readers whether or not I should risk the 100km race by going all out for a marathon PB. The results were unanimous: go for it and to hell with the consequences.

As a result, just seven days before the 2014 London Marathon, I decided to run it 'properly' rather than use it as a training event. It was an unorthodox approach but I was quite relaxed about it all. My attitude was one of, 'Let's just go for it and see what happens.' I quickly settled into a really fast pace, one that I knew I was capable of sustaining but which was unlike any pace I'd ever previously run in a marathon. All I kept thinking was, 'Keep this up and you're on for a new PB.' The Commonwealth Games wasn't in my thoughts.

At least not until the final few miles, when I realised I was actually going to run close to 2:17, which was the minimum qualifying time required to go to Glasgow.

As it happened, I crossed the line in just over 2:16, which made me the third fastest Brit that year behind Mo Farah and Chris Thompson. The thing was that neither of them wanted to run the marathon in Glasgow. Mo wasn't planning to take part in the Games and, for Chris, London was his first marathon and I knew he was still completely committed to the 10,000 metres at that point.

What I didn't know was that this meant I was in if I wanted to be in. The rules stated that, so long as they met the minimum qualifying time, the first Brit to cross the line in the 2014 London Marathon who wanted to race in Glasgow got a place.

It wasn't until I got home later on, when I finally sat down and read all the qualifying information and criteria, that it dawned on me that I was going to be a Commonwealth Games athlete. I re-read it, and re-read it and re-read it. It was ridiculously surreal. Neither my wife nor I could believe it. The next morning, I got the call officially offering me the slot. It was so funny. Literally twenty-four hours earlier, I'd been chasing a marathon PB. Now, here I was being invited to represent England in one of the world's most important international sporting events. For what it's worth, I didn't screw up my 100km bid either because, three weeks later, I managed to break the British record for the distance. I'm not quite sure how my body coped with it all!

Getting a medal in Glasgow was always going to be a tall order. I was going up against some of the best marathon runners in the world who had previously clocked times that I just couldn't sniff. Instead, my dream scenario was to go there, post a PB, try to finish in the top ten and pick up the British 'Vet 40' marathon record for athletes aged forty and up which had remained unbroken since 1979. Much to my amazement, all of that happened. I ran the race of my life, completing the course in 2:15:16, finishing tenth and leading my English teammates home. It was brilliant. Just brilliant – and I'd never have had that opportunity had it not been for the London Marathon.

In the summer of 2014, I hit the dizzy heights of athleticism that, even now, I still can't believe I reached. To think that I ran 26.2 miles in London that year at a rate of one mile every five minutes and nine seconds, and then three weeks later I covered sixty-two miles at a rate of one mile every six minutes and six seconds, makes my head spin from time to time. If I do nothing else in my running career, I've already got more than I could ever have hoped for from the sport. I'd be lying if I said it wasn't hugely satisfying.

I know that not everybody will be able to run the times that I've run but what I hope they can take from what I've done is realise that you're never too unhealthy to start running. I was fat, hooked on cigarettes and loved a weekend session down the pub far too much. If you'd seen me in my twenties, you'd have said there was no way I could ever run a marathon. Fact is, nothing's impossible. I know that sounds cheesy but it's the truth. If you put your mind to something and you commit to doing what it takes, there's next to nothing you can't do. And if you're looking for a place to challenge yourself, I don't think you need to look any further than London. Just go easy on the takeaways in the build-up!

CHAPTER SEVEN

DAVE HOWARD

Worcestershire man Dave Howard completed the London Marathon in 2014, just over a year after losing one of his best friends Matthew West to suicide. It was Dave's first London Marathon and he ran it in Matthew's memory, raising over £2,000 for The Samaritans.

I CAN still see it, Matt and I sitting in his front room watching the television one April morning in the early nineties. The London Marathon is on. Out of the blue, Matt turns to me and says, 'You know what? You should run that.' I used to do a bit of running at school. I ran at county level and in the National Schools Championship and so on, which he'd remembered, and so for some reason he thought the London Marathon would be a good fit for me.

'No way,' I tell him. He jokingly presses the point a little bit more but I'm adamant I'm not going to do it and, soon after, the conversation turns back to music. It inevitably did at that time in our lives.

I thought nothing more of running the marathon until the spring of 2013, shortly after Matt took his own life.

He and I had been friends most of our lives. I met him when I was about five years old, soon after my family moved from West Bromwich to Evesham in Worcestershire. We went through school together. First school, middle school, high school, the lot. We basically grew up together. However, it was when we left school that we became very close.

'Westy', as we called him, was a real character. He was one of those people who was larger than life, very popular. Everyone knew him. Everyone liked him. His biggest passion in life was music. He absolutely idolised bands like The Stone Roses, The Charlatans and all the other Manchester bands who were big around then. He had their posters on his wall, dressed like them and basically wanted to be just like them. That's what led us to form our own band. Matt sang, I played the bass, another best mate of ours, Shaun, played guitar, and we all used to mess about on the drum machine.

Those were great days. We had the time of our lives pretending to be rock stars. Don't get me wrong, it's not like it ever amounted to anything. We occasionally played in people's front rooms, village halls and spent hours in a shed we built specifically for practising. But we had a lot of fun doing it.

Matt was our frontman and he was a natural. He was heavily influenced by Ian Brown, the lead singer of The Stone Roses. He had the swagger, the attitude and the confidence to stand out front and sing our songs.

At that point in our lives, the only time we were apart was when we went to bed. All three of us even worked together. The band and our friendship became a way of life. That's how close we were. We used to see each other up until about midnight, go to bed and then, at six o'clock in the morning, we'd be back at work where the whole cycle would repeat all over again. That's how it was for a good four or five years. We did absolutely everything together. Sadly, in later years, we drifted apart. I got married and my view on life changed. As I'm sure many people will be able to relate to, Matt and I still talked occasionally as if we were still best mates but, unfortunately, years started to pass where we never made the time to simply hang out. It's ironic that we started to become close again in the last six months of his life only for me to lose him again.

It was when Matt lost his parents that he really started to change. For as long as I can remember, his mum, Elaine, had been unwell. I genuinely can't remember a time when she wasn't ill. She had kidney problems, which meant she was quite often on dialysis, and I can remember the family doing some fundraising to install a Portakabin onto the side of their house with a kidney dialysis machine in it so that she didn't have to go to the hospital every day. She sadly passed away in 2002 and, as terrible as it was, nobody was surprised when she died. To be honest, we had all been expecting it, even Matt himself. What was a shock, however, was when he also lost his father, John, two months later. He was diagnosed with lung cancer shortly before Matt's mum died; within weeks, he was buried next to her. Matt had also lost a sister who had been stillborn some years earlier and he often thought about her. It was an awful time when his parents passed and the combination of all the losses he'd gone through really knocked Matt for six.

He grew up as an only child and the three of them were really closely knit, so losing his parents really affected him in a big, big way. Fact is, I thought he was never the same after that.

He also started to have some health problems of his own, which, again, ate away at his confidence. In his teenage years, he had been such a confident, good-looking, cool guy, the sort of kid who never had any trouble with the ladies. That was in stark contrast to the final few years of his life when almost the opposite was true. He didn't like to venture out very much. He seemed to be ashamed of his appearance and I remember he was very self-conscious about his teeth in particular. He also had some issues with his eyes and it transpired that he was developing some of the same issues that had affected his mum. Some of the things she had suffered with appeared to be hereditary and had passed to Matt. That really worried him.

The long and short of it is that he was the kid that had everything but, over time, slowly lost it all and turned into a person who was the opposite of what he had been just fifteen years or so earlier.

The one good thing he had in his life was his son. Matt had various girlfriends when we were in the band. He got quite serious for a while with one of those girlfriends and they ended up having a little boy together, called Liam. He's in his twenties now and is the spitting image of his dad. It's quite uncanny, the resemblance. When you look at him, it's a lot like having a young Matt looking right back at you.

Still, as much as he loved Liam and in spite of all that he had to live for, nothing was enough to prevent Matt from taking his life at the age of thirty-eight.

He had a strange relationship with suicide, in the sense that he almost idolised it on some levels. His heroes included the likes of Jim Morrison of The Doors and Kurt Cobain, the lead singer of Nirvana, and part of his fascination with them – and respect for them – was the fact that they had both killed themselves. He would talk with admiration about how they had died at their peak and how they'd never since faded, got old or been forgotten. Matt thought that was cool.

Suicide is something that he always seemed to like the idea of but I don't think any of us who knew him thought that he had the guts to commit. He was one of those people who would occasionally say something like, 'Sod this, I'm going to kill myself,' or 'Stop the world, I'm getting off,' – a favourite Stone Roses lyric of his – but none of us took it seriously. We just thought it was Matt being Matt. That's just the way he was. A bit dramatic, a bit highly strung.

That's what made it difficult in the end because there were certain things he did in the last week of his life that you can't help but look back on and think, 'Was he trying to tell us something?' For example, he started talking a bit differently. He seemed to spend more time with the people that he cared about and reassuring them that things – whatever things they were dealing with – were going to be okay and not to worry.

He also stood up when he was out for dinner with a group of friends a few days before he took his own life and declared to everyone that this was the 'Last Supper'. Again, we thought nothing of it. We'd heard this kind of thing from him plenty of times before and, with it being around Easter time, it seemed like Matt having a laugh more than Matt trying to warn us. He was quoting various dark song lyrics which, again, didn't seem weird because music was his life. He often quoted lines from his favourite songs by his favourite bands. It didn't seem unusual at the time but now you can't but wonder if, in a roundabout way, he was asking for help. Hindsight's both wonderful and terrible in that way.

When I got word that Matt had committed suicide, I couldn't believe it. It was hard to take in. His parents had left him a very good inheritance. He had a house, money and, by all accounts, he was in a good place as far as being comfortable goes. It just didn't make sense. What could have gone so wrong?

A mate posted on Facebook that he'd found Matt hanging. That's how I found out, believe it or not – on Facebook. At first, I didn't believe it because the person who posted it has a reputation for being a bit of a joker, so my initial reaction was, 'Yeah right! Pull the other one.' But no. It was true.

So, what happened? A bunch of the guys had been down the pub. I wasn't there but Matt was and his behaviour was a bit odd. He was apparently being overly friendly to people, saying goodbye, 'See you in the next life,' and all that kind of thing. The guys who were there have since described him as being almost over-compensatory in his behaviour, as if he knew that this was going to be the last time he'd see everybody.

Anyway, some of the crowd from the pub went back to Matt's house afterwards where they had some more to drink, ate some pizza, the usual stuff. Nothing out of the ordinary. The two guys who lived with Matt went off to bed and everyone else slowly trickled away home. The last person to leave the house did so at about 2 a.m. Five hours later, just after 7 a.m. on 29 March 2013, Matt was found hanged.

He killed himself with the other two guys sleeping upstairs in the house and it was when they came down in the morning that they found him. By that point, there was nothing that they nor anybody else could do for him. He was gone.

He left a suicide note but it was a load of gobbledygook. He picked his own songs for his funeral but I'm told the rest of it didn't really make much sense.

The last time I'd seen him was two days earlier. He had some things on his mind but that wasn't unusual. Matt was the sort of guy who always had worries. He was always in the midst of a drama of some kind. Don't get me wrong, I could tell something was bothering him and, looking back, maybe I should have prised it out of him a bit more, but at the time it wasn't unusual. Put it this way, I never got the feeling that he was about to kill himself. He never gave me the impression when he said goodbye that he was saying goodbye once and for all.

When I found out he was gone, it was so hard to take in. I'm not sure why but I'd always felt a responsibility to look out for Matt. If he ever had any problems, I'd try to help him. We were more like family than friends. There's nothing I wouldn't have done for him. Sure, we had drifted apart in later years but there was still that bond between us.

I had nothing but questions after he died. Why have you done this? Why didn't you come to me? Why didn't you ask me for help? When I think of all the times that I helped Matt down the years, it almost means nothing to me because the time that he most desperately needed my help, he never came to me and I never knew he needed it. That's a horrible feeling and, believe me, it can linger.

I spent a lot of time in the days and weeks that followed Matt's death thinking about our time together and one thing that sprang to mind was the stuff he'd said in his front room years earlier about me running the London Marathon. Immediately, I knew I wanted to run it for him. In a situation where not much made sense, that did. I needed to do something. It's hard to explain but, when someone close to you takes their own life, you feel utterly helpless and useless. You feel like you haven't been able to help them and, in a sense, like you've let them down. Running the marathon was the 'something' I needed to get the peace of mind that I'd been missing since he passed.

It was in November 2013 that I put the wheels in motion. I contacted every charity I could think of that might have been able to help Matt or, likewise, that could help other people in a similar position to him in the future. Depression-related charities, suicide prevention charities and so on. However, by that point, none of the charities had any places left. It was just by pure luck that, at the end of January 2014, I got a phone call from The Samaritans to say that they'd had a person drop out and would I like to run for them? Without hesitating, I said yes.

Of course, the only issue was that it didn't leave me a particularly huge amount of time to train. I had just over two months to prepare, which is about half the recommended amount, but I did as much as I could. During my training, I'd listen to music that Matt and I had both enjoyed, including songs from our old band and his new one. Hearing him sing whilst I ran kept me going and focused on the task in hand.

Ultimately, though, my lack of preparation told on the day of the race. I had a bad marathon in terms of how well I was able to run it. I was flying when I made it to the halfway marker at Tower Bridge. My wife and a friend were waiting for me there, so getting to see them and knowing the lift I would get from that kept me moving for those first thirteen miles.

It was when I got to the Docklands area that things started to go wrong. I had to stop to go to the toilet. Unfortunately, there was a massive queue and, by the time I got to go, I had really started to cramp up. It was crazy: I'd spent so long in the queue that my bloody legs had gone! I actually had to get a massage from the St John's Ambulance people and, luckily, that got me going again – but only after 45 minutes of them working on my legs. It was bloody murder after that. It was like a totally different race. The whole stretch from the Docklands to Big Ben, I was hanging by a thread.

The thing about the London Marathon is that it's psychologically tough, but that's also part of what makes it such an incredible experience. You can't just turn up and do it. You can't bluff your way through it. You have to work seriously hard and dig deep physically and mentally if you're going to complete it. You earn the right to be called a marathon runner. That's what makes it so special.

Anyway, the whole of the section after you turn right at Big Ben all the way through to the finish was just amazing. I don't know if it was the realisation that it was almost over or if I was feeding off the energy of the crowds but all the pain that I'd been feeling for much of the previous ten miles or so started to lift and I was able to pick up my pace all the way to the finish. I crossed the line in a time of just over five hours.

I thought of Matthew virtually the whole way round. It was all for him. I'd never have run it had he not suggested it all those years earlier. I sometimes wonder what he would have made of me doing it. I expect he would have called me an idiot, to be honest! He was quite sporty and loved his football but he wasn't much of a runner.

Above all, though, I hope he'd have been proud of me, as much for the fundraising as the running. I think he'd be really touched that so many people care about him and miss him.

The fundraising itself was quite a cathartic experience. It gave me an opportunity to speak to a lot of people who knew Matt and to hear all of their favourite memories of him, all of their stories about him. That was really nice and, in the end, we managed to raise more than £2,600 in just two months. That, to me, just goes to show how popular a guy Matt was. He was a fantastic friend; genuine, talented, funny, caring, loving and loved.

He was my best mate and I miss him very much.

CHAPTER EIGHT

NELL McANDREW

As well as being one of the UK's most recognisable models and TV personalities, Leeds-born Nell McAndrew is also an accomplished amateur athlete. After signing up for the London Marathon in 2004 to raise money for charity, she discovered a talent for running that led her, in 2012, to attempt to do what fewer than 100 British women managed in the previous calendar year: running a marathon in under three hours . . .

I CAN still picture sitting in the front room of my grandma and grandad's house, watching the London Marathon on television for the first time.

It really made a lasting impression on me. Not just the race but London, too. To a young Yorkshire girl, it seemed like such a faraway place, so big, bright and busy. I remember wondering if I'd ever see it with my own eyes. Maybe my school would organise a trip there and I'd get to see it that way.

I didn't know it then but, not only would I end up living there for a while, the London Marathon would also become a massive part of my life.

It was in 2003 I signed up to run it for the first time. I had always run to keep fit but mainly just on the treadmill in the gym. As a model, you are always very conscious of your body image and do what you can to stay in shape.

Still, it wasn't until I met Jonny Kennedy that my journey to the marathon's start line really began. Jonny was a remarkable man who was born with a condition called dystrophic epidermolysis bullosa, or 'EB' for short. It's a rare disease that makes the skin extremely fragile and, in Jonny's case, meant it blistered at the slightest touch. His story was made into a TV documentary on Channel 4 as he wanted to make everyone more aware of EB and its devastating effects and, at the same time, raise more funds to support sufferers and, one day, find a cure. I met him not long before he passed away from skin cancer in 2003 and he and his family made a huge impression on me and my family.

It was around the same time that my dad, Ted, was diagnosed with non-Hodgkin lymphoma, which required him to undergo surgery to have a large tumour removed, followed by chemotherapy. It was a scary, difficult time for the whole family.

All of this made me realise that, as somebody who was in the public eye, I was in a position to help raise both money and awareness for a variety of worthy causes; causes like DEBRA – the national EB charity – and Cancer Research UK. Running the marathon seemed like a good way to do that, so I signed up in 2003 to run the following April.

The prospect made me feel both excited and nervous. It was such an unknown quantity. Anyway, a friend of mine called Ali Tingle recommended I join her running club, Thames Valley Harriers, to help prepare myself for it. At first, I wasn't sure. It was a bit daunting. Going to a proper athletics track to join in with lots of proper runners just felt too 'professional' for me. Still, I decided to give it a go. What did I have to lose?

I pulled up in the car park in my normal jogging pants and a cotton T-shirt. By comparison, everyone else was in Lycra and all the proper running kit. The sprinters were gathered on one side of the track, the middle-distance runners were in another group, and I just felt totally out of my comfort zone. Fortunately, everybody was so friendly and happy to share some of their own marathon experiences with me. I really appreciated that. They were all very encouraging. I only went to the club for a short time but I got a lot out of it.

I didn't follow a 'training plan' as such for the 2004 marathon. I just ran when I could, fitting in runs around work. In fact, the only real 'long run' I did beforehand was a race called SPEN 20, which a friend called Andrew Wiggins recommended to me. It takes place every year in Cleckheaton in West Yorkshire, and is a popular event over a twenty-mile course that is seriously hilly. The day I ran it was wet and windy and there was no crowd there to cheer you on. It was really, really tough but I told myself, 'If you can get through this, you can do the marathon no problem.' I did pretty well, finishing in 2:38

and won a medal for being in the top three Yorkshire women. Not bad for a first attempt at that distance!

That set me up nicely for my first London Marathon, which I ran in 3:22:29 – and, believe me, I was as shocked as anybody that I was able to do it that quickly. I had never been a particularly great runner. Even going back to my school days, I was more enthusiastic than talented when it came to athletics. So, managing to record that good a time on my marathon debut, with less than perfect preparation, was a very pleasant surprise. Truthfully, though, I imagine I felt no different to most other people taking part: relieved just to finish!

More important than all of that was the fact that I managed to raise over £50,000 for the charities I was supporting. That felt amazing. It's one thing finishing a marathon but handing over an amount of money like that to worthy causes really is the icing on the cake.

I had such fabulous support. The British tabloids with whom I'd worked down the years donated a sizeable chunk, which was fantastic. I also remember writing letters to Sir Richard Branson and a few other well-known people asking them to sponsor me. I remember thinking that a handwritten letter would make more of an impression and, in turn, make them more likely to respond, so I was delighted when Sir Richard replied to say that, if and when I completed the race, he would donate £100. He did, too. I will always be grateful that he responded.

I ran again the next year and completed it in 3:10:51. I didn't know it at the time but that was fast enough to qualify me for a place in the 'Championship Start' at subsequent marathons. It's not 'elite' as in 'Paula Radcliffe elite' but it's the next level down. Again, that was just incredible. I couldn't quite get my head around it at first. My first instinct when I got into that category was that I'd take my training more seriously the next time and really push myself to see how much faster I could get. However, I didn't end up running in 2006 because I was pregnant with my first child, Devon, who was born in August that year.

I did take part in 2007 but, rather than go for a really quick time, I ran with my mum, which was both brilliant and awful. Brilliant because running a marathon with your mum is a really nice thing to do; awful because she really struggled. To be honest, that was largely her own fault. She didn't take her training seriously enough. I was on her case regularly, saying, 'Mum, you really need to clock more miles,' but I don't think she ran anything longer than a half-marathon before the day of the race, which is really no preparation at all. In that respect, she did amazing just to finish! Looking back, I don't actually know how she did it. She looked grey and complained of feeling sick more or less throughout.

I remember she was feeling particularly ropey as we approached one of the water stations. I said, 'Why don't you stop and take a sip of water or an energy drink?' but she couldn't face it. She was literally too sick to drink! Eventually, my Yorkshire 'straight-talking' influence took over and I said to her, 'Why don't you just be sick so we can get on with it!' It sounds terrible but, in a way, I thought it would be good for her to get whatever it was out of her system. Looking back, I do feel a little bad about saying that to her but we laugh about it now and do you know what? She refused to give up and got all the way round. I'm really proud of her and have told her that many times since.

There was actually a really funny moment at the end of that race. Mum was feeling very stiff from her exertions and was struggling just to put one foot in front of the other. We'd arranged to meet one of my friends, who was looking after Devon whilst we ran, but, by the time we found her, my mum was adamant she couldn't walk another step. Her legs had totally seized up and she wasn't moving – so we ended up taking Devon out of his pushchair and squeezing my mum into it instead! We wheeled her about like that until we found somebody pedalling a rickshaw that we were able to put her in. We all went back to the hotel, where my friend had to peel my mum's socks off her feet because she was so exhausted! It's funny looking back on it. It made us all giggle at the time and still does to this day.

Although my mum found completing the London Marathon a seriously tough experience that cost her most of her toenails, she has always said that she is really glad that she did it. That's the kind of event the London Marathon is. It demands absolutely every ounce of strength and willpower that you have got but rewards you with a huge feeling of satisfaction.

In 2009, I ran on my own again, improving by around half a minute on my 2005 time. I got quicker still in 2011, finishing in 3:08:25. It was only after that I started to think getting under three hours might be a realistic possibility. I didn't feel like I'd trained as well as I could have in any of my previous attempts. I knew that if I could try and focus more on my running then I could potentially run faster.

I started Googling 'sub-three-hour marathons' for more information. I found lots of online discussions recommending that the combined total of your long runs should add up to 100 miles. Most people said that it was only possible to achieve a sub-three if you were doing high mileage in your training. It was around about this time that I discovered a book called *Marathon Running: From Beginner to Elite* by a man called Richard Nerurkar. It was the cover that drew me in. It looked like a proper running book. I had a flick through, saw that it had some training plans and thought to myself, 'Right, I'm going to give this a shot.'

I decided that I was going to train for a faster race time than my target time. I reasoned that I'd have a better chance of getting under three hours if, for example, I worked towards a 2:20 race plan. I knew I couldn't do the marathon at that pace but I certainly felt that I was more than capable of clocking the increased mileage on the plan, which, in turn, would improve my chances of beating my intended time.

Immediately, training appeared on my 'To Do' list every day. It was a case of, 'Get the shopping, do the washing, tidy the house, run six miles.' By treating it as part of my daily routine, it became something I just did as opposed to something I had to make time for. At the end of every week, I was able to look back at what I'd done and say to myself, 'Excellent, that's another week logged.' It really kept me motivated.

When I got to the start line on the morning of the 2012 race, I was feeling good but I wouldn't say I was overly confident. There are a lot of factors in a marathon that you have no control over. You might need the loo, you might get a stitch, you could slip and hurt yourself, somebody could accidentally trip you up – you basically need a lot of things to fall into place to get the result you want. The only thing you can control is how you prepare and, having followed my plan, I knew I had done that part as well as I could. I really felt more ready than I'd ever been for a marathon.

I got to Greenwich nice and early. I always like to be one of the first ones there so that I can prepare myself mentally, go to the loo as many times as I like and, basically, just hang around feeling nervous! The thing about the 'Championship Start' is that everybody looks super-fast. I watched them all that morning, wondering what they were doing, what they were drinking, what they were thinking. I got chatting to a lovely lady called Victoria Perry. She actually

RUNNING THE SMOKE

completed the race in 2:59 that year, which ranked her first in the women's 50–54 age group. She's a fantastic role model and somebody I really admire. Anyway, that morning she reassured me that I would be fine and not to put too much pressure on myself, which proved to be great advice.

When the race got underway, I felt fantastic from the start. Sometimes when you go for a run, you feel lethargic and, really, you just want it to be over but that day was the total opposite. I felt light and bouncy on my feet. It was amazing. That's not to say it was easy. I don't think there's such a thing as an easy marathon. I just felt better conditioned that day than I'd ever felt before.

It was around twenty-one miles in that everything started to take its toll. I was just inside the three-hour mark at that point but I could sense my pace was slowing. I remember thinking, 'This is going to be pretty close – I need to just hang on in here and not give up.' I tried to convince myself that I was just going for a short five-mile run and I focused really hard on picturing that in my mind. That really helped and, fuelled by endless cheers from the crowd, I was soon at Buckingham Palace and turning the corner up The Mall. As soon as I heard the music blaring from the finish line up ahead, I knew I was home and dry. I could see the time on the clock read two hours and fifty-three-and-a-bit minutes and, honestly, I was overcome with emotion. I remember punching the air and beaming during those last few hundred metres. I'd made it. I'd managed to achieve what I had set out to do, but even better than I had expected.

My official time was 2:54:39 and I was ecstatic, so much so that I burst into tears. I was so overcome with emotion that there was no way of holding them back. It was such a buzz. All of the training over the three or four months leading up to that day had paid off. I was so happy. I was overcome with joy, pride, happiness and relief. I felt such a huge sense of achievement – I was absolutely thrilled. I had done it!

I later found out that only eighty-eight British women managed to run a sub-three-hour marathon during the whole of 2011. I couldn't believe that when I first heard it!

I'm not finished yet, though. I'd like to run a sub 2:45 marathon before I turn fifty. That's currently seven years away, so I'd like to think it's possible.

I do sometimes wonder what I might have achieved had I taken up running at an earlier age. At the same time, though, I quite like the fact that I don't do it professionally. I'm not sure I would enjoy it so much if I did. I remember reading an interview with Yuki Kawauchi, who is widely regarded as the world's best 'fun runner'. He holds down a full-time job for the Japanese Government but has a marathon personal best of 2:08. When you consider the men's world record is less than six minutes faster than that, he could quite easily compete full-time. In the interview, though, he explained why he doesn't, saying: 'Unlike professional runners, amateur runners never retire.'

I love that. It sums up exactly how I feel. In my mind, I'm only just beginning my running journey and I truly believe that my best years are still ahead of me. As my children get older, I'll have more time to commit to it and that really excites me. I genuinely feel like I'm only going to get faster because I'll be in a position to dedicate more time to training. Don't get me wrong, I'm not trying to wish my life away or anything like that. I just like the fact that I'm going to be able to keep doing the thing I most love to do and, hopefully, get better at it as time goes on. It's good to have a positive mindset. Why not believe you can get fitter and stronger with age? Believe and you will achieve. Getting older is mostly associated with loss. In the case of running, though, I think the opposite can be true. You just have to want it enough and take care of your body.

It's no exaggeration to say that signing up for that first London Marathon changed my life, and changed it for the better. I feel most like myself when I'm running. It's a time when my appearance doesn't matter. I can look like a red, sweaty mess and nobody bats an eyelid.

I also do it for the psychological benefits as much as the physical benefits. It's so good to just get out in the fresh air, have time to think, listen to the birds and improve your health and well-being. Whereas others might prefer to sit and have a cup of tea if they've got a spare twenty minutes, I'd much rather use that time to lace up my trainers and go for a run.

I also like the fact that you have to work hard to prepare for a marathon. You can't just turn up on the day and do it. That really suits my personality. When I do something, I like to give it my all, whether it's cleaning the house or running a race.

The London Marathon really is a one-off event. It's everything I imagined it would be the first time I watched it in my grandparents' house, and so much more besides. It's a once-in-a-lifetime experience. Give it a go. Who knows, you might just surprise yourself and realise that you were destined to be a runner?

CHAPTER NINE

KANNAN GANGA

Kannan Ganga ran the London Marathon in 2015 in memory of his partner, Satori Hama, who passed away on the morning of the 2014 race. Running with his friend Tom White, Kannan completed the race in a time of 6:31:18 and, in doing so, raised over £5,000 for Bowel Cancer UK.

IT is early in the morning of Sunday, 13 April 2014. The skies over London are clear and bright as tens of thousands of people of all ages, from all walks of life and from all over the world, make their way to Blackheath for the start of the London Marathon.

By contrast, I'm in Charing Cross Hospital. It is there at 12.51 p.m. that my partner, the love of my life, the beautiful Satori Hama, has lost her long and courageous battle with bowel cancer.

It's an impossibly sad day. My heart is broken. My mind is racing. All of my emotions are rushing to the surface; a grief-infused stampede of feelings. I'm angry. I'm distraught. I'm relieved that her suffering is over. I'm bereft. I'm in shock. I'm lost. And I miss her. I miss her so much. I wonder, 'Can this really be happening?'

The fact that the London Marathon is taking place this morning isn't lost on me. The finish line is only a few miles east of Charing Cross Hospital. I stand there in the ward, desperately trying to gather and organise my thoughts, that I make a silent but solemn promise to Satori. I pledge that, next year, I will run the London Marathon in her honour.

Like many who commit to the race, I'm not a runner, nor have I ever been. This, though, feels like something I can do and must do. My resolve hardens. It will be tested many times over the coming months. Life will become difficult in ways that I could never have imagined it could and, at times, I'll struggle to see a way out of the darkness that will engulf me. However, I will do this for Satori. I will run the London Marathon for her. I can and I will. After all, she never gave up, no matter how tough things got.

It was in North London that we met in November 2012. My friend Delphine was throwing a party and she persuaded me to come along on the promise of having 200 single ladies to introduce me to! Delphine, I should add, is a dancer and artist, exceptionally talented and very sociable. For a single guy, like I was at the time, it was too good an invitation to turn down and so I went along. The odds seemed good and Delphine was right; there were indeed lots of women there. However, only one lady caught my eye. Satori.

She was just so beautiful. Like 'words-can't-describe' beautiful. I plucked up the courage to talk to her and tried my best, complimenting her name, which I later learnt means 'Enlightenment' in Japanese, but I guess my nerves must have got in the way because I was a bit awkward and she walked off!

I figured that was it and that I'd blown my chances but, the next day, I went back over to Delphine's place and, sure enough, Satori was there again. This time, I was a bit more relaxed and it went much better. As well as being beautiful, I was pleased to discover she was really down to earth and easy to talk to. Very modest and incredibly smart. She had it all.

I remember her dropping into conversation that, as well as being a dancer, which is how she knew Delphine, she also taught piano. Sensing an opportunity, I mentioned – as casually as I possibly could – how I had always wanted to learn to play and that maybe she could teach me. To my absolute and devious delight, it worked. Over the next few weeks, she gave me a series of lessons, which, of course, I paid for. There was nothing romantic to it at that stage. I mean, we both liked each other but we just took the time to get to know one another. We spoke about everything and it was during one of those chats in the early days that she told me she had cancer. She was open and honest about it right from the start.

I felt terrible for her and tried to be as much of a support as I could. Working in HR, as I did at the time, I was accustomed to hearing all kinds of deeply personal and often deeply upsetting news. So, she talked, I listened and we tried to make sense of the situation as best we could, together.

Shortly after that chat, I was due to go to Denmark but the thought of not seeing her for a few days tore away at me, so I asked her to come with me. We took separate flights and met in the airport in Copenhagen, where we kissed for the first-ever time. It was every bit as good as I'd imagined it would be. I was utterly smitten.

That whole trip was brilliant and I got to see the full extent of Satori's vivacious personality. We rode the city's equivalent of London's 'Boris Bikes' to all the main tourist attractions. She even made me dance in front of the famous Little Mermaid sculpture down by the harbour front! You know how they say that, when the right person comes along, all your inhibitions take off? That's how it was for me meeting Satori. She brought out the best in me. She brought out the *real* me.

Still, cancer was always there, always a part of our lives. It was in March 2013, during a dance class, Satori turned to me and mentioned that she had a pain just under her ribs. It wasn't something she'd experienced before so we decided to get it checked out straight away. It was then that we discovered that the cancer had spread to her liver.

When it had been originally diagnosed, a couple of years before I met her, it was in her ovaries – which they had to remove, cruelly leaving her unable to have children – and had spread to her intestine. However, she was dealing with that and she was determined she would deal with this latest news, too. I couldn't believe her strength. She was so immensely brave. Here she was, receiving terrible news, the kind that would break most people, but she was unwavering in her commitment to fight it every step of the way.

She started fortnightly chemotherapy sessions and was diligent in her treatment, watching what she ate and so on. However, as well as taking good care of herself, she also looked out for others. For example, she would have her chemo sessions on Wednesdays; the next day, she volunteered at a local school, where she taught kids to play the ukulele.

That summer, we went away together for three weeks, attending a few weddings and that sort of thing. That meant that Satori missed a chemo session. When we returned, the doctors told her that the cancer had got progressively worse. Until that point, we hadn't been that aware of just how aggressive it was. The news rocked us both.

However, it didn't stop us moving in together, in Highgate, North London, in October 2013. Whilst we couldn't just wave a magic wand and remove cancer from our lives, we also didn't have to give in to it and let it consume us either. That's something Satori was very big on. She just wanted as normal and as happy a life as possible, so we did everything we could to give her that. After her chemo sessions, for example, we'd go to a nice restaurant to take her mind off it. She was a seriously big 'foodie'. It was one of her big passions.

Christmas that year was fantastic. Truly joyous. We got a real Christmas tree, spent lots of time with our families and friends and, generally, just made the most of things. At New Year, we went ice skating at Canary Wharf for the first time and decided that was going to be our thing, our ritual that we'd do together every year. That's the way we thought. I honestly believe that at no point did Satori think she was going to die. That wasn't her way. She attacked life. She was such a strong character.

On 25 February 2014, we celebrated her thirty-sixth birthday with all her family. Her father presented her with a vintage bottle of wine from the year she was born. As it turned out, that was to be the last time she tasted alcohol. It was a great evening, though, filled with fun, laughter and, of course, karaoke. Coming from Japan, Satori and her family loved karaoke! I'm not much of a singer but, that night, I got up and performed a rendition of 'Come Fly With Me'. It was so much fun.

It wasn't long after her birthday that Satori started saying that she felt bloated. She constantly felt full and her abdomen was disproportionately bigger than the rest of her body. We didn't know it at the time but her liver was starting to fail. It was devastating and very surreal.

She subsequently developed an infection and ran frequent high temperatures. We knew things were bad, so we contacted her consultant who re-admitted her to Charing Cross Hospital. True to form, Satori made some good friends on the ward. She was the youngest patient there by some distance but she enjoyed the company of the other people and they, in turn, warmed to her.

It was a Wednesday morning when the doctors sat Satori, her father and I down and told us that the treatment they were giving her was no longer working and that there was nothing more they could do. The focus, they said, would now switch to end of life care.

The words hung in the air. For the briefest of moments, she was very upset. Suddenly, though, she composed herself. She turned to me and asked if I was okay. Clearly, I wasn't – I was crying like a baby! All I wanted was to take her pain away and make her better. I'd have given anything for that but I couldn't. There was nothing I could do. I felt completely and utterly helpless.

What happened next amazed me. When we left the room, Satori danced for all of the other ladies on the ward. She danced. She had just been told she was dying and she danced. It took me a second or two to realise that this wasn't for her benefit – it was for the benefit of the other women there. She was being brave for them. So very, very brave.

Her last weeks were spent with her loved ones by her side, listening to music and talking to her friends on Skype. Her mother arrived from Japan and they were able to see each other, whilst her best friend, Priya, flew from San Francisco to see her.

On 12 April, we were told that she had just hours to live. I couldn't believe this was it. It felt like my world was slipping away. I guess it was, in a lot of respects.

I decided that I would ask her to marry me. I actually had to propose twice as, the first time I tried, she passed out on me. The second time, though, she gave her assent. We agreed that we would meet in another lifetime. After that, we listened to all of her favourite music: Chopin, Etta James, Michael Jackson, The Ronettes and so on. It was a beautiful, peaceful evening. Even though I was emotionally drained, it was the most significant night of my life.

The following morning, on 13 April 2014, Satori passed on.

I think it is testament to how wonderful and warm a person she was that her many friends around the world celebrated her life with memorial services in San Francisco, London and Tokyo. She loved completely and was completely loved in return.

After her funeral, I went travelling for three months. It wasn't just that I needed to get away; I had a promise to fulfil. I'd told her that, one day, I would take her to India, which is where my family is originally from, so I took her ashes there. Her older sister, Naoko, accompanied me and it was very special.

When I returned, I had to set about preparing for the other promise that I'd made to her – that silent promise in the hospital ward on the morning that she passed.

The London Marathon.

I have to be honest, I turned up to the race very under-prepared. I didn't really stick to any sort of training plan or anything like that. I found it hard to focus on even the simplest task, let alone prepare for a race, such was my grief. However, I knew that I could and would complete it. It was a big challenge but precisely the kind of challenge I needed to take me forward.

I also had my friend, Tom White, for company. Tom is super-fit, one of those guys who eats these kinds of challenges for breakfast. Just having him there was a major confidence boost.

We stayed with one of Satori's best friends, Alison, and her family in Greenwich the night before the race. That was particularly nice as Alison had asked Satori and I to be the godparents to her son, Joshua. I think we were in bed by 9.30 p.m. and woke early, ready – if not exactly raring – to go. Before we knew it, we were at the start line and it was time to run.

For the first two miles or so, I was going well. I was keeping pace with everyone and feeling fine. However, soon enough, my lack of training started to take its toll.

Tom, by comparison, was doing great. He found his stride and was moving well. I knew I couldn't sustain his pace and didn't want to hold him back so I told him to push on. 'It's fine,' he insisted, 'I want to stay with you.' I was adamant, though. I wanted him to go at his own pace. He'd enjoy it more and, to be honest, I knew I would knowing that he wasn't having to run within himself for my benefit. So, off he went and I ambled along.

Things were fine for the first half of the race when you're on the south of the river. You've got so many people there cheering for you and you just kind of get swept along by good wishes.

I also had Satori's name on my vest. Because it's an unusual name and I'm of Indian origin, I guess people just assumed it was my name and I could hear them shouting 'Go on, Satori,' 'You can do this, Satori,' and so on. That was really nice.

It was in the Isle of Dogs – or 'D-*oh*-gs', as Satori pronounced it – that I hit the wall. In fact, that's not entirely accurate. I didn't just hit the wall; I properly collided with it!

I remembered that I had Satori's iPod with me, which I'd pre-loaded with some songs. 'Eye of the Tiger', the theme from *The Karate Kid* and things like that. They helped to keep me moving.

However, it was listening to it that the weirdest thing happened – Satori's voice came through the earphones. Her *actual voice*. She had recorded some voice notes and other little clips of her playing the ukulele and I just kind of stumbled upon them during the race. I can't even begin to tell you how wonderful it was to hear her. Just when I needed her the most, there she was.

As we reached the bit where you go back under Tower Bridge, I actually dropped the iPod and cracked the screen. I remember that making me laugh as I could just imagine her giving me a telling-off for that one!

Around about the Embankment, I really started to struggle. One guy must have noticed my pain because he offered to let me use him as a crutch for the rest of the way in. I politely declined, though. I was determined to get there myself, even if that meant walking across the line. I appreciated the gesture all the same. It was so kind and so genuine. Characteristic of the race, in many ways.

I finally crossed the line in just over six-and-a-half hours. The few hours after that are still all a bit of a blur. I went and met up with friends and family, had a beer and a massage, and then went home and slept. My muscles ached and I was so unbelievably tired but I achieved what I had set out to. I kept my promise to Satori. I ran the London Marathon for her.

I think it's also important to point out how generous people were in sponsoring Tom and I for the race. We raised in the region of £5,000 for Bowel Cancer UK, which was great, but it was amazing where some of the donations came from. Satori and I's story featured in the press in the run-up to the race – in places like the *London Evening Standard*, *The Independent* and so on – and it must have struck a chord with some people because we got some remarkable donations. One has stuck with me: 'Man on the Train'. It's so humbling to think that people who had never heard of Satori and I cared enough to contribute to this important cause.

It's still difficult without Satori. It's not like the London Marathon was a 'silver bullet' cure for my grief. It doesn't work like that. I miss her every single day and I've pretty much prepared myself for the fact that I may not have a family of my own. If I can't have that with Satori, then I'm not sure that I want it at all. We had such an incredible romance and, even though she's gone, it's still continuing. I still love her. She has changed me completely and forever. I have a totally different view on the world just from having met her and, now, I try to see it as best I can through her eyes.

For Satori, life was never about wealth or ego. It was about loving life, living life, enjoying the people you meet and trying to make a positive contribution to society. This is what I will carry forward with me for the rest of my days.

People ask me how I feel about our time together. 'Is it bittersweet?' Things like that. The truth is that I'm so thankful to have been given this glimpse of happiness and I'm hopeful that we will have it again.

In the case of the London Marathon, I hope she's proud of me for completing it. I'd like to think that she is but she was such a hard taskmaster that I wouldn't be surprised if she'd have told me I should have done this or that better! That's one of the many qualities I loved and miss about her.

What helped me get to the finish line was knowing that she never gave up. She fought and battled this awful disease with every ounce of her being, so what right did I have to give up on a race?

Another thing that people ask me is how I feel about cancer. They want to know if I'm angry at the disease. The truth is that I'm not. Truly, I'm not. In my mind, Satori conquered it. Despite the outcome, her spirit endures and that's something that cancer could never break nor take. She beat the disease, both in the way she lived with it and the way that she lives on even though she's gone. Truth be told, Satori saved me. I just wish I could have saved her, although I truly cherish the glimpse of happiness we had.

She's my hero and the best thing that ever happened to me. I'm a better person for having met her and it was my privilege to run the London Marathon in her memory.

It's a memory that will live forever.

CHAPTER TEN

JAMIE ANDREW

Edinburgh man Jamie Andrew lost his hands, his feet and his friend, Jamie Fisher, during a climbing accident in France in 1999. However, he defied the odds to run the London Marathon in 2002.

WHAT'S your biggest passion in life? For me, it has always been mountaineering. It's something I've loved since my teens and, at university, I met a kindred spirit in Jamie Fisher. He shared my love of the great outdoors and, together, we scaled numerous great peaks. It was in January 1999 that we set out to conquer one of the main mountains on our 'tick list' – the imperious Les Droites in the French Alps. It is there that my London Marathon story begins.

Jamie and I were very experienced climbers, so when the opportunity arose to climb Les Droites during a skiing holiday with other friends in the Mont Blanc region, we leapt at it. We told the rest of our group that we would see them in a few days and set off together for what we thought would be the adventure of a lifetime.

We were well equipped, well prepared and more than capable of getting safely up and down within a few days. What we weren't prepared for, however, was a very big, vicious and unforecasted storm that arrived in the French Alps during the second day of our climb just as we were approaching the summit. We did the sensible thing, which was to dig in, carving ourselves a tiny little icy ledge right on the crest of the mountain. It was around 4,000 metres above sea level and the immediate drop below us was around 1,000 metres. Still, we reasoned that it was the safest place to be in the event of any avalanches, so we holed up for what we thought would be one night.

One night turned into two. Two nights turned into three. In the end, we spent five nights trapped on the side of the mountain, pinned to the spot and desperately clinging to survival. It was grim but we were strong, capable mountaineers. We kept each other going, too. We didn't really dwell on morbid thoughts or anything like that. We were more preoccupied with the business of surviving and making sure each other was comfortable. We discussed possible escape strategies and, at other times, tried to keep the mood light. We tried our best to laugh at our predicament and focus on the sort of things we were going to do when we got back down the mountain. Hot baths, warm beds, huge meals, that kind of thing.

Our provisions quickly ran out. The main issue was not being able to get our stove lit because of the wind and, even though we had a packet of biscuits, we couldn't eat them because there was no liquid and so they would only make our mouths even drier than they already were. Thankfully – and this probably saved my life – we managed to get a brew going on the fourth day, which enabled us to make some tea to go with the biscuits but that was the last of what food we had. We survived on more or less nothing for five days.

Ultimately, though, there's only so much that the human body can cope with and we did, eventually, start to succumb to the effects of hypothermia and frostbite.

It was during the fifth night – the fifth and final terrible night – that Jamie lost his battle for survival. For whatever reason, he started to fade faster than me. He quickly became delirious, then unconscious and finally just stopped moving altogether. It was awful. Devastating, to be honest. I felt so helpless and, at that point, I was pretty certain that I, too, was going to die soon on this mountain. I was aware that I was in the advanced stages of hypothermia, which is the beginning of the end, really. It's a bit like drifting off to sleep. Everything becomes very dream-like and surreal. I felt like I was looking down on Jamie and from above. It was an almost 'out of body' experience. Still, I was aware of our predicament. I was severely frostbitten and my hands and feet were, quite literally, frozen solid. It seemed as though there was only one inevitable outcome. A lot goes through your mind when you find yourself on the brink of death. In the main, I felt regret that I was not going to live a full life and sadness at not getting to say goodbye to the people I was leaving behind. Equally, though, I felt a strange sense of peaceful release. I knew it was close.

Miraculously, however, I was still alive a couple of hours later as dawn broke around me and, with it, came a fresh attempt to save us by the mountain rescue team. On this occasion, they managed to pull me off the mountain in a very spectacular and daring rescue. I was remarkably conscious throughout it. I remember that the winds were too powerful for the helicopter to fly anywhere near us. All of the updraughts were throwing it about the sky. Fortunately, though, they managed to make a passing drop, whereby, in essence, one of the crew was put onto a peak just above Jamie and I where the updraughts were at their least severe. The helicopter then had to pull back for safety, leaving the guy there on the mountain. Straight away, he sprang into action. He got his ropes out and abseiled down to where we were trapped, reaching us very quickly and efficiently. It was pretty obvious that I was alive and Jamie wasn't, so he dealt with me first. He forced some hot tea from a flask down my neck, got me strapped into a rescue harness and radioed the helicopter.

Still, because of where we were positioned, the helicopter couldn't hover anywhere near us and its winch line was only forty metres long, which was nowhere near long enough to reach down to where we were. So, they added another fifty metres of rope to the line, onto which they attached a hook and made one pass right over the summit of the mountain, trailing the line beneath them. The pilot managed to guide it with such precision that my rescuer was able to reach out with his hand, catch the hook and, as it swung past, he clipped it straight onto my harness and, instantly, I was yanked off the mountain. Suddenly dangling high above the glacier floor, I looked back to the ridge to see my rescuer Julio standing in his blue uniform and hunched over the lifeless body of my best friend. It's an image that is etched permanently in my mind.

I blacked out shortly thereafter but, before I did, I can remember thinking, 'I've made it. I'm going to live.' It was just so bittersweet. Jamie was gone. As for me? Well, I was very much aware that in no way was this going to be a happy ending. On the contrary, I was going to be returning to a very different world to the one I'd left behind.

I was taken to Chamonix hospital where I was very well taken care of. The staff were just brilliant and it was wonderful to see my girlfriend, Anna, as well as some other family and friends at my bedside. Even so, it was evident that I wasn't going to get away from all of this completely scot-free. The doctors were hopeful that they could save something and so they wanted to leave as much time as possible for my body to naturally regenerate but, to do that, they needed to fight the infections that were entering my body through the dead tissue in my frozen hands and feet. Within about ten days, I became very ill with septicaemia and started to fall into septic shock. That's basically when the septicaemia reaches a stage where your major organs start shutting down and, of course, that's not survivable. At that point, the doctors had to take a very difficult decision. They had intubated me, put me on a ventilator and sedated me, so I was unconscious. It was whilst I was unconscious they had to decide whether or not to amputate both my hands and my feet – which they did.

Looking back, my journey only really began when I woke up after the hospital and I looked down the bed to see that my hands and feet were gone. Gone forever.

Several things occurred to me in that instant. For one, I recognised that this was my fate now and that my life was never going to be the same again. It was going to be a much more difficult life. However, I also had a strong sense that this could be a new beginning. I had an opportunity to acknowledge this as the lowest point in my life and, from here on, start an upwards trajectory. Compared to Jamie, I was the lucky one. I'd been given a second chance and I owed it to him to make the most of it.

Still, thoughts do cross your mind and you mourn for the future you always thought you'd have. You think, 'I'll never get to do this,' and 'I'll never get to do that.' The list goes on and on to the point that it becomes difficult to think of anything you *can* do. In the end, the only thing you can do is push those negative thoughts away and begin to reconstruct your life. Put it this way, I didn't get back into the mountains again by clinging to the hope of climbing in the mountains. I got there by accepting I might never get there again and making room in my life to rebuild.

So, that's how it went: step by step. Each day, I would set a new goal. One day, it would be to brush my teeth by myself. The next, it would be to put on a T-shirt unassisted, or drink from a glass on my own. All these small things might not seem like much but each one would absorb me for the day and, if I achieved it, it was a victory, another step down the road towards rehabilitation and independence. It was like winning back a piece of my self-esteem.

In the early stages of my recovery, time seemed to pass slowly. It was a bit like being a child again. Your childhood seems to drag out for ages because, every day, there's something new. You're learning new things, seeing new things and such like. Everything seems so large in your mind compared with being an adult where it all feels like it flashes by in an instant. To that point, I'm not sure I could have done any of it without the help and support of a lot of people: doctors, nurses, surgeons, physiotherapists and prosthetists, as well as my family, my friends and, of course, my girlfriend. I had an amazing network of support and they provided me with the patience I needed.

So, how and where does the London Marathon fit into all this? Well, things like it and climbing in the mountains again sit in my mind as the icing on the cake of my recovery, but the cake itself was the much more important business of learning to do all of the things that the vast majority of us do every day and take totally for granted. Things like getting up out of bed and washing myself. It was a detailed and important process, one of the final parts of which was learning to walk again. It was quite a long, difficult journey to, quite literally, get back on my feet. Standing for the first time and looking down on my new, prosthetic legs was an amazing experience, likewise walking for the first time on my new feet. It was a truly rewarding and, for the first time, led me to believe that I could, one day in the near future, lead a near-normal existence.

I tried to normalise my situation as much as I possibly could. For example, during the hospital visiting hours on a Tuesday, I announced to my friends that we were going to have our visits at a local pub around the corner. They'd come and collect me, we'd go and have a good time, and then I'd go back to hospital, literally legless! It was so important. Physical recovery is one thing but just as important is your emotional and psychological recovery.

Once I learned to walk, I became utterly focused on going home, which I finally got to do four months after the accident. That coincided with a major shift in direction. I was then no longer so geared towards the mundane, everyday things; I was starting to set my sights further afield. I became obsessed with setting myself new challenges which, inevitably, diverted my focus to the outdoor pursuits and activities that I had previously loved so much.

A big part of that was getting back into the hills again, starting off with Blackford Hill in Edinburgh. It's pretty much the smallest hill in Scotland but I had to start somewhere. After that, it was just a question of working my way up from there one step at a time until, about a year later, I climbed Ben Nevis. That was a major milestone for me.

It was about six months after the accident that I realised I was strong enough to begin running again. It was probably no more than a mile into my first run that I decided to make it a goal of mine to run the London Marathon.

I'd never taken part in anything like it before but, about a year after my accident, I went to watch friends compete in the Edinburgh Marathon. It was so incredibly inspiring, seeing all of these people pushing themselves and their bodies to the absolute limits. Plus, the atmosphere was out of this world. At that stage, I didn't really believe I could do it but I'm quite good at talking myself into things and so, in the autumn of 2001, just over two years after the accident, I signed up for London. I just told myself, 'Right, I'm going to do this.' I got a charity place through the Red Cross and that was that.

Because of the media coverage my story attracted, the sponsorship pledges rolled in thick and fast. Before I knew it, tens of thousands of pounds had been raised, which was fantastic. There's nothing quite like a lot of money riding on something to really galvanise your commitment!

A lot of people have asked me what it was like to train for the marathon without full use of my limbs. The truth is that, yes, it was a daunting prospect but I expect that would be the case no matter what. Getting your body ready to cover twenty-six and a bit miles as fast as you can on foot is a serious business.

From my point of view, I just tried to approach it in as logical a way as possible, starting with shorter distances and building up. The problem, if you want to call it that, was that as I built up my distances, I built up the muscles in my legs which meant that my prosthetic legs had to change regularly. Ironically, if you put on muscle, your legs can stop fitting the sockets that they're in. I also had problems in my stumps with bone growing where it shouldn't be and stuff like that. So, the training was hard going and I didn't actually get up to nearly the amount of distance that I wanted to. I only made it up to fourteen or fifteen miles and, naturally, that caused me to have some doubts. In fact, at one stage, I seriously considered pulling out. However, I had some heart-to-heart conversations with some of the guys who were advising me with my training and one of them – I can't remember who – said to me, 'I know what you're like, Jamie. On the day, you will find a way to keep going, so just go for it. Don't worry about your time or your speed. Just go out and do it.' I took that advice and, sure enough, that's how it turned out.

I think my mountaineering background really helped me. It's a sport that often calls on you to dig deep, push through the barriers of pain, fatigue and suffering and have faith that there's something better waiting at the end of it all. So, whilst I'm not a great runner, I do have an innate understanding of how to push my body to keep going.

Anna, who was by that stage my wife, accompanied me to London the night before the race, where we stayed in Islington with some friends. The following morning, I made my way to the start line where I met up with a couple of people who I planned on running with; another amputee – also called Jamie – and a long-term friend, called Geoff.

Waiting to get started, I was pretty nervous. I knew that, once I got going, I'd be fine but my biggest fear was the bone pain in my leg becoming unbearable and leaving me unable to finish.

The early stages of the race were hard at first because you kind of had to just do what the crowd did. If they walked, you walked. If they ran, you ran. For the first four miles, it was a bit like being stuck in a traffic jam on the motorway. After that, it starts to thin out and you are able to set your own pace and start to enjoy yourself. I managed to go slowly enough that Jamie, Geoff and I could chat to each other, other runners and, of course, engage with the crowds. The support really was just phenomenal. I had the wit to write my name on my vest, so people were shouting and yelling and calling out to me which was really encouraging. It was a great atmosphere.

It was as we reached Tower Bridge that I started to feel invincible, as though I could do this all day. It was an incredibly empowering feeling. It was short-lived, though. By the time we reached the Docklands area, the pain had really started to kick in and my lack of training began to show. There were spells where I had to walk for a short period of time, then run, then walk for a little longer, then run again. It was a sequence that repeated a few times but I was fine with that. I wasn't fussed about running within a particular time. I just wanted to finish, so it was just a case of keeping on trucking on.

It was when I first saw Big Ben that I started counting down the miles rather than counting them up. I knew at that point that the finishing line was within reach and that was a great feeling. That's not to say I wasn't exhausted. Of course I was. I was feeling it all over. It was complete body and mind exhaustion, so I was delighted to finally see Buckingham Palace, The Mall and the finish line after more than six hours of running.

What is it like to cross that line? Quite simply, it's euphoric. It's unlike anything else. You feel this deep and intense camaraderie with everyone around you. In that moment, you know you've become a member of a truly special, exclusive club.

By the time we went back to our friends' flat in Islington, I was hobbling around like an old-age pensioner but the feeling of pride at what I'd just accomplished was worth the physical pain. The thing about completing the London Marathon is that it's something that nobody can ever take away from you. Whatever happens in your life from that moment on, you will always have run the marathon. It's yours forever.

It would probably be a little disingenuous of me to say I thought back to being stuck on Les Droites whilst running the marathon. Fact is, I carry that with me everywhere I go. I don't really think that much about it or dwell on it a great deal anymore but it goes without saying that I ran London that day in memory of Jamie. He was one of my main motivations and I hope I did him proud.

Since London, I've run other marathons, as well as an Ironman, mountain marathons and completed all sorts of other challenges. It's been quite a journey. The way I see it, you can either rest on your laurels for the rest of your life or you can set yourself a challenge and take full advantage of the wealth of opportunities that life brings you.

It's a life I nearly lost and a life I'm so grateful to have.

CHAPTER ELEVEN

JO-ANN ELLIS

After losing their five-year-old son Jake to cancer, Cumbrian couple Jo-ann and Nick Ellis launched 'Team Jake' from within the Children's Cancer and Leukaemia Group. Their fundraising efforts included Jo-ann running the London Marathon for the first time in 2014.

MOST people probably haven't heard of rhabdomyosarcoma. My husband Nick and I just wish we hadn't. Instead, we live with its devastating consequences every day of our lives. It is a rare but particularly aggressive form of cancer which took our son Jake from us in November 2008. He was only five years old and had bravely battled this God-awful disease for most of his short life.

Jake was born on 30 September 2003, and both Nick and I were overjoyed when he came along. We had been married for a couple of years by that point and were so ready to start a family. Jake was every inch our little bundle of joy.

For the first ten months, things were great. Then, one night, we noticed a lump had appeared underneath his belly button. Immediately, I had a feeling that something was seriously wrong. Call it mother's intuition, parental instinct or whatever – I just couldn't shake this nagging doubt that my little boy was really unwell.

We took him to hospital where, after numerous tests, he had a biopsy on a tumour on 30 September 2004 – the day of his first birthday. Three days later we found out it was a rhabdomyosarcoma.

It's hard to describe what it was like receiving that news. As a mother, all you want to do is protect your child and keep them from harm. To hear that there is something hurting them and that you are absolutely powerless to stop it is one of the most heartbreaking and helpless feelings there is. And the timing of the operation, on his first birthday, was just so cruel. We should have been celebrating his special day with friends and family. Instead, we were sitting in a hospital.

I remember it hit my dad particularly hard. It took some time from Jake's symptoms first appearing to receiving the news that he had cancer, during which I think Dad had convinced himself that he would be okay. Cancer, in his experience, was something that happened to older people or people who smoked; not little babies. I don't think he could quite get his head around it at first. To be honest, none of us could.

After the initial biopsy on his tumour – where the rhabdomyosarcoma was identified – Jake took really ill. The doctors found E. coli in his blood and he spent a few days in the High Dependency Unit at Royal Manchester Children's Hospital. Things got so bad that the nurses even told us to prepare for the worst. It was just horrific.

Fortunately, he pulled through, only to go straight into successive bouts of chemotherapy. Usually, you get a break in between sessions but the doctors wanted to blast the tumour to give him the best chance possible. It was a very intense period and we probably spent around two months effectively living in the hospital. Even that was difficult, as only one parent was allowed to stay in the family accommodation provided, so there were nights when Nick slept in the back of the car in the car park. It really took its toll. I gave up my job to become Jake's full-time carer and both Nick and I lost a lot of weight through not eating properly and generally not looking after ourselves.

Jake, though, was incredible. He showed such courage. He fought and he fought and he fought. He astounded us all and we were delighted in May 2005 when we were told that he was in remission. By chance, I fell pregnant around the same time. It seemed as though the clouds above us were beginning to clear.

That Christmas, they rolled back in. I was around seven months pregnant when Jake got poorly again. It soon became clear that his tumour had returned, this time in his lung, and the whole horrible process began all over again.

Suddenly, giving birth to our second child wasn't something to look forward to – it was something that I had to fit in around Jake's chemo sessions. In fact,

I remember it got to the start of March and I was fifteen days overdue. My midwife was phoning me and saying, 'Jo, you have to come in and have your baby,' but it wasn't that straightforward. In the end, and as crazy as it sounds, I managed to find a spare forty-eight hours where I figured I had to give birth. I literally had to make room for it in my diary.

In the end, our second son, Luke, was born in the midst of a truly crazy, distressing spell for us as a family. Not only was Jake having a terrible time with his chemo – he ended up needing an urgent blood transfusion after it destroyed his white blood cells – Nick's stepfather was also admitted to hospital after falling from a roof and seriously injuring himself. Honestly, it sounds like the script from a soap opera but it was all real . . . and it was awful. How we coped, I'll never know. I guess it must have been adrenaline or something.

Again, Jake was a star. He battled his way into remission for a second time and, over the next eighteen months or so, we had some really nice times as a family. Nick and I took the boys to Disney World in Florida – although only after finding somebody willing to provide the £7,000 cost of Jake's travel insurance – as well as Alton Towers and several other places in the UK. Luke was a really early walker, too, taking his first steps at around ten or eleven months old, so he and Jake went everywhere together. They were a great little double act. Proper brothers in every sense.

It was just before Luke's second birthday, in March 2008, that we noticed Jake's heart was beating on the opposite side of his chest. We booked an urgent appointment with the doctor and our worst fears were quickly confirmed: Jake's tumour had grown back and had pushed his heart to the right-hand side of his chest. I'll never forget the doctors telling us that, at best, he probably only had another six weeks left and that the only option available was to treat him using a trial drug. We simply had to try it. We went ahead with the treatment and, incredibly, it shrunk Jake's tumour by around fifty per cent. He lived for a further nine months.

Those days were bittersweet. We knew things were critical but we still got to have some wonderful moments with him before he passed. We did all the things he wanted: went to Euro Disney, visited a farm, those sorts of things. We never told him what was happening. He didn't need to hear any of that and, besides, he kept pretty well up until his last two or three weeks. He never complained. There was only one moment towards the end when he was at home in bed and was really poorly. He pointed to the corner of the room and told me that he wanted to go over there and play. It was almost as if he knew what was happening; as if there were other children waiting for him to play with. It was devastating and beautiful all rolled into one. You know when you see your child falling off their bike and you run to catch them? It was just like that but there was nothing either Nick or I could do to stop cancer from hurting him. Put it this way: if love could have saved him, he'd have lived forever.

Losing Jake turned our lives upside down. He was only with us for a cruelly short space of time but, despite all of the sadness, it was the happiest time of my life because he was there. He was such a great little person. He loved cars – especially red ones – and enjoyed doing jigsaws and watching films. One of his favourite movies was *Jurassic Park*. It was probably too advanced for him but he was crazy about dinosaurs, so we let him watch it. He even made Nick and I buy *The Fast and the Furious* – which was *definitely* too advanced for him – because he couldn't get enough of cars. He was a real chatterbox, too. Smiley. Polite. A real gem. At times, it was as though he had been here before.

It's fair to say both Nick and I fell to pieces a little bit after he passed. It was traumatising. I can't even describe how painful it was. It was a desperately tough time and, when my sister invited us to stay with her in Michigan for a month, we gratefully accepted. We were able to play with Luke and try to come to terms with what had happened to Jake away from other people's judgement. It was just what we needed.

When we returned home, it wasn't long before reality hit us hard. The bills started to pile up and we both had to go back to work at a time when, frankly, neither of us was ready for it. It hit Nick especially hard and he suffered with a spell of depression. If it hadn't been for Luke, I don't know how we'd have got through it. He wasn't planned and we were using contraception when I fell pregnant with him, so the fact we had him is a miracle. I truly believe he was sent to save us. We've now got Poppy, too, and she's so much like Jake. They're just wonderful kids.

Not long after we lost Jake, I decided I wanted to do something in his memory, so I signed up for the Keswick to Barrow Walk, a long-standing, forty-mile charity walking event close to where we live. I had done it once before when I was at school and it was so tough that I'd vowed never to do it again. However, when Jake passed, something just sparked inside me making me want to do some things to honour him. So, after the walk, I organised a charity ball in his memory, which is still going today.

It was only after speaking to our consultant, Dr Brennan, that the idea for 'Team Jake' came about. She mentioned that she was a member of the Children's Cancer Leukaemia Group, a charity for those involved in the treatment and care of children with cancer. She told me that, if we wanted, we could name a charitable trust after Jake within the charity which would, in turn, raise money for research into cancer amongst young children. That immediately struck a chord with me and, to date, through a variety of fundraising activities, 'Team Jake' has raised over £120,000 for this great cause.

It was in 2014 that I ran the London Marathon for the first time. It was a daunting challenge in many respects but particularly because I wasn't especially fit. My weight has always been a bit up and down and, when Jake was especially ill, I turned into a bit of a comfort eater. However, I was determined to get fit, not just for Jake, but for Luke and Poppy. I figured that I owed it to them to be healthy.

Nick was really supportive, too. He's always been quite fit and so, when I signed up for the marathon, he helped me with my training. It was hard going at first. I couldn't run very far at all. However, I gradually built up my distance and, before long, I was running five miles, then ten miles, then fifteen miles. I could see myself getting thinner and fitter, which made me even more determined.

On the morning of the race, I arrived at the start line with really mixed emotions, to be honest. On the one hand, I was excited, if a little nervous, at the prospect of the race; on the other, I felt pretty emotional and thought a lot about Jake.

Anyway, off we went, and it was just fantastic. Those first few miles really flew by and I found myself really enjoying it. Around ten miles in, my stomach started to churn and I really had to dig deep. Luckily, when I got to Tower Bridge – just short of the halfway mark – I spotted my family and, after a few hugs from them, I went off on my way again with a bit more of a spring in my step. Seeing them really helped spur me on.

Between miles eighteen and nineteen, I found myself beginning to flag. The finish line felt so far away and exhaustion was really beginning to take hold of me. It was at that point that I started thinking of Jake again. I would have done anything for a hug from him right then.

After a tough few miles, I found myself closing in on the finishing line and the atmosphere really started to build. It had been great the whole way round, of course, but it was as if it just intensified over those last few miles. It got noisier and the crowds just got bigger and bigger. It was simply incredible. I've never seen or heard support like it.

Finally, I was on The Mall, running those last few hundred yards to the finish. I crossed the line with tears streaming down my cheeks and my face looking up to the sky. I truly believe Jake was looking back down and smiling. I like to think he was proud of me.

Interestingly, the same day as the London Marathon, my sister in the United States ran a marathon of her own, beating my time of 5:20 by around half an hour. The following year, in 2015, we ran the London Marathon together, which was just amazing. By the halfway mark, I was really struggling with terrible stomach pains but she kept me going. The pains lifted almost completely around seventeen miles in and I was able to run the last eight or nine miles pain-free. We crossed the finish line together hand in hand and as though we didn't have a care in the world. That's a memory I'll always treasure.

I love that I'm now able to call myself a 'marathon runner' but deep down I know that I would never have been one had we not lost Jake and so, for that reason, it's tinged with a bit of sadness. The only thing I can take any comfort from is the hope that the money we've raised through 'Team Jake' will help prevent other families going through what we've gone through. If just one child's life is saved from the London Marathon and the other fundraising events we've done, great.

As for Jake, there's not a day that goes by that I don't think of him. He was a beautiful, extraordinary little boy. He was our little boy. He is our little boy.

He's our hero and the reason I run.

CHAPTER TWELVE

JOHN FARNWORTH

Not content with just participating in the London Marathon in 2011, John Farnworth – a football freestyler, entertainer and four-time Guinness World Record holder – decided he would make it extra-challenging by doing kick-ups the entire way around the course. His goal? Complete the race without dropping the ball once.

IT started with an innocent conversation between my friend Ivar and I early in 2010. Ivar is from Iceland and is a seriously good runner, one of these guys who seems as though he's always training for his next marathon. We were talking one night about running when he said to me, 'Do you think you could manage to do kick-ups with a football for a full marathon without dropping the ball?' Me being me, I replied, 'Of course I could.' Just like that, my London Marathon challenge began.

I've been a football freestyler since my teens, although I wasn't really into football much as a young kid. It wasn't until I was about nine or ten years old, when my grandad bought me a Manchester United hat and scarf set, that I showed any interest in it.

Around the same time, my dad took me to my first United match at Old Trafford. It must have been 1994 or 1995 and I was totally blown away. It was around the time that Eric Cantona and Ryan Giggs were at their best and, from that moment on, I was a football fanatic. I was at my happiest when I was kicking a ball around. It didn't matter if I had any mates to play with. All I needed was a ball.

I started to play for my school team but, if I'm being totally honest, I wasn't an especially good player. I was average at best but that didn't bother me. I never really had any dreams to become a footballer. I didn't really enjoy the training or the tactical side of it. I wasn't fussed about winning or losing matches. I just wanted to kick a ball around. So, when I was told by one of the coaches that I wouldn't ever make it as a professional, mainly on account of the fact that I was too small, I wasn't especially bothered.

Anyway, like most young boys, my mates and I were really competitive with one another. We were always challenging each other to see who could juggle the ball in the air for the longest without it hitting the ground. We called it 'kick-ups'. Every day, it was a case of 'how many kick-ups can you do?' At first, I could only do two. Then three. Then five. Then ten. Then twenty. It just built and built and I became quite obsessive about it. Other kids liked running around and scoring goals but not me. I liked tricks.

I remember, in my early teens, getting a Ryan Giggs skills video. There was a bit on it where he kicked the ball in the air and caught it on the back of his neck. Instinctively, I wanted to master it. It's as though something just lit a fire inside me and I had to learn to do it as quickly as possible. Of course, it didn't happen straight away. It took a lot of practice but I got there in the end. That was the first real 'trick' I ever learned.

Sometime after that, Michael Owen appeared on the scene for Liverpool and England. Like me, he was quite small and skilful and, because of the success he had so early in his career, he ended up getting his own TV show called *Michael Owen's Soccer Skills*. I remember watching it and seeing loads of kids about the same age as me doing all of these mind-blowing tricks. Never mind Giggs catching a ball on the back of his neck; these kids were doing things that were ten times cooler and, technically, much more advanced. I was completely transfixed by it.

I was desperate to become as good as them, so I went out and bought a book called *Learn to Play the Brazilian Way*. As anybody who follows football knows, the Brazilians are pretty damned good at it, not to mention extremely skilful, so that book became my bible. I studied it from cover to cover and made it my goal to learn one new skill every day. I practised and practised and practised until I finally got it right before moving onto the next one.

At that time, freestyle football wasn't really a thing. These were the early days

American Dick Beardsley, left, and Inge Simonsen of Norway cross the finish line together to win the first-ever London Marathon in 1981. *Getty Images*

Lloyd Scott poses near Tower Bridge during his attempt to complete the 2002 London Marathon wearing a full deep-sea diving suit. *Getty Images*

Sir Steve Redgrave, wearing the No.1 bib, waves to the crowd during the 2001 London Marathon. *Getty Images*

Sadie Phillips and her boyfriend, Jon, ran the 2015 London Marathon after Sadie defeated cancer not once but twice.

Claude Umuhire, a survivor of the Rwandan genocide as a child, ran the 2015 London Marathon only a matter of years after sleeping rough on the streets of the capital.

Steve Way weighed close to seventeen stone before he discovered a talent for running.

Steve Way finishing the 2014 London Marathon. He was the third fastest Brit that year and, as a result, qualified for the Commonwealth Games in Glasgow later that year.

Nuneaton Library

Customer ID: ****790

Items that you have borrowed

Title: Eleanor Oliphant is compl
ID: 0142582821
Due: 27 April 2023

Title: Running the smoke
ID: 0141430610
Due: 27 April 2023

Title: The night circus
ID: 0136629468
Due: 27 April 2023

Total items: 3
Account balance: £0.00
Borrowed: 3
Overdue: 0
Hold requests: 0
Ready for collection: 0
06/04/2023 15:58

Tel: 0300 555 8171
www.warwickshire.gov.uk/libraries
Follow us on: @warkslibraries
Thank you for visiting Warwickshire Libraries

Dave Howard ran the 2014 London Marathon in memory of his best friend, Matthew West, who committed suicide a year earlier.

Kannan Ganga, right, ran the London Marathon in 2015 after his partner, Satori Hama, left, passed away on the morning of the 2014 race.

Nell McAndrew with her mum, Nancy, ahead of the 2007 London Marathon which they ran together. *Getty Images.*

Jamie Andrew ran the 2002 London Marathon, just three years after having all four limbs amputated following a climbing accident in the French Alps.

Jo-ann Ellis ran the 2014 London Marathon in memory of her son, Jake, who died from a rare form of cancer aged just five.

Jake Ellis.

Football freestyler John Farnworth completed the 2011 London Marathon whilst juggling a football the entire way. He didn't drop the ball once, kicking it an estimated 90,000 times! *piQtured*

Dale Lyons is one of a small band of runners to have completed every single London Marathon since its inception in 1981.

Guy Watt, pictured here with his daughters, ran the 2015 London Marathon just over a year after he was almost killed in a horror car crash.

Andy and Elaine Rayner with their son, Sebastian.

Liz McColgan takes the tape to win the 1996 London Marathon. *Getty Images*

Former Army major Phil Packer defied doctors' expectations when he completed the 2009 London Marathon.

Watching the 2014 London Marathon put novice runner Rob Young on the path to becoming one of the world's top ultra-marathon runners. *Chris Winter*

Look closely – Luke Jones (No.27588) ran the 2014 London Marathon . . . barefoot. *MarathonFoto*

Australian rugby union legend Michael Lynagh, left, completed the 2013 London Marathon alongside Sky Sports rugby presenter, James Gemmell. *MarathonFoto*

Claire Lomas closes in on the finish line during her London Marathon challenge in 2012. *Robin Plowman*

Dave Heeley has completed the London Marathon more than a dozen times since 2002, despite being registered blind.

Paul and Laura Elliott had a wedding day to remember when they tied the knot during the 2015 London Marathon.

Former boxer Michael Watson crosses the finish line after completing the 2003 London Marathon in 6 days, 2 hours, 27 minutes and 17 seconds.

A delighted Charlie Spedding crossing the finishing line to win the 1984 London Marathon.

Jill Tyrrell ran the 2006 London Marathon, just a matter of months after being caught up in the 7/7 terrorist attacks in London. 'I had the motivation of wanting to prove to the bombers that they didn't, couldn't and never would win,' she said.

of the internet and sites like YouTube and so on hadn't really taken off. Instead, it was just seen as something people did to practise their skills. However, that all changed when Nike ran a campaign called 'Nike Freestyle', which was fronted by the Brazilian footballer Ronaldinho. The first time I saw an advert for it on the television, it was like somebody switching on a light bulb. It was as though I was staring at my future and, in turn, it was staring right back at me. I didn't know how I'd be able to make a living from trick shots, or if that would even be possible, but I knew I wanted to at least try.

My mum and dad were supportive but probably also a little sceptical that I could make a career out of it. They were quite pragmatic and urged me to stick in at school and college to get good grades. Still, I was becoming obsessive about it and, in 2003, I attended an event in Manchester where I saw freestylers up close for the first time. It was like a shock to the system. They were so good. The stuff they were able to do just shouldn't have been possible and made me want to get even better, so I started working harder to develop my repertoire.

It was around a year later that my uncle, who's a huge football fan and was in charge of running a kids' football club at the time, asked me to come along to training one night and do some tricks for his team. It seemed like a great idea but I wanted to do it right, so I decided to mix a couple of songs together: 'Samba de Janeiro' and 'A Little Less Conversation' by Elvis Presley vs JXL, which had featured in that Nike advert. I then devised a little routine of tricks and skills to do in time to it. The kids all absolutely loved it and their parents were, I think, dumbfounded more than anything else. That's when I knew I was on to something.

At the time, I was working part-time as a pot-washer. I'd wash up all night for £20, so I thought to myself, 'Why don't I just charge £20 for my trick show instead?' I knew a few football coaches who asked me if I'd come along and do the routine for their teams and so, before I knew it, I had made a part-time job out of my hobby.

I went street-performing most days in Manchester city centre. The money I made from that paid for business cards and a website and I ended up setting up my own business as a sole trader. I then went around every school in Preston to tell them what I was doing and to see if they would be interested in having me come in and perform for their pupils. One school in particular, a place called Broughton High, was especially supportive and, when they took notice of what I was doing, other schools soon followed. I started to get quite a good flow of income.

Word soon spread and, before I knew it, I was getting invited to perform in lots of cool, overseas places, like Holland, Malaysia and Hong Kong. It was incredible. Here I was, this nineteen-year-old kid from Lancashire, and I was flying around the world to do tricks with a football. It was a dream come true.

Why is freestyling so popular? Well, for one thing, it looks cool. It's like magic but with a football rather than a deck of cards. It gives people that same 'wow factor'. On top of that, I think a lot of kids, in particular, are fed up with the old-fashioned ways of training. Coaching methods, certainly in the UK, are quite restrictive. There's a lot of emphasis placed on tactics, which is fine. However, there still needs to be an element of letting skilful players express themselves. No kid wants to spend all of their time dribbling around cones. They want to be able to learn new skills and new tricks. Quite often, these days, they have the skill coached out of them. That's true even at the top level of the game. There are a lot of professional teams who have had their edge blunted by being forced to stick religiously to tactics. I've been fortunate enough to be invited in to work with some top clubs and you can't help but watch them train and think to yourself, 'Why are they doing that? They'd never do that in a match.' You then compare them with probably the best team in the world right now: Barcelona. Again, I've done some work with them over the past few years and the way they train is brilliant. Every player has a ball at their feet and they're encouraged to get as many touches on it as they can. There's no 'stop, start, stop, start'. Their training ground is more like a playground. Their players are trained to feel comfortable kicking and dribbling a ball. That's why they all have such good composure and, in my opinion, is why they're the best team in the world. It probably also explains why most of the people who play there look so happy. They're not coached to fit a particular mould. They're coached to be the best they can be.

Anyway, my business grew and grew. Things were going great – and that's when Ivar asked me if I thought I could manage a whole marathon doing kick-ups without dropping the ball.

I loved the idea pretty much straight away. It appealed to me on two different levels. One, it was totally unique. And two, it seemed like a great challenge. I was immediately up for it. I got in touch with a charity – a fantastic organisation called Kick4Life, which uses football as a vehicle to deliver social change in Lesotho – and they got me into the 2011 London Marathon. If I recall correctly, that was probably just under a year out from the race and so, from then on, it was a case of committing to lots and lots of training.

My first session was awful. I went out into the country, where I'd planned a nice easy five-mile route around some quiet roads. About a mile in, I was knackered. My knees were killing me, the wind was blowing hard and cars were beeping at me to get out of the way. I remember thinking, 'What have I let myself in for?' I honestly wondered if it was even going to be possible. I was pretty demoralised.

At that point, I sat myself down and decided to go right back to when I first learned to freestyle. I didn't become good at it overnight. It took lots of practice and required focus, patience and dedication. So, I told myself to take things slowly. Start off doing a mile at a time and gradually build it up from there. When I broke it down like that and looked at how much time I had to master it, I felt my confidence rushing back. In no time at all, one mile turned into two; two miles turned into four; four miles turned into eight. I made really good progress.

The trick to doing kick-ups is to not kick the ball too high. You want to nudge it gently into the air. That way, you are able to maintain better control over it. Adding in a forwards motion, such as walking or running, makes it a little bit more complicated but it's essentially the same idea: gentle nudges up and forwards. It's all about having good coordination and balance. Kick, walk, kick, walk, kick, walk. After a while, you start to do it subconsciously. It's like learning to drive a car. It's tricky at first and you really have to focus but, soon, it becomes second nature.

After that initial false start, my training went really well and I managed to get up to doing around nineteen miles, so I felt quite prepared when the race finally came around. I actually spent most of the week leading up to it in London. Because what I was doing was quite unique, I got a lot of media coverage. I made several television appearances and did a number of radio and newspaper interviews. I made sure to get all of that out of the way during the week, so I could just relax on the Friday and Saturday and be properly rested in time for Sunday. In fact, on the Saturday, I did absolutely nothing. I just sat and watched Manchester United lose in the semi-final of the FA Cup to Manchester City. That part wasn't in the script for my marathon weekend!

On the morning of the race, I got up, got ready, pulled on my trainers – a pair of indoor football shoes, for feel, lined with running insoles, for cushioning – grabbed my football and headed to the start line. I got quite a few funny looks from people when I arrived there carrying a ball under my arm. I think they maybe thought I'd got the wrong day!

It's hard to describe how I felt as I got ready to start. I was definitely nervous, in part because I'd done so much press. It felt like everybody knew what I was doing, so I was quite anxious about failing or letting people down. At the same time, just looking around the start line filled me with such a massive surge of positive energy. I took a minute or two to take in all the people who were there and contemplate all the good that they were doing for their various charities. You can't help but be inspired.

I was lucky in the sense that I got to start in a smaller group towards the back of the pack, so it was a little bit quieter and meant that I didn't have anybody barging into me or knocking me off balance. If that had happened, my challenge could have been over almost before it began.

It was a few miles into the race that we hit big crowds of cheering spectators for the first time. Everyone was just like, 'Whoa, look at that guy!' All of the people lining the sides of the road and other runners were just so encouraging. It made me quite emotional, to be honest, but really spurred me on.

I kept my mind busy by talking to my brother, my mum and a couple of friends, who walked alongside me. We talked about everything and nothing. Things like the weather, what was on television and so on. We tried to keep it as relaxed as possible.

You often hear people talk about the amazing landmarks you go past and all the incredible sights you see during the London Marathon. I didn't get any sense of that. I had my head down the whole way. It's the first rule of football: keep your eyes on the ball. I reckon that if you were to take me around that route again, I genuinely wouldn't recognise it. It would be like seeing it for the first time. That's how little I was able to look up.

In terms of keeping myself fuelled, I was careful not to drink too much because, well, if you think it's difficult doing kick-ups and walking at the same time, just imagine how difficult things get when you need to answer a call of nature! I drank when I was thirsty and snacked on sweets and bananas to keep my energy levels up.

There were only a couple of times that people tried to kick the ball. Luckily, though, my brother had assumed the role of 'bodyguard' and dealt with both of them pretty quickly. The first was a guy on rollerblades who came flying straight at me but my brother just clotheslined him. He stuck out an arm and stopped him right in his tracks. Not in an aggressive way; just in a 'watch where you're going' kind of way. Then, with about half a mile to go, some drunk guy tried to swing a kick at me but, again, my brother was right on the case.

Those two incidents aside, I had absolutely amazing support virtually the whole way round. There was an incredible moment just after Tower Bridge where you make a right turn and you head out towards the Isle of Dogs parallel to people running in the opposite direction. It's a strange experience; they're almost finished and you've only made it as far as halfway. Anyway, there was a huge crowd there cheering on the people going the other way when it was almost as if they all noticed what I was doing behind them and spun around as one to cheer me on. That was unreal. I'll remember that buzz as long as I live.

There was another cool moment towards the end where we encountered a group of kids. They had seen me on TV in the run-up to the race and were waiting for me to come past. They ran up, all excited, so I told them just to follow me for a bit. I said to them, 'I'm really tired and my legs are hurting but I want to finish, so come on, talk to me about football, tell me who you support.' They were such nice kids and really helped keep me going at a time when I needed a major pick-me-up.

Finally, after twelve hours, I made it to the end. By that point, it was dark and they were packing up the finish line. Still, it was an amazing, incredible feeling. I was relieved, exhausted, delighted and a bit emotional. I'd dedicated so much of my life to it for almost a whole year that I just felt overcome with this amazing sense of accomplishment. It's what I imagine it must be like to stand on top of Everest. I sat down on the side of the road and this lovely woman came up to me with a plastic bag and said, 'Congratulations – here's your finisher's pack and medal!' That was really nice.

In terms of the total number of kick-ups, I worked out that I probably did around 90,000. More importantly, I didn't drop the ball once. It's funny because now, when kids come up to me and say, 'How many kick-ups can you do?' I can say, 'Ninety-thousand – what about you?'

It was an incredible experience. I wouldn't trade it for anything. Not even another Champions League win for United!

CHAPTER THIRTEEN

GUY WATT

Coventry man Guy Watt had run the London Marathon four times and was preparing to do it for a fifth when, in January 2014, he was involved in a car crash that nearly cost him his life. Just over twelve months later, and after battling back to health, he belatedly took his place at the start line.

I CAN remember the very first London Marathon in 1981. I watched it on television that year and made a promise to myself that, one day, I would run it. Well, never mind 'one day' – I've run it five times since then!

The most recent of those was in 2015, although it was supposed to have been 2014. I had got a place for that year's race through Phab – a charity that means a great deal to my family and I – and I was training hard, stepping up the distances of my long runs and getting excited about taking my place on the start line when, on Friday, 31 January 2014, my world was turned upside down.

It was shortly before 3.30 p.m. and I was driving home from work, looking forward to the weekend. I am a self-employed homelessness officer and so I do a lot of work with various councils and other bodies trying to re-home those in need of shelter. I had been working that day in the Huntingdonshire District Council in Cambridgeshire and was driving home to Dunchurch via Northampton, where I went to see a colleague who was going off on maternity leave. I've been driving for over twenty years and that particular journey is one I'd done countless times before. All in, from door to door, it takes around an hour.

It was raining heavily that evening and I can remember getting around five minutes from home. Then, blank. The next thing I knew, it was two weeks later and I was coming round from an induced coma in hospital.

Whilst nobody knows for sure, the belief is that my car hit water and aquaplaned, subsequently rolling over and only coming to a stop when the driver's side – by this point, facing the wrong way down the carriageway – split a tree in half. Ultimately, I believe that tree saved my life because the car didn't roll again. If it had, well, I might not be here today.

Unbeknownst to me, a long-standing friend of our family had heard the crash. He didn't see it, nor did he know I was involved. He just knew somebody had crashed nearby and so he called 999. The operator asked him how he knew it was an accident if he wasn't able to see it, but he was insistent. He told them, 'Look, if you don't come, you're going to find a body.' Little did he know, it would have been mine.

The call then went through to the Warwickshire & Northamptonshire Air Ambulance who, because of the time of year and the difficult conditions, could have said they were unable to assist and left it to attending paramedics instead. They can't compromise their own safety, after all. But they didn't. Rather, they jumped in one of their land vehicles – deciding it could reach the site of my accident quicker than the helicopter – and came rushing out. Had the call come just ten minutes later, there's a good chance they might have been finished for the day. It's funny how fate works.

When the medics found me, my pulse was so weak they couldn't get a blood pressure reading. I was also unconscious and in the back seat of the car. I should add that, mercifully, it was just me in the vehicle that night. Fortunately, I had no passengers. Anyway, my seatbelt was still engaged. Experts believe that, when the car rolled over, I slipped out of the seatbelt onto the roof and then, when it spun back over again, I was thrown into the back of it.

The damage I suffered was extensive. I broke most of the bones in my right foot; snapped my femur in half; broke my pelvis; damaged my lower back; and broke six ribs in multiple places. I also punctured both my lungs. In fact, my right lung was so badly flailed that they thought I would lose it. In addition to all of this, a piece of bone punctured my bladder, I lost six pints of blood and I had a head injury, a broken shoulder and more. I was, quite simply, clinging on to the very sinew of life.

As I was being rushed to hospital, the police went round to my house. My wife, Cathy, answered the door to see two officers standing there, one holding my car's number plate. They asked if it belonged to somebody at the address. She said, 'Yes, that's my husband's car.' They told her that I'd been involved in a serious traffic accident and that she had to go with them immediately.

When she got to the hospital, the doctors sat her down and gave her the prognosis. It wasn't good. They didn't expect me to survive the next twenty-four hours. Against their expectations, I did, although I still wasn't out of the woods. The doctors said that the next seventy-two hours would be absolutely crucial as to whether or not I'd pull through. Again, I did, and they next explained that it was highly likely that anything I had been before the accident would be gone. In other words, my brain injury was so severe that my memory would be wiped and I'd have to be re-taught even the most basic things. As for ever walking again? Forget it.

So, when they brought me out of my induced coma two weeks after the accident and I knew who my wife was, who my mum was and I was able to respond to what they were saying to me, they were both stunned and delighted.

Put bluntly, it was a miracle. I had been at the very brink of death but had, against all the odds, made it back. I guess it just wasn't my time and, for that, I have to thank all of the first responders, paramedics and medics who attended to me in those first few days. People are quick to mock the National Health Service but, if you ask me, it's one of our greatest triumphs, not to mention one of the best things about being British. Is it perfect? No. But the care it provided for me – and, equally, my family – in the aftermath of my accident most certainly was. I'm a father, a husband, a son, a brother, an uncle, a friend, all of those things, because they never gave up on me.

People often ask me if I was aware of anything whilst I was in my coma. The answer is no – with one exception. I don't know if it was a premonition, or a dream, or even me teetering on the fringes of consciousness but I had this vision of the emergency services at the scene of the accident. In it, I heard one of them say, 'Anything that's left here is dead.' I was standing there amongst them, watching all of this happen and screaming, 'Please don't leave me, please don't go, I'm not dead,' but it was as though they couldn't see me. It was like I wasn't there, invisible, floating shapeless and colourless in the air. As I screamed, one of the medics shouted, 'Hang on, we've got a pulse here.' I turned around in time to see them dragging me unconscious from the wreckage of the car. At that point, watching as they fought to keep me alive, I made a promise to fight with every ounce of my soul to pull through.

I don't honestly know when this vision occurred. I suspect it was early on. It may even have been in the immediate aftermath of the accident. It was just so clear, so vivid. It is the one thing that is etched in my brain. I don't remember any of the accident itself – but I remember that.

Another thing that contributed to my survival was, believe it or not, the car I was driving. It was a Ford Focus, probably around twelve or thirteen years old. The two pieces of glass that made up its windscreen were held together by a very thin piece of plastic. When the accident happened, that piece of plastic prevented the glass from shattering and peppering me with sharp shards that would, most likely, have shredded me to bits. At the time, I believe that technology was unique to Ford. My wife actually saw the car the week after the accident and remarked she couldn't believe that, although the screen was shattered, it was held together in one piece. It's remarkable all of the little things that add up to survival.

One day, as I lay in the hospital recovering after coming out of the coma, my wife said to me, 'I've got something to show you.' She pulled out her phone and loaded up the fundraising page I had set up for the marathon. Before the accident, I'd mainly been concentrating on my training and, as a result, had only raised about £500 for my nominated charity. However, in the two weeks I had been lying unconscious in the hospital, it had grown to over £2,000. People had heard about what happened to me and I guess they must have felt the need to do something – anything – to help. Donating to the marathon cause must have seemed like the best option.

As Cathy showed me that, she said, 'You do know you're not going to be able to run it, don't you?'

I was in the hospital, wearing a 'Beckham boot' on my right leg, and I hadn't even attempted to walk, far less run. Still, I looked at her and said, 'What do you mean? Why not?'

She said, 'Guy, look at your leg.'

I said, 'Okay. I'll do it in a wheelchair instead.'

She said, 'You won't be able to. You've broken your shoulder in two places. How are you going to be able to push yourself in a wheelchair?'

I thought about it for a second. 'All right,' I said. 'I'll just do it next year.'

Right then, that became my goal, the foundation on which I would rebuild myself, my body and my life.

I was discharged from hospital on 27 February, four weeks after the accident. Much like my survival, elements of my recovery were also miraculous. The doctors don't know how but my pelvis healed itself. No joke. They had expected to have to operate on it but, when they looked at it again some weeks after the accident, they were amazed to discover it had healed. They then looked at my bladder and discovered the hole in it had also healed. As for my lung, which they thought I might lose, it, too, was working again. It was incredible. Simply incredible.

Getting home? Well, it was a huge relief, particularly for my two daughters, Bronte and Bailey. There was a point at which they must have thought I'd never cross the front door again, so it was fantastic to get back to them. They'd put up banners and all sorts. It was really lovely.

Soon after, I got in touch with a very good friend of mine called Spencer Brown. Spencer is a strength and conditioning coach and, when he found out what had happened to me, he told Cathy, 'Whenever he needs me, I'll be here to help.'

I knew I couldn't make it to the start line of the marathon without him, so I called him up. At that point, my mobility wasn't great. I could get around the house pretty well using crutches but anything outside required a wheelchair. As far as Spencer was concerned, my goal was to regain my independence.

He told me, 'I can guarantee you two things, Guy. One, that I'll get you walking again and, two, that it's going to hurt like hell.'

I said, 'Okay, that's fine but here's a question for you: can you get me running again?'

He looked at me for a moment before saying, 'Yes, but only if you listen to what I tell you and do what I tell you to do.' That's how it started.

We both knew what we were letting ourselves in for and that there would be a lot of terrible, tough, challenging days ahead – but we were both up for it, Spencer in particular. He wasn't interested in what I couldn't do; only what I could. In addition to having poor mobility, my flexibility initially wasn't great either. I had a lot of scar tissue around my knees, not to mention a titanium rod that had been inserted in my leg from just above my knee right into the head of my femur. But Spencer wasn't fazed. He said, 'We can deal with that. It's just going to take time.'

Luckily, in the context of the 2015 London Marathon, time was something I had plenty of. On the day of the race in 2014, which I was meant to have run, I wanted to celebrate the fact I was still alive and, at the same time, do something to take my mind off the fact that I wasn't running it. By then, it was almost three months after my accident and, with help from Spencer, I was able to walk largely without the aid of crutches. So, I set myself a challenge of walking around the reservoir that I used to run round during my training. It's just under five miles from start to finish and, to my delight, I managed it. That in itself told me that, with the right application and plenty of hard work, I could get myself into a position to be able to run the marathon in 2015.

My charity, meanwhile, had said to me that they would defer my place until the following year if I felt up to it. That gave me a dream to work towards.

The weeks and months that followed were very difficult at times but I persevered. I dug deep, trained hard and listened to Spencer. Consequently, on Sunday, 26 April 2015, I took my place at the start line of the London Marathon along with almost 38,000 other runners.

Standing there was the beginning of one really long road but, equally, the end of another, so I didn't feel particularly nervous. More than anything, I was excited to finally get to achieve something that had been almost two years in the making.

Before we got going, I just took a few quiet moments to compose myself and take it all in. It was huge just to be there and, as soon as I started running, a flood of emotion hit me. It was difficult to keep my feelings in check for those first few miles. I actually had to tell myself, 'Guy, if you don't gather yourself, you're not going to be able to do this.' I knew I was wasting valuable energy and for no good reason. There was no pressure on me. I had succeeded just by getting to the start line and I wasn't aiming for a particular time. I was there just to celebrate being alive and to show my appreciation for all the people who had looked after me. The only thing I needed to do was relax, enjoy it and soak up the atmosphere.

And what an atmosphere it was! It didn't seem to matter whether you were fast or slow, the crowds cheered everybody the same. For a normal man like me, I truly believe it's the greatest feeling you can have participating in a sport.

It's when you look around and there's just this sea of people flanking you, people who you've never seen before and who you'll probably never see again, and they're willing you on, telling you, 'Come on, mate, you can do this, you're nearly there.' That's a very powerful, gratifying thing.

I thought back to what my doctors said when I told them, before I was discharged, of my plans to run the marathon the following year. Whilst they were supportive, they also said to me, 'What are you doing it for? You've got nothing to prove.' To a point, they were right. Against the odds, I was alive. However, it's one thing to be alive – it's something very different to live. And what's the point of being alive if you don't live? That was what motivated me.

It was shortly after crossing Tower Bridge, around halfway, that I had my 'marathon moment', if you like. I knew my family were going to be waiting there and when I saw them – wow! It was overwhelming. Just thinking about it actually brings a lump to my throat.

I had been starting to hurt a little by that point and, when I didn't see them at first, I thought I'd missed them. Immediately, my mind started to play tricks on me. *What if they're not here? What if nobody has come to cheer you on? What if it's just you on your own? What are you doing this for anyway? Why are you still running? Stop!*

That's when I saw them: my wife, my daughters, my mum, my dad, all my brothers and their partners. They were all there for me, cheering, smiling and waving. It was just wonderful. I couldn't help but burst into tears. It was one of the most special moments of my life. To think that, just over a year earlier, they had all been gathered around my hospital bed, hoping against hope that I might wake up, to now, having them all waiting to greet me as I tackled the London Marathon, it was incredible. There's no other word for it.

I cried again when I finished. The race had meant so much to me in the context of my accident and my recovery that, when I saw the finish line, I just broke down. It felt like the line of a circle joining up with itself.

There is one more little story I'd like to share that, in my opinion, sums up the beauty of the marathon. It involves a charge nurse from University Hospitals Coventry and Warwickshire, where I was treated. His name is Bert and he's a wonderful man. On the day I left hospital, he said to me, 'Do you remember your promise?'

I said, 'Sorry? What promise?'

He said, 'You promised me a couple of weeks ago that you were going to get well enough to run the London Marathon next year.'

'Oh yeah,' I replied. 'Don't you worry about that, I'll definitely do it.'

He smiled at me and said, 'Good. A promise is a promise after all.'

Fast-forward to the day of the race. The BBC had heard about my story in the build-up and so, when I was on Tower Bridge, I was interviewed live on TV by Denise Lewis, a former Olympic gold-medal-winning heptathlete who has been a mainstay of the marathon coverage for some years. Just as the interview was wrapping up, I said, 'Can I just pass on a message to a friend of mine called Bert? I just want to let him know that I'm here, I've fulfilled my promise and I'm running.'

I had no idea but, at the time, he was working a shift in the hospital's Critical Care Unit. One of his colleagues, who had seen the interview, went to find him and said, 'Do you remember somebody called Guy who was in here last year?'

He said, 'Yes, I do.' He later told me that, as soon as they asked him, he knew I was running the marathon and that I'd mentioned his name. When he told me about it, he said, 'You don't know this but I wasn't feeling especially great that day. However, to hear that you had taken the time to mention my name really lifted my spirits so very, very high.'

That's the power of the London Marathon for you. It unifies, it inspires, it lifts and it gives.

It means the world to me.

CHAPTER FOURTEEN

ANDY RAYNER

On 22 November 2014, Andy and Elaine Rayner's first child, Sebastian, was born almost four months prematurely. Keen runner Andy subsequently ran the London Marathon the following April to raise money for King's College Hospital in London, who cared for the couple's little boy in the first few months of his life.

RUNNING has been a part of my life for almost as long as I can remember. I joined Blackheath & Bromley Harriers Athletics Club in south London when I was eleven, competed regularly in events, and reached sub-international level whilst on a running scholarship in the USA. These days, I work in the running industry in retail.

It was through the 'Harriers' that I met my wife, Elaine. She joined from another local club and we were properly introduced on the night of her twenty-first birthday party in 2007. She'd invited a friend of mine, who asked if I could come along too. She said yes and we hit it off more or less straight away. Not long afterwards, she started working for the London Marathon and, in 2012, I ran the race for the first time, just a few months after I turned thirty. I'd taken part in the London Mini Marathon as a kid and used to compete against people like Mo Farah and Scott Overall in my age group, so I suppose you could say it was inevitable I'd run the main race one day.

That actually proved to be quite a significant year as, in addition to turning thirty and running London, I proposed to Elaine whilst we were on holiday in Morocco. We married almost a year later in November 2013 in Kent.

We pretty much decided to do everything all at once: get married, buy a house and start a family. We just didn't expect all three to happen in the same year. We moved house in the January of 2014 and, by November, our first child was born. The only thing was that he wasn't due to arrive until March.

We'd always planned on having a couple of kids and so we were absolutely delighted when Elaine fell pregnant in the summer of 2014. It was the July when we found out and, as you'd expect, we were absolutely thrilled. I remember having what I'm sure are all the standard reactions to the news that you're going to be a dad: excitement, panic, jubilation, the works.

Everything went really well at first. It was a textbook early pregnancy. Elaine had ultrasound scans at twelve weeks and twenty weeks as standard and everything appeared to be going great. We also found out at twenty weeks that we were having a boy, which was no great surprise as boys run in our family.

It was at twenty-four weeks into the pregnancy that things changed suddenly and drastically. I remember it as clearly as if it were yesterday. It was the morning of Thursday, 20 November. I woke up as normal and was getting ready to go to work when Elaine said she had a sore stomach. I told her to take it easy, keep an eye on it and let me know if it got worse. With that I went off to work. It was later in the day, sometime in the afternoon, that I got a phone call from her saying she was sure something was wrong. The pain had got worse, her stomach was tense and she was feeling really sick.

After I tried to reassure her, she phoned her brother and described what she was feeling. Her sister-in-law was listening in the background and said that it sounded as though she was having contractions. Elaine's first reaction was, 'No way, that can't be possible.' She called me back after speaking to them and was quite upset by this point but in my head it just wasn't possible she was going into labour. I just never considered it. Anyway, I rushed home and, together, we made a dash up to the hospital where we were seen pretty quickly. To cut a long story short, the doctors did all of their examinations and came to the conclusion that she probably had an infection. They gave her some antibiotics and sent us home. Whilst the antibiotics helped with the pain, they also made Elaine really unwell. She was up most of that night being sick but, again, we didn't think much of it. We figured it was just the drugs flushing the infection out of her.

Things eventually settled down and we managed to get some sleep. I took the Friday morning off work to make sure everything was okay and, when she woke up, Elaine felt a lot better, although she was still being quite sick. About 11 a.m., with things improving, I went into work but told her to phone me if anything changed. I also called my parents to explain what had happened and to ask my mum to pop in during the afternoon to make sure everything was okay.

It got to tea-time and I called my mum who assured me everything had seemed fine when she saw her. Elaine had still been in a little discomfort but nothing major. It was almost immediately after I ended the call with her that Elaine phoned me in a lot of distress. By this point, things had taken a turn for the worse again and she was convinced she was in labour. That's the first time I felt properly scared. I told her to stay there and that I'd send both my parents and her parents round to the house. Whoever got there first was to take her straight to the hospital, where I would meet them.

After an interminably long train journey, I eventually arrived at the hospital. Both my parents and Elaine's parents were there and directed me to the room where she was being treated. Before I even got to it, I could hear her screaming. It was clear she was in a bad way. She was being constantly sick and they were struggling to get IV lines into her. All of her veins were collapsing on account of how dehydrated she was as a result of not being able to take on any fluids.

As was the case the previous night, a couple of doctors checked her over and, again, they were adamant she wasn't in labour. However, I just couldn't see how that was possible. By this point, she was having what seemed like quite obvious contractions, so I told them I wanted a second opinion. Another doctor soon arrived and, thankfully, they quickly realised that, yes, she was indeed in labour. I say 'thankfully'. Truth is we were absolutely terrified.

The doctors took us to one side and explained that they were going to give Elaine a drug that would stop things in their tracks, which wasn't entirely true. It actually only delayed it long enough to give them time to arrange for us to be moved to a specialist unit. The hospital we were at could only take babies after thirty-five weeks, so we needed to be taken to King's College Hospital instead.

It was around midday on the Saturday that we were transferred and, by that point, the drugs the doctors had given to Elaine had taken effect. She had stopped having contractions and her sickness had more or less completely gone. As far as we knew, she was no longer in labour.

However, our relief was short-lived. When we got to King's College Hospital, the doctor immediately took Elaine off her medication. I asked why and was told that this particular medication could only be taken for a maximum of forty-eight hours. I said, 'Oh right, so what happens now?' but the realisation started to dawn on me almost before I'd finished asking the question.

The doctor said that, when somebody goes into labour, you can only delay it; you can't stop it. When the baby decides it's coming, it's coming and that's that. I said, 'So, you're telling me that we're having the baby?' She said, 'Yes, and you'll be having it today.'

It was a surreal moment. Everything seemed to stop. The doctor asked me if I knew what this meant. 'Your baby is going to be very sick when it comes out,' she said. I felt this wave of pragmatism wash over me and I said to her, 'Okay, so are we talking about a life and death situation here?' She replied, 'Yes. At twenty-four weeks, there's a fifty per cent chance the baby will live. And, if it does, there's a much higher chance it will have real long-term problems.' Well, that was almost impossible to take in.

They took Elaine off the medication and, not long after, the contractions started again. I remember us being taken into the ward where she was going to give birth. It was a small room but was packed with people. There were two or three doctors and about eight nurses. Your first instinct when you see that is, 'Oh my God, they must be expecting something bad to happen.' As it turned out, a lot of them weren't there for any reason other than to observe. It's very rare for a baby to be born at twenty-four weeks so they came in to see how the doctors handled the situation.

Standing there in the room, I felt completely useless. Elaine was in a lot of pain and was really worried about what was going on. I was trying my best to put a brave face on it but it wasn't easy. I was every bit as scared.

Before we knew it, the baby was coming and, as if things weren't already complicated enough, he ended up being breech, which meant he came out feet first. I can still remember seeing him for the first time. He was so tiny. A little purple creature. He weighed only 724 grams, or one pound and nine ounces. He would easily have fitted in the palm of your hand but there was nothing abnormal-looking about him. As far as I could tell, he appeared to be perfectly formed. However, his skin was very shiny and almost see-through, a bit like a little baby bird.

I know this is going to sound terrible but, at first, I didn't feel any great emotion towards him. Don't get me wrong, he's absolutely the best thing that's ever happened to me but there wasn't that immediate overwhelming sense of gushing pride like you hear other parents describe. Instead, my immediate concern was for Elaine. I just wanted to know she was okay. She was my top priority.

As soon as he came out, the baby was taken to an adjacent table in the room where the medical staff set about keeping him alive. They had to get a ventilation tube down his throat and various lines into him. They also covered him in what looked like a plastic sandwich bag to keep him warm. Elaine was asking me, 'Is he okay? Is he definitely okay?' and I was saying, 'Yeah, he's fine,' although I didn't really know whether he was or not.

After they put him into an incubator, they paused for a moment and asked us if we wanted to take a photo. We weren't allowed to hold him but there was time for a quick picture if we wanted. Truth be told, I didn't really want to but I decided I had to. Something told me that it was important that I had something of him just in case anything bad happened.

He was then taken to intensive care. The nurses asked that I follow them so that at least one of us knew where he was. That wasn't easy as it meant leaving Elaine. She had just given birth but, unlike other new mums who get to hold their baby, hers had been whisked away from her, so she was understandably upset. It really didn't feel right leaving her like that, no matter how briefly, but it had to be done.

It was only when I returned to Elaine's bedside a few minutes later that the emotions poured out. There was shock, fear, panic, heartache, worry – a bit of everything really.

That was the beginning of what would prove to be a long stay in hospital. We were taken aside and told that most babies that arrived as prematurely as ours would get out by their due date if they were lucky. Our due date was 11 March 2015; he was born on 22 November 2014 – almost four months early. Consequently, we always had in the back of our minds that we'd be in hospital for at least that long. We were also under no illusions that there were going to be a lot of bumps in the road over the coming weeks and months. We knew it would most likely be a case of two steps forward and one step back. It was never going to be a smooth run, with the very real possibility that he might not actually pull through.

Again, that's so tough to come to terms with. You try to tell yourself that it'll all be fine and that the worst won't happen but the intensive care unit soon shakes you back to the reality of your situation. You see babies that don't make it and that's so incredibly and desperately hard. Believe me, there is nothing worse than hearing the alarms going off in the ICU. Its machines all have a particular sound. Even to this day, I can hear the noise of them and it haunts me. You know immediately what it means and it's just – well, it's heartbreaking.

In any case, time moved on. Each day, our little boy had to have X-rays on his chest so the doctors could monitor his lungs, which had been in quite a bad way and made it difficult for him to breathe independently. He also had a brain scan once a week where they checked for any blood vessels bursting. That, I'm told, was a real possibility because they were so under-developed and burst blood vessels in the brain is one of the main causes of cerebral palsy amongst premature babies. There were a lot of things that could have happened to him. It's a miracle that he came through relatively scot-free. He had kidney failure, pulmonary bleeding and a hole in his heart – all sorts of issues – but nothing that will pose him any real long-term problems.

The weeks that followed his birth were difficult but there were some really nice moments, too. One of those was the day we named him. We didn't do that straight away because we hadn't settled on anything by that point. We hadn't expected to need to choose a name so quickly, so, for a few days, the medical team referred to him only as 'Baby Rayner'. However, that didn't feel right to us, not least because the other babies in the ICU all had names. We wanted him to have an identity and so, a couple of days after he was born, we decided to call him Sebastian.

Telling that to the staff at the hospital was a really proud moment, as it had been a name I'd always really liked. It was very special seeing them changing all his charts from 'Baby Rayner' to 'Sebastian'. It was right then that the emotional 'father and son' bond that hadn't been there right at the moment he was born hit me for the first time. I remember seeing him lying there, 'Sebastian' written on the chart above him, and him fighting away, desperately trying to survive. I thought to myself, 'That's my little boy.' I was fit to burst with pride and love for him from then on.

It's funny, some of our friends actually thought that we'd named him after Sebastian Coe because of my passion for running, so I want to take this opportunity to categorically state that we didn't! We honestly just liked the name. We do, however, have a cat called Bannister, after Sir Roger . . .

Another nice moment came shortly before Christmas when we were allowed to hold him for the first time. It was 19 December and he was just under a month old, so of course he was still very small, very fragile and hooked up to a lot of wires. Because of that, only one of us was allowed to hold him initially. I was adamant that should be Elaine. She had missed out on that when he was born, so I wanted her to have it then. It was an incredibly precious moment. God knows how many pictures I took. A few weeks later, I got the opportunity to hold him for the first time, too. Words can't do justice to how special that was.

Tuesday, 31 March 2015 was a fabulous day as we were finally allowed to take Sebastian home. We were so fortunate that the people who looked after him in those first few moments, hours, days, weeks and months of his life were just fantastic. I can't speak highly enough of all of the doctors and nurses who were there for us, particularly at King's College Hospital. They were so good, so caring and so supportive.

It was during our time in hospital that I found out the cost to the NHS of looking after a baby in intensive care is £1,500 per day. That's £10,500 per baby per week. That really resonated with me. It just brought it home how fortunate we are to have an institution like the NHS, with such amazing people working in it. Immediately, I felt the urge to raise some money for them to give something back and running the London Marathon just seemed like the perfect fit.

The idea came to me around Christmas 2014, which I figured would give me plenty of time to train. That, though, was wishful thinking. Being at the hospital took up so much time and emotional energy that, when I did get a spare few hours to go out and clock some miles, I was too exhausted. Still, I tried to make the most of the situation. For example, my work was about four miles from the hospital, so, two or three times a week, I'd finish my shift, put on my trainers and run there. Don't get me wrong, it wasn't nearly enough preparation but it was better than nothing. Throw in a little 'panic training' in the final few weeks and I figured I could complete it.

Problem was, just completing the marathon wasn't enough for me. I was determined to do it in under three hours. Not so much for me; more so for everybody who had sponsored me and, in particular, for Elaine and Seb. It's hard to describe but I almost felt as though I wanted to prove something. I don't know what – personal pride maybe – but I figured I could go a long way towards accomplishing it with a sub-three hours time.

I wasn't in sub-three hours shape, however. I was nowhere near it, if I'm being honest, so it's an absolute miracle I managed it with a few minutes to spare. I think it was just sheer stubbornness that got me round.

I was also fortunate that I had a couple of friends running with me, one of whom, Alex, would have reasonably expected to finish in around two hours forty under normal circumstances. However, because his training hadn't gone very well, he sacrificed his own race to help me break the three-hour mark. He ran with me every step of the way, which helped enormously.

Running under three hours means a mile every six minutes and fifty-two seconds, so I became almost religiously obsessed with sticking to it. I had my GPS watch on my wrist and that became my focus. So, when the calf cramps that unexpectedly appeared about five kilometres in cleared up, I decided to try and put some time in the bank for the second half of the race, expecting it to be quite tough. We improved our speed down to a mile every six minutes and twenty or thirty seconds.

Around nine or ten miles in, my knees started to hurt. It was exactly the same pain I'd experienced on one of the few long training runs I did, during which I was forced to stop and walk, so, I was a little worried that, having got over the cramps in my calves and having built up some good surplus time, I was going to have my race knackered by knee pain. I tried to block it out and just gritted my teeth, dug deep and pushed on as hard as I could.

It was around the eighteen-mile mark that I hit a short sharp hill – a new part of the course introduced that year to accommodate some building work – and, as I reached its crest, I remember thinking, 'There's no way I'm breaking three hours here.' I was in a world of trouble. Luckily, there were loads and loads of spectators right at that point. They must have been three or four rows deep on both sides of the road, all banging together their inflatable 'clappers', blowing whistles, shouting and cheering and willing us on. That kept me moving in spite of myself.

It was at mile twenty-two that I felt the wheels really beginning to come off.

I looked at Alex and gasped, 'Are we still under three hours?' I had no concept of what time we were on and lifting my wrist to look at my watch felt like too much effort. He said, 'Yeah, but we can't afford to lose any more time.' That was the kick up the backside I needed and, with him shepherding me along for those last few miles, we finally arrived at the foot of The Mall staring down the final couple of hundred metres.

Coming up it, I remembered that Elaine had told me she'd managed to get tickets through her work to stand in the VIP section at the front of the grandstand on the left-hand side. I knew she was going to be there with Sebastian, so I made a beeline to the left – you're meant to go right – where I found them both. I stopped quickly to give them a kiss and a cuddle before running the final twenty metres to the finish line. I had actually been planning to take Sebastian from Elaine and carry him over the finish line but, when I saw them there, I said to her, 'I'm in no fit state to take him!' I was scared I'd drop him because I was so exhausted!

Crossing the line was more a feeling of relief than anything else. I had finished in less than three hours as planned and, in my mind, had managed to justify all of the support people had given me. I raised just over £14,000 – or, to put it another way, a week and a half's care for a baby in ICU.

These days, Sebastian's doing great. He's a real bundle of energy. As I write this, he's almost walking and I expect he'll be running around before Elaine or I know it. He's up to a good weight, eating solid foods and his first words aren't all that far away. It's just wonderful to see him developing after everything he has been through.

I'd love to think that one day we'll run the London Marathon together. Because he was born prematurely, he will likely always have chronic lung disease and I remember people in the hospital telling us that, while his lungs would improve as he got older, he'd 'never run a marathon'. I'd hear them say that and think, 'He bloody well will, just you wait and see, he'll prove you wrong.' I feel like I can almost guarantee he will run a marathon one day – and I would absolutely love to be there with him when he does.

CHAPTER FIFTEEN

DALE LYONS

The irrepressible Dale Lyons is part of an exclusive group of runners who have completed every single edition of the London Marathon. The retired master chef and university lecturer has, in fact, completed close to 100 marathons and, as he closes in on his eighties, he's still going strong . . .

OVER one million people have taken part in the London Marathon since it launched in 1981. Only twelve, however, have run it each and every year.

It's not something I ever aspired to. Truth be told, I'd only ever intended to run one marathon, which is something that I'm sure many other runners will be able to relate to. I actually only took up running in my forties and, even then, it was just a means to an end. I wanted to get fit enough to play squash and running seemed like the best way to do that. At that time, in the late 1970s, I had just moved to Solihull and so my running was restricted to pounding the streets of the town. I found that very boring, though, so I decided to join a club: the Centurion Joggers.

I turned up that first night and was told we'd just do an 'easy five miles' to break me in gently. I remember thinking, 'Five miles? The furthest I've ever done is two!' They pointed me towards the group I'd be running with. They looked like a bunch of geriatrics and I figured they'd never be able to keep up with me. As it turned out, it was the other way around – they left me standing!

Anyway, I enjoyed it and continued going to the club. In 1980, the man in charge of it, John Walker, organised the first People's Marathon in Chelmsley Wood, Birmingham. It was the first real mass participation event of its kind in the UK, with over 5,000 people taking part, so I decided to sign up. It would, I figured, be my one and only marathon. Of course, what did I know! It was tough but I enjoyed it, particularly the feeling of accomplishment at the end. It was a real buzz and, despite hitting 'the wall' with just over a mile to go, I still managed to finish in 2:58.

Some months later, I was out for a run with some of my friends from the club and our conversation turned to this new marathon we'd heard about in London.

'Are you going to enter it?' one of them asked.

'I might,' I answered.

'Yeah, me too,' said my friend, Geoff. 'Tell you what, I'll do it if you do it.'

That was it. That's how we decided to take part in the first London Marathon.

Now, back in 1980, there was no internet or anything like that, so the only way you could enter was to turn up at the Post Office when entries opened to try and get a place through the ballot. Chris Brasher, the brains behind the race, had done such a good job of publicising the event that a lot of people wanted the very few spaces that were available, so you had to be quick to the Post Office to give yourself the best chance – and by 'quick' I mean queuing up outside Birmingham's Mail Box at midnight like my friends and I did! Luckily, our efforts were rewarded and we got in.

The morning of the race dawned and it was a wicked day weather-wise. It was cold, wet, windy and generally unpleasant. In any case, we gathered at the start line where Chris himself gave us a small pep talk before sending us on our way. He told us we were the lucky ones. They had received more applications to take part than they could ever have anticipated and he promised us that it would be the first of many London Marathons.

With that, off we went. I had become quite a decent runner by that point and so I had set myself the target of going round in under three-and-a-half hours. I'd prepared well and had stocked up on glucose tablets. They really made a difference in terms of keeping my energy up. Funny story about that, actually. At the Tower of London, about four miles from the finish, I saw Peter Duncan, the *Blue Peter* presenter, sitting on the ground. He was knackered and suffering from serious glycogen depletion. I recognised him straight away and so gave him a couple of my glucose tablets and told him that they'd help get him to the finish line. Well, wouldn't you know it – he only went and passed me in the final few hundred metres! I watched *Blue Peter* the next day and he talked a little about taking part in the race but, funnily enough, he made no mention of the stranger whose special tablets helped him to finish! I wasn't that fussed, though. What mattered to me was my time. I beat my target, completing the race in 3:10, which I was very satisfied with.

Despite the weather, I really enjoyed that first race and, deep down, I think we all knew it had the potential to become something really big. It was well organised, the route was fantastic and, even though it was raining and bitterly cold, the public turned out in their thousands to cheer us on. Put it this way, it was no surprise when they announced it would be taking place again the next year.

By the time it came around again, I had a friend who knew somebody who worked in the Post Office, which meant they were able to help ensure we got our places, so I ran in 1982. Then again in 1983. And again in 1984, although on that occasion I only got in through the 'Good for Age' category after initially receiving a rejection letter.

Before I knew it, it was 1990 and I was getting ready to run my tenth consecutive London Marathon!

Shortly after that, Chris Brasher considered creating an 'Ever Presents' club in order to make those who had run every single marathon up to that point exempt for future races, provided they kept up the sequence. However, there were too many people who fitted that bill; I believe there were around ninety people who would have been eligible at that time. So, Chris and his team waited until 1995, when they revisited the idea around the time of the fifteenth edition of the race. By then, the number of us who had run every one had reduced to forty-two, so it was a much more manageable number.

At the end of the 1995 race, each of us was presented with a special commemorative medal, sweatshirt and guaranteed acceptance for future London Marathons, which was a real honour.

In the time since, we've got to know one another pretty well. We've clocked up some pretty good times, too. The vast majority of us have done at least one sub-three-hour marathon, whilst a couple have even shaded the 'two hours and twenty minutes' mark. When you consider that the world record is just seventeen minutes quicker than that, it's really fantastic running by anybody's estimation! One of the guys, Mick McGeoch, has actually run forty marathons inside two-and-a-half hours. He's an international-class runner. Meanwhile, in

2011, Chris Finill ran across America, from California to New York, in under eighty days. He's the 'baby' of the 'Ever Presents' and has run every London Marathon in under three hours, with just one exception.

Now, I'm not in Chris's league when it comes to running. My best-ever time is 2:57:15, which I ran in 1984. However, I've still managed to accumulate three Guinness World Records whilst running in the London Marathon.

The first came in one of the early editions of the race when I became the first person to complete a marathon whilst tossing a pancake from the start to the finish. I used to work as a patisserie chef and I just thought it would be a bit of a laugh. My friends even gave me the nickname 'The Galloping Gourmet'! During the race, I was overtaken by a guy dressed as a waiter carrying a bottle of Perrier water and a glass on a silver tray. These things weren't even glued down. They were sitting loose on the tray and yet he still managed to finish in just over three hours. I got chatting to him later. He was a really nice chap from Switzerland called Roger Bourban. He told me that he had run in lots of races carrying a tray of drinks and that his efforts had got him into the *Guinness Book of World Records*.

'You should try to get in for your pancake flipping,' he told me. 'That's not a bad idea,' I thought, so I decided to give it a try.

I trained carrying a heavy rock to mimic the weight of the frying pan and ultimately completed the race in 3:09:30. After some very thorough checks, I was included in that year's *Guinness Book of World Records*, with a picture no less – a proud moment! People often ask me if it was a real pancake that I was tossing. You better believe it was! The pancake was actually a special recipe that I developed to counteract the effects of cross-winds on the Isle of Dogs. I wrapped it in two rolls of cling film to make sure that it would last the distance.

I repeated the pancake tossing in a future London Marathon where I was sponsored £50 by a friend to try to get the TV presenter Harry Carpenter – the team leader for Muscular Dystrophy, the charity I was running for that year – to eat it at the post-race reception. I told him the deal and he said he'd be up for it. 'Here, that's not too bad,' he told me as he took a bite.

However, the thing about tossing a pancake in a marathon is that it's 'fraught with danger' shall we say. At any point, somebody could grab it or it could disappear with a sudden gust of wind mid-toss. That's why I always carried a spare tucked down my shorts and that, I'm afraid to say, is the one that Harry ate! Ah well – at least he enjoyed it!

I also hold the world record for the fastest marathon completed with an egg and spoon, which I set in 1991 with a time of 3:34:50. I was kindly assisted before the start that year by Chris Brasher and John Disley, the race founders, with Chris signing the guinea fowl egg to verify that it was the same egg that finished the race. That record has stood for over twenty-five years and, to be honest, I can't imagine anyone breaking it any time soon. Anybody who's capable of running a marathon as quickly as I ran it that year isn't going to be seen dead carrying an egg and spoon. There's one guy I know of who is desperate to break it. He's an Australian and has emailed me a number of times over the past few years for my advice on technique. To my knowledge, he has come within three minutes of breaking it and, to tell the truth, I'd be disappointed if he did. Let's be honest, being a Guinness World Record-holder is quite something, isn't it?

The third and final record I hold is shared with my good friend Dave Pettifer from Leamington Spa: the world record for the fastest three-legged marathon. This was back in the early to mid-nineties when we were both a lot fitter. We used to be very similar in terms of stride length, speed and height – important things to consider when you're tied together – so we decided to give it a go whilst flipping pancakes. That was in 1992 and we didn't do too badly, completing the course in 4:18. However, Guinness World Records wouldn't accept our entry. They said we weren't fast enough. 'How fast is fast enough?' I asked them but they said they couldn't tell me. So, in 1995, we decided to try again but this time without the pancakes. Tied together in a single suit, we finished in a time of 3:58. That, as it turned out, was fast enough!

However, none of the records have given me my favourite London Marathon memory. Instead, that came in 1998 when I ran it three times in the one day. That's right: three times, one day.

I'd previously done a couple of 'Double Londons', when I ran from the finish in time to get to the start to take part in the official run. The first time I did it, in 1987, it took me 8:59 I clipped eleven minutes off that time when I did it again the following year. This was in memory of my best friend, Pat Churcher, who was tragically murdered.

I decided to up the ante a little to try and raise more money for charity, which is how the 'Triple London' came about. I attempted it for the first time in 1997 and managed sixty-one miles – almost two-and-a-half marathons – before I ran out of steam at 9 p.m. on the Sunday night. However, that only made me more determined to do it the following year. So, on Blackheath Common, at 10 p.m. on Saturday, 25 April 1998 – just as most runners would have been getting ready for bed in anticipation of the race the next morning – I was setting off at the start line just two months after my sixty-first birthday. I ran through the night to the finish line and then back to the start again, getting lost twice, and arriving just thirty minutes before the main event. That gave me enough time for some food, a quick shower and an interview with Clare Balding from the BBC before joining the back-markers to return to The Mall again.

Overall, my split times averaged about eleven minutes per mile. I ran the first marathon in 5:14, the second in 5:23, and the third in 6:35. All in all, I ran for a total of 17:12. For a few miles, around the sixteen-mile mark, I was also accompanied by my daughters, Kyla and Iona, who are both good runners in their own rights.

I completed the challenge at 3.12 p.m. on the Sunday afternoon. I was exhausted but the adrenaline kept me wide awake until I arrived back in Birmingham that evening. I think I'll cherish that particular London Marathon forever. I also think that I would have been faster but, two weeks prior, I cracked a wrist bone in a snowboarding accident and had to run with my right arm in a sling.

So, what does the London Marathon mean to me? It's simple, really. It's changed my life, not to mention that of my wife, Janet, my 'ever-present' supporter. I've now got a totally different perspective on what's important and what's not, and that's something that has come to me through running. Going out for a jog or a race has become my favourite thing to do, which is quite surprising when you consider it was a sore part of my secondary sports education. My PE teachers used running as a punishment in that, if you didn't behave, football was cancelled and replaced with a one-and-a-half-mile cross country run. It should have put me off running for life but, instead, it has given me a life interest and a status that's hard to define. Since 1979, I have logged over 43,000 miles and run in some of the world's most famous cities, races and events. I've completed the New York Marathon, Boston Marathon, the Berlin Marathon, the European Ironman and, believe it or not, the World Triathlon Championships in Manchester in 1990, where I finished thirteenth in my age group. I've crammed a lot in, run in many places and raised upwards of £50,000 for more than twenty-five different charities. But, for me, nothing compares to the London Marathon.

As for the future, I fully intend to keep on going for as long as I can, although with increasing age and debility, it's getting harder every year, especially as I've had arthritis in my knees. That resulted in a knee replacement in 2009 and I also had a total ankle replacement in 2013, so I feel a little bit like the 'Six Million Dollar Man'! But I won't stop, primarily because I'm still an 'Ever Present'. Unless my body physically can't make it, I'll keep going. I'm sure it's the same for the other guys. We are part of an extremely exclusive club – one that you can only leave, never join – and so we'll buck the pain barrier for as long as we possibly can to remain a member. For example, I broke my leg in August 1992 and ran the 1993 race with the aid of a crutch. For the same reason, I competed in a wheelchair in 2015 because my new ankle wasn't strong enough to cope with the rigours of the race that year. Because of my 'Ever Present' status, I was given special dispensation by race director Hugh Brasher, the son of Chris, to compete in the 'Standard Wheelchair' category and I finished in my best time for ten years in 4:36. I know I may not end up being the last man standing of the 'Ever Presents' but it won't be for the lack of resolve. 'No pain, no gain' – that's my mantra.

Without question, the London Marathon is an event that is, quite simply, one in a million.

CHAPTER SIXTEEN

LIZ McCOLGAN-NUTTALL

After establishing herself as a dominant middle-distance track runner, Dundee-born Liz McColgan-Nuttall turned her attention to the marathon in 1991. It proved to be an inspired decision and set her on the way to becoming one of the UK's greatest-ever athletes.

NEVER tell a young Scottish girl, who has grown up in a council house, with next to no money, what she can or cannot do.

That's exactly what Lisa Martin and Rosa Mota did in a press conference promoting the New York Marathon in 1991. They were two of the top female marathon runners of the day and, when they were asked if they thought I could make the step up from successful middle-distance runner to marathon runner, they dismissed the suggestion as if it was the most ridiculous idea ever.

They basically said that, whilst I was a good track runner, the road was a good few steps up. They also suggested that I wasted too much energy when I ran to sustain a competitive pace for a whole marathon.

Well, that was all the motivation I needed.

Other people might have taken these critiques on the chin but I've never really been 'other people'. I'm determined and competitive. I knew I had it in me to prove them wrong. That's why, six weeks before the New York Marathon, I accepted an invitation from the organisers to take part.

It was to prove to be the start of my transition from middle-distance runner to marathon runner and ultimately, in 1996, the winner of the London Marathon.

I got into running for one very simple reason – it was accessible. I grew up in Dundee and, like I mentioned, my family wasn't rich by any means. Running was great because it didn't cost anything to do. All I had to do was open the door and off I went. As I got better and started to train with a local athletics club, the Hawkhill Harriers, I would even run to training to save on bus fares. Running gave me an opportunity to participate and be competitive and I loved it for that.

I can't say I was especially good at it at first. However, a combination of a stubborn personality and a strong work ethic made up for any shortcomings in natural talent. I grafted and grinded and never gave up. The harder I trained, the better I became.

It was when I was around sixteen years of age that I was taken to one side by my coach, Harry Bennett, and told the ingredients required to compete at the top level. By that point, I was doing a lot more sports. Things like netball and badminton and so on; I was a real tomboy. Harry, though, insisted that I give them all up and concentrate on running. It was time to start taking it seriously.

Now, long-distance running is not everyone's cup of tea. I get that. However, all the things that other people hate about it, I absolutely loved. The longer the race went on, the more comfortable I felt. It requires a good degree of physical strength but, almost as importantly, mental fortitude. I like to think I had plenty of both.

Back then, of course, there were tight restrictions on how far kids of a certain age were allowed to run in competition. In fact, the first time I ever ran 10,000 metres competitively was in a qualifier to make the Scottish team for the 1986 Commonwealth Games in Edinburgh.

Making that team was the real start of my career. Not many people had heard of me by that point. I was still only twenty and had spent the previous three years on a scholarship at a US university. However, I won the women's 10,000-metre race in a time of 31:41.42, a new British record. I ended up finishing more than ten seconds ahead of the runner-up, a very talented runner from New Zealand called Anne Audain.

As it turned out, that was the only athletics gold medal won by Scotland during those Games and to be the one to do it in front of a home crowd was an incredible, almost indescribable feeling. I'll never forget the pride I felt standing on a podium in the middle of Meadowbank Stadium, the rain hammering down onto the track but the stands full of supporters, as the medal was hung around my neck. The hairs on the back of my neck still stand up every time I think about it.

The five years that followed were fantastic. I retained my 10,000-metre Commonwealth gold medal in Auckland in 1990 and won bronze in the 3,000 metres at the same Games. I also won a silver medal in the 10,000 metres at the 1988 Olympic Games in Seoul, silver again in the 1987 World Cross Country Championships in Warsaw and, just for good measure, another silver in the World Indoor Championships in Budapest in 1989. Just as importantly, my times were getting consistently better.

It was shortly after my second Commonwealth victory in 1990 that I fell pregnant with my first child, Eilish. She was born in the November of that year and has grown up to be a very talented athlete and Olympian in her own right. After she was born, I made a quick return to the track and, in 1991, won bronze at the World Cross Country Championships. In June that year, I ran my lifetime best for the 10,000 metres, with a time of 30:57.07 in Hengelo in the Netherlands. It was, back then, the second-fastest 10,000 metres time ever clocked by a female. Two months later, I won gold in the 10,000 metres in the World Championships in Tokyo. I was in the best condition of my life.

That's when I found out that, apparently, I wasn't good enough to convert my form from the track to the road and from middle-distance to marathon.

The organiser of the New York Marathon called me up to tell me what Lisa and Rosa had said about me and he invited me to take part to try and prove them wrong.

The race was less than two months away but what was I meant to do? Sit back and take it or strive to prove them wrong? There had been so many things that I couldn't do when I was young because, as a family, we couldn't afford it. That's why nobody was going to get away with telling me that I couldn't win a marathon. Only I got to decide that. So, I accepted the invitation to take part and, six weeks later, took my place on the start line in the 'Big Apple'.

I completed the course in a time of 2:27:23, winning by almost a minute from Olga Markova. It was, by just over three minutes, the fastest time ever clocked by a female marathon debutant as well as the sixth-fastest time in the twenty-two-year history of the New York women's event.

Naturally, I was thrilled to win but the funny thing was that I actually felt as though I could have gone faster. I had prepared myself to run a time of 2:24, so I ended up outside of my target time by almost three-and-a-half minutes. That gave me the belief that I hadn't really scratched the surface as a marathoner.

The other good thing about the marathon was that it was quite lucrative, certainly compared to competing on the track. At that time, I was the principal breadwinner in my family. Running was my career, it was how I supported my family. After Eilish, I had another four children and it was important to me to be able to look after them and provide for them. It soon became clear that the road was the best way to do that.

If I'm honest, I also preferred the training. Track training is typically very intense. By comparison, the road is easier; at least, it was for me. I felt more at home, more comfortable.

In 1992, I won the Tokyo Marathon and, the following year, entered London for the first time, finishing third. It was the first defeat of my marathon career, so I can't say that it holds many particularly good memories! The next two years, in fact, were really tough. I spent the vast majority of them on the sidelines with a serious knee injury. For a while, it actually looked as though my career was over and, naturally, it was a really difficult, testing time. You start to wonder if your best days are behind you, if you've peaked. It's hard to explain just how hard that is to process. Try to imagine somebody coming up to you and telling you that you've done the thing you love doing more than anything else in the world for the last time. I couldn't accept that – so I chose not to.

I worked my way back to fitness, put in the training, banked the miles and got myself back into a condition where I was ready to take my place at the start line of the 1995 London Marathon.

I can't even begin to tell you how good that felt. Just a few months earlier, I'd been told by doctors that I might not run competitively again and now here I was getting ready to take part in one of the world's most iconic, most special and most demanding races. I felt like a winner before I even set off.

I finished fifth that year, clocking a time of 2:31:14. That was almost a minute-and-a-half slower than I ran two years earlier and the competitor inside me didn't like that. However, I had to see it for what it was: a return to the road, and a decent one at that.

The next year, I arrived in London feeling fresh and pain-free. I was in far better condition than I had been the year before. I'd been able to get all my training done uninterrupted and had managed to get consistency back into everything I'd been doing. So, I felt fit, ready and, most importantly, confident.

My pre-race routine was always the same. I never drastically changed anything, so I got up on the morning of the race, had a big bowl of porridge and got myself down to the start line. About an hour before it started, I had a mug of strong black coffee, again just like I always did. To some people, that might sound strange but coffee is actually a really good thing to take before you run a marathon. Studies have shown that it slows down the use of muscle glycogen, which is the carbohydrate that the body uses for energy. Generally speaking, the less glycogen you can use, the better and longer you will be able to perform. It also makes you feel more alert. It was an essential part of my race day preparation.

I hadn't just prepared physically, though. I'd also prepared mentally. That included getting myself a game plan for how to approach the race. It was pretty straightforward. Get through the first ten miles in the most efficient way possible, position myself in the middle of the pack and try not to do anything silly. A big part of running a marathon is being disciplined. You will be tempted to push on and run harder. You will feel as though you're running within yourself. But it's not about how quickly you run the next mile; it's about how quickly you run twenty-six of them back to back.

I stuck to my plan, which enabled me to perfectly execute the final part of it over the closing six miles: attack, push, run for home.

My main competition was the Norwegian runner Anita Håkenstad. She hit the front after ten miles and, by halfway, was two minutes ahead of me. She stayed out in front until twenty miles in – and that's when I made my move. I gained on her and gained on her and gained on her until I'd overtaken her.

Suddenly, I was in the lead and found myself closing in on victory.

Those final few miles passed in a bit of a blur. I didn't really hear anything, see anything, feel anything. I was just focused on the line. The thing with a race is that you haven't won until you've taken the tape ahead of everybody else.

And that's exactly what I did.

I crossed the line in 2:27:54, over two minutes ahead of Joyce Chepchumba from Kenya (who, incidentally, succeeded me as the winner the following year).

It was an incredible moment. Surreal even. You are hit with a tidal wave of emotions and feelings. Exhaustion, euphoria, relief, pride. They all surge through you.

The first thing I can remember thinking was, 'I've done it. I've finally done it.' For a British long-distance runner, there's nothing much that compares to winning the London Marathon. Doing something like that in front of a home crowd – it's just magical.

I was only the third British winner in the history of the race by that point, so it was quite a big deal and there was a lot of attention that came with it. It's funny, when you're out there trying to win, you think it's just you, the road and the race. It's an individual sport, after all. It's not until you meet people afterwards and they tell you, 'I ran up the Embankment alongside you when you went past,' that you realise you were never alone. You were actually part of something much bigger than yourself. That's the beauty of the London Marathon. It's not about individuals running races. It's about people coming together and achieving extraordinary things together.

I don't think it's any exaggeration to call it one of the biggest sporting events in the world. It attracts a whole cross-section of people who create something that is arguably more of an event than a race.

It is slickly organised, brilliantly supported by the local people and, best of all, the course is absolutely amazing. There's only one part of it that I never particularly enjoyed and that's the area around the Isle of Dogs. Psychologically, it's really tough because you're running in the wrong direction from the finish line. Plus, it comes at a time in the race when the physical effects are really starting to take their toll. It takes all of your strength to really dig in and get through that stretch. If you can, then you're soon rewarded with the incredible atmosphere of Canary Wharf and the Embankment all the way along to the Houses of Parliament and the final miles of the race.

The 1996 London Marathon proved to be my final major marathon victory. I finished second in 1997 and 1998, and on both occasions I actually ran faster than I did in '96. In '97, for example, I was more than a minute quicker than I'd been the year before – go figure!

Even so, I look back now on 1996 as one of the high points of my career.

It's right up there with everything else I achieved. I have nothing but great memories of it.

My best advice for anyone thinking of doing it? Get ready to spend a lot of time on your feet! That means putting in the miles during training and getting mentally prepared for the task in hand. It's a long way to go – but it's great fun doing it. Believe me.

CHAPTER SEVENTEEN

PHIL PACKER

A former major in Her Majesty's Armed Forces, Phil Packer defied expectations when he completed the London Marathon in 2009, having sustained devastating injuries just over a year earlier whilst on operational duty. He has subsequently become one of the UK's most prolific fundraisers and charity campaigners.

LIKE thousands of others, I started the 2009 London Marathon from Greenwich Park on 26 April 2009. However, whilst the majority of them completed the race in under six hours, it took fourteen days for me to reach the finish line on The Mall. Still, given that less than a year earlier I had been told it was highly unlikely I'd ever walk again, I was just delighted to be able to take my place at the start line.

It was on 19 February 2008 that I sustained catastrophic injuries whilst serving on operational duty. An incident following a rocket attack left me with bruising to my heart, ribs and most significantly, spinal cord damage. In medical terms, I suffered a T12/L1 spinal cord injury. Initially, I was paralysed from the waist down. However, over a lengthy period of time, I regained some mobility.

I can still remember the doctors giving me the news that I was paralysed. The words hung in the air. It was devastating. Countless thoughts raced through my mind, amongst them the grim, shattering realisation that my military career was over. That was particularly tough to take. I had enrolled at twenty-one and the fifteen years that followed, right up until the accident, were the best of my life. It gave me everything I ever wanted. The duty, the service, the people – serving in Her Majesty's Forces was one of the most amazing privileges I've ever had. I had fully planned to do a full career, right up to my retirement, but suddenly, because of one horrible incident, I was left facing the unexpected reality of early retirement. It was a crushing blow.

I lay there in the ward at the Royal National Orthopaedic Hospital at Stanmore and felt as though my world was falling apart. I was surrounded by fellow patients who had also sustained spinal cord injuries, but in my mind I felt completely alone. It was, by some distance, the hardest time of my life.

Plans were subsequently made to prepare me for becoming a wheelchair user. It wasn't easy but, through a wonderful charity called The Back Up Trust, I met a lady called Paula Craig, a senior police officer, who had sustained a spinal cord injury some years earlier and gone on to become an elite wheelchair athlete. Speaking to Paula gave me hope. I felt as if I had lost much of my independence as a result of my injuries but she was incredibly inspiring and, from speaking to her, I decided to explore the opportunity of becoming a wheelchair athlete.

We arranged for a race wheelchair to be brought into the hospital for me to try with a view to participating in the 2009 London Marathon. I also attended a Paralympics selection day where I was given the opportunity to pursue fast-track training in fencing, archery and basketball. I desperately wanted to feel valuable again. It's hard to explain but losing my army career, trying to cope with life in a wheelchair and dealing with the psychological trauma of it all destroyed my self-confidence, self-esteem and self-worth. For so long, I had been part of a remarkable organisation that I took great pride in being part of. Then, in the blink of an eye, it was gone. It was horrible. I felt that I was unable to contribute to anything worthy and convinced myself that's how other people saw me, too. It felt like a crushing blow and so pursuing a Paralympic journey seemed like a great way to try to reclaim at least some of what I'd lost.

Then, late in 2008, something extraordinary happened. Post-surgery and with the help of my medical team, physiotherapists and occupational therapists, I stood for the first time since the accident. Shortly thereafter, I took my first few steps. They were slow and unsteady but they were steps nonetheless.

That left me with a decision to make: take part in the London Marathon in a race wheelchair and pursue the prospect of competing in the 2012 Paralympics in London, or learn to walk again?

I wanted to walk again.

Of course, by that point, I had my heart set on participating in the London

Marathon and, knowing that continuing to train for the event would help my rehabilitation, I asked the race organisers if they would allow me to walk it instead. Fortunately, they gave their consent. My consultant, Dr Angela Gall, also agreed on the strict condition that I completed no more than two miles per day. So, if I was going to complete the London Marathon in 2009, it was going to take me fourteen days.

In hospital, when I did manage to stand and start to walk again, I was acutely aware of how fortunate I was. I felt a sense of duty to try to use my 'second chance' for some good.

That's how my £1 million fundraising effort for Help for Heroes came about. I committed to do three challenges in 2009: row the English Channel, climb El Capitan in the USA and walk the London Marathon.

The London Marathon, in particular, was an extraordinary experience. I watched all the runners pass the start line and then that's when I started. As I walked round the second bend on my crutches, the cordon was being taken up, the road was being re-opened and I had to move onto the pavement.

Other people who have completed the marathon talk enthusiastically and appreciatively about the support of the crowds and the masses of people running with them. Due to the nature of my attempt, however, I never really sensed that. Even so, the support I received was very special. People on the streets going about their everyday business were just incredible. We raised approximately £650,000 over those fourteen days from the generous support of the public. It was just remarkable.

Each day, when I completed my two miles, I left the route to recuperate before returning the following day to pick up where I'd left off. It was a long, slow process but I had a wealth of support from family, close friends and former colleagues.

Finally, a full fortnight after I started, I found myself just a few hundred metres from the finish line on The Mall. It was a very emotional experience; a time of joy and also a time to reflect on where I was personally – both physically and mentally.

I was met at the finish line by Sir Steve Redgrave, who presented me with my finisher's medal. I recall giving him a hug and the emotions really just hit me at that point. It's when you cross the finish line that the enormity of what you've accomplished really sinks in.

As a side note, Sir Steve was also the person who presented me with the Helen Rollason Award at the *BBC Sports Personality of the Year* ceremony in 2009. On top of that, he joined me on Mount Snowdon in support of Sport Relief and met me on the finish line of my 2015 marathon in London when I reduced my time from fourteen days to fourteen hours. Together with Sir Ranulph Fiennes and Baroness Tanni Grey-Thompson, he has been an absolute inspiration to me and donated a great deal of his time and support in all of my fundraising and charitable endeavours. I consider myself very lucky to have met and been assisted by so many inspirational figures.

Soon after the marathon, I flew to the USA to scale El Capitan. I had a great team that comprised some of the country's best climbers including Andy Kirkpatrick and Ian Parnell. After more than 4,250 pull-ups and three nights sleeping on the side of the mountain, we reached the summit, which was a fantastic feeling. On returning to Great Britain, the initial fundraising target of £1 million was reached and then exceeded by more than £300,000. I am truly indebted to everyone who made that possible and especially to the public who donated so generously.

The following year, I decided to tackle the London Marathon again but this time I wanted to complete it in twenty-six hours. I nominated a different charity for each mile, for the duration of which I walked alongside a young person benefitting from its work or promoting their charity as an ambassador. It was a very emotional experience and, as I made my way up The Mall, people from all of the charities lined the way. It was a wonderful occasion.

Since then, my challenges have been ambitious and continued to push the boundaries physically. For example, in 2012, I completed 2,012 miles walking through every county of Great Britain and Northern Ireland. Adjusted to account for my spinal injury, it was the equivalent of completing 310 marathons in 331 days. Then, in 2015, I completed a full marathon distance through the City of London in fourteen hours, which was fantastic. I have used each of my challenges to raise awareness of charities. However, not only that, they have also tested my physical limitations and assisted me in dealing with my own psychological trauma.

Taking on all of these challenges has certainly helped to give my life some purpose. I felt an enormous sense of duty serving in Her Majesty's Forces and I guess the charitable work has helped to provide a different kind of duty that

I need in life. Whatever the case may be, I am enormously grateful for the life I have now and for the many people who have helped me live it.

Physically, I still have my limitations, such as the lack of bladder and bowel function and other associated challenges caused by the spinal cord injury, together with walking with the aid of a stick. The psychological wounds haven't healed completely, nor do I think they ever will. There are days where I have a wobble or feel a bit low. I think that's natural, though, and I draw a great amount of strength from having unconditional friends whom I can talk to and be open with. They are my lifeline in those occasional dark moments. As much as possible, I try to look forward but, even so, I think that one sometimes cannot help but cast the occasional backwards glance and reflect. I don't think there is anything wrong with that. It is those sobering moments that really help you to appreciate the good in your life.

Working within the charity sector reminds me regularly of just how lucky I am and I think that's very important. After experiencing any kind of trauma, it is important that you give yourself time to heal, both mentally and physically. When you've had a medical condition or a disability, there's a grieving process that comes with it and it's important that you allow that process to take place, no matter how hard it might be.

For me, even if I didn't realise it at first, the London Marathon was a vital part of that process. It wasn't about finishing it in fourteen days – it was just about finishing it, about re-establishing some of the self-esteem I'd had previously but which had diminished. It showed me that, irrespective of what happens to you in life, there are major goals you can set yourself and major achievements you can accomplish. I used to view my injuries as a disability but not any more. These days, I look at my life from the perspective of what I can do, not what I can't.

Completing the London Marathon isn't easy. It's not meant to be and nor is any physical challenge. It helps, however, if you have something or someone to do it for. I have found that combining my physical challenges with fundraising for worthy causes makes them more special and also goes some way to rebuilding and retaining my self-belief. In that respect, the London Marathon was one of the first opportunities I had to do this and it will always be a memory that I treasure.

CHAPTER EIGHTEEN

LUKE JONES

A keen environmentalist, Hampshire businessman Luke Jones decided to run the 2014 London Marathon to raise money for the World Wildlife Fund. However, not content with just taking on the streets of the capital, he decided to add an extra element of difficulty to his challenge – by completing the distance in his bare feet . . .

SO you think long-distance running is tough? Try doing it without any shoes. That's the challenge I set myself when I ran the 2014 London Marathon barefoot. That's right: no socks, no shoes, nothing.

You're probably wondering why anyone would choose to put themselves through such a treacherous ordeal. To be honest, my motivation was pretty simple. I had been keen to run a marathon for some time. Plus, I'm a passionate environmentalist, so I wanted to do something to try and raise money for the World Wildlife Fund (WWF). It has always been one of my favourite charities and, one night, I was watching TV when an advert for a new campaign of theirs came on. They were teaming up with Sky to try to save one billion trees in the Amazon rainforest from deforestation and, immediately, I thought to myself, 'That's an amazing idea – what can I do to help?' The rainforest, after all, is one of those things you can't get back. When it's gone, it's gone.

So, raising money for WWF was my motivation – but why do it barefoot? Well, in addition to running a synthetic eyelash company called Flutter Eyes Ltd with my wife, I'm also a personal trainer. Fitness is a big part of my life but not just the act of keeping fit; I'm very much into the theory and science behind it, too.

Barefoot running was something that had intrigued me for a while. I had read a lot about it and it really challenged the way I thought about running. It requires a considerably different technique to running in trainers. When you are wearing something on your feet, it is much easier to strike with your heel first. That collision between the ground and your foot sends a large shock wave up through the body via your bones. However, running barefoot encourages you to strike more with your mid and forefoot, which generates very little impact force and, in turn, reduces the stress and strain on your body, particularly the muscles, tendons and joints in your lower leg. In simple terms, running barefoot promotes a better running form.

Additionally, there's a lot of evidence that wearing shoes, particularly the closed-toe shoes that bind your foot into one single fixed position, weakens the foot structure. Biomechanically speaking, the foot is the most complex part of the human body. There are loads of bones, movements and planes of movement that the ankle and the foot move around.

The simplification of the theory is that, if you stop the foot from being able to move on the planes that it naturally would, the muscles atrophy and the body compensates by forming an unnatural gait, just like any part of your body would if you didn't use it the way it should be used.

I see that a lot with the people I train. Many of them have sat in an office for thirty to forty hours a week for years and years on end. As a result, they've developed all kinds of problems. They've essentially immobilised their body and held it in one bad position for long periods of time. Nearly all of us do a similar thing with our feet. Most of us wear shoes to work all day and the only time we take them off is when we get home which could be five, six or seven o'clock at night, even later if you work in central London. We bind them into an unnatural position but convince ourselves that it must be good because 'it feels comfortable'. It's not, though. Yes, it's cushioned – but it's very restrictive. I've seen the repercussions of it myself. I've trained people who have suffered the effects of over-training in running shoes. They've hammered the roads, logged the miles and covered a serious amount of ground, and more often than not with a counter-productive running style.

So, all of that got me thinking. I wanted to see if it was possible to condition myself to run a full marathon distance barefooted; to see whether or not I was capable of converting myself from running in trainers to running without them – and where better to attempt that than London?

My friends and family all thought it was a great idea, although my dad, Robert – Bob to all his mates – said I was nuts. He'd done the London Marathon quite a few times, despite only taking up running in his mid-fifties as a way to stay fit, and so he knew better than most what I was getting into. It wasn't going to be easy but I was determined to do it.

In my favour was the fact that I already had a good running history. I competed at county level when I was younger and my body is quite naturally predisposed to being good for running. I've got good biomechanics for it. Strong arches and things like that. However, in many ways, this was like starting from scratch and I was determined to do it properly. I couldn't afford to try too much too soon. I had to be patient and take my time if I was ever going to be able to do it.

I started off by wearing Vibram Fivefingers, a minimalist shoe designed to replicate the effects of running barefoot. It has a thin, flexible sole that is contoured to the shape of a human foot. It even has individual sections for each toe. It's a really impressive product and I wore the shoes for about a year before I first went barefoot. Any opportunity I got, I put them on and the results were instantaneous. The muscles around my calves went insane because they were suddenly being used the way they're meant to be.

I found running in them absolutely excruciating at first. After a 5km race, for example, I could barely walk the next day. I was okay with that, though. It told me that I was using my feet properly. No pain, no gain, right? So, I persevered and gradually increased my distance.

Finally, they came off and I went out barefoot for the first time. Initially, it was a pretty surreal experience and it's fair to say I got some funny looks from other runners, dog-walkers and pretty much everyone else I encountered.

Also predictably, it took quite a bit of adjusting to. When you first go barefoot, one of the main problems you have is that you quite literally tear the skin off your foot when you run. The 'flicking' action when you kick back to propel yourself forward wears the skin off your toe-pad and works through your calluses very quickly. That's unless you've got really strongly callused feet – which I didn't and which you just won't have if you wear shoes.

At the time, my wife, Kathryn, and I were living in New Malden in south-west London, so I did a lot of my training around there, specifically in

Richmond Park. I also found a fantastic flat piece of road from Leatherhead to Dorking, which was perfect for barefoot running. The tarmac was nice and smooth, with very little debris on it, so I was able to really develop the calluses and the toughness of the skin on the soles of my feet. I also had my brother-in-law, Andrew, for company. He was a tremendous support throughout and managed to keep me focused. He wore the Vibram shoes and, most importantly, was okay with running at my speed. That's the other thing about running barefoot: you have to run a lot slower than you would normally. You can't run fast when you're doing this type of training because you'll just wear through the soles of your feet in next to no time. You have to make a conscious effort to slow yourself down.

After about a year of training, I had worked up to half-marathon distance. That's how long it took. A typical marathon training plan will get you ready for the start line in around sixteen weeks if you have a good base level of fitness. But nothing about running barefoot is 'typical'. It's a long, slow process that requires patience and discipline. I managed to work up to running twenty-one miles on two separate occasions before the day of the London Marathon itself, which I thought was pretty good, so I was in good shape and feeling quite confident when the day of the race arrived.

Fortunately, my charity place meant that I started in a different wave to everybody else. I set off with around 3,000 people as opposed to around 20,000, which was great. Imagine if I'd been in amongst that large group: my feet would have been trampled on. It would have been horrible. As it was, when people got too close, I just gave them a gentle push out of the way because, when someone stands on your foot when you're running, it can really hurt and even rip off your toenails. Going in the main wave would have been a total hazard, so it was a blessing that I was in with the charity runners.

In the end, I completed the race in just under four-and-a-half hours, which wasn't bad. I'd have liked to have done it in under four but, given the circumstances, I was happy with it. Most people can't appreciate how much harder it is to run with nothing on your feet. Don't get me wrong, some do but many don't. They'll ask me what my time was and, when I tell them, they'll say 'Oh, that's rubbish, I know someone who has done it in under four hours and they're not even fit.' There are wildly varying ideas of what constitutes a fast time and what doesn't. Honestly, though, my time wasn't my motivation; I was just trying to see if it was possible to do it barefoot or not – and it was a thrill to find out that it was.

For the most part, it went well. There were some tough parts, of course. The bit around the third mile where the two different start waves coalesced, for example. Suddenly, the roads became really crowded and I had to, quite literally, shove people out of the way otherwise they would have run all over me.

Water stations were also quite tricky. People just toss the bottles aside when they're done with them, so it was a delicate operation weaving through them. I probably looked like I was doing some kind of Irish jig!

The discarded energy gel packets were horrible, too. I'd stand on them and they'd stick to my feet which, as well as being really disgusting, was quite hazardous. Plus, my legs went into cramp any time I bent over to try to pick them off, which obviously affected my cadence. Little stones would stick to the gel, too, which meant that, unless I removed them, I had a sharp, searing pain every time my foot hit the ground. Try to imagine standing on a plug over and over: that's what it's like.

I knew to expect those sorts of things, though. On one training run through Richmond Park, for example, I landed with my full weight right on a thorn branch. The spikes went about half an inch into the sole of my foot, and not the soft bit, either. They went clean through the hard, callused part and, believe me, that hurt a hell of a lot. It was extremely unpleasant. I remember reflexively pulling my foot back off the ground and this giant thorn branch was rammed right in there – it looked like something from a cartoon! I'd been really paranoid about standing on glass or a needle or something like that but it ended up being a thorn bush that hurt me the most. After that, I think I was pretty much prepared for anything.

The other thing about running barefoot is that it is mentally draining. You continually have to look at the ground and watch where you're going, which, when you're trying to move at a decent pace, gets pretty tiring after a while. Your eyes are scanning the ground and collecting a lot of information. It's a bit like watching a full conveyor belt at the supermarket on a fast setting – eventually, you get exhausted looking at it.

However, the goodwill and fantastic atmosphere of the London Marathon helped to keep me moving. It's an incredibly emotional thing and I wasn't prepared for that at all. My previous running experiences had been mainly competitive, where there were just a few significant others spectating. I'd never been in an environment where there were thousands and thousands of strangers, ten deep on either side of the road, screaming and willing you to do well. It's simply amazing.

I was singled out for a lot of attention from the spectators. I hadn't really expected that, to be honest. I didn't think many people would notice me running barefoot in amongst all of the other runners, so it was a surprise that the whole way round, and almost without any let-up, I got shouts of, 'Go barefoot man!' or 'Go Tarzan!' and so on, which was fantastic. My fellow runners were great, too. They'd pat me on the back and tell me that what I was doing was amazing. Their encouragement really helped me.

Even so, I found the last six miles particularly tough. By that point, all the muscles in my feet had become really fatigued. You use a lot more muscles when you run barefoot but they hadn't been conditioned enough for running that distance, so that was tough. Also, my whole body was just hurting generally from running the distance. I'm fit but I don't have a typical runner's build. I'm quite tall and weigh nearly ninety kilos, so it really did take its toll.

On top of that, the pain in the soles of my feet was searing. More or less the entire London Marathon route, you run on tarmac and it's a particularly poor quality surface for the majority of the second half of the race. It's not that big a deal if you're wearing trainers but, if you're not, it's hard going. It feels a bit like having sunburn on your feet. You know when you scrub your hands really hard and you take off the outside layer of skin? It's like that, but with a side serving of being pummelled with a cricket bat all over! So, yes, you could say I was relieved to finish. Exhilarated, but relieved.

For most of the final few miles, I had serious cramps in both my hamstrings, my feet were in real pain and my entire body ached. Each stride fired a shock wave through me that I could even feel shooting down my arms and into my hands and fingers.

People who would never normally overtake me – old men bent double and people dressed as cans of Coca-Cola, for example – were cruising past, which was quite demoralising. I could feel myself getting mentally eroded. As a fit guy, I'm not really accustomed to that. I'm more used to being near the front of the action. At the same time, though, I was really proud of what I was doing and that I'd be able to face my friends and say, 'I did it.'

As soon as I crossed the finish line and stopped running, the cramps took over. I tried to get as much salt and sugar in me as quickly as I could and lay on my back with my feet up against a fence to drain out the lactic acid. I stayed there for about ten minutes and, incredibly, felt fine when I stood back up.

I reclaimed my bag, put on a pair of shoes and went to meet up with some friends and family in a pizza restaurant. It's funny, the first thing Kathryn said when she saw me was, 'You're totally burnt – did you forget to put on sun cream?' That made me laugh. I'd just run in my bare feet for over four hours through the streets of London but she was more interested in the fact I hadn't worn any sun protection! She was fantastic, though. She was so supportive of me throughout. I couldn't have done it without her.

When we got home, one of the first things I did was clean the dirt off my feet. To my surprise, they just looked the same as they normally do. The skin was a little worn but, apart from that, they were fine. They felt great the next day, too. I knew several other people who ran that year and who told me they'd had blisters, or couldn't walk, or had muscle pain for days afterwards. By comparison, I went out the next day and trained four clients. I had some muscle fatigue but my feet were absolutely fine. Honestly, I could have quite easily gone for a 10km run if I'd been so inclined – I wasn't, though!

So, what does the London Marathon mean to me? More than anything else, it reminds me of my dad. He was my inspiration for doing it. It was through him that I got into running. I can remember being around nine or ten years old and trying to keep up with him when he went out for a jog. More often than not, he'd leave me in his dust but that just made me more determined to get better so that I could accompany him the whole way. I'm not sure I'd be as into fitness if it wasn't for him.

There's also a part of me that looks at it from the point of view of a personal trainer and fitness enthusiast. It's just an amazing event. Look at the elite end of the scale: it has some of the most incredible athletes in the world taking part. If you want to get an idea of just how fast they are going, get on a treadmill, turn the speed up to 22kph and try to run at that pace for one mile. It's unlikely you'll last much more than 200 or 300 metres. But the elite participants in the London Marathon, the men and the women, sustain that speed for twenty-six consecutive miles, incorporating twists, turns, elevation changes and more. They are truly remarkable. It's almost incomprehensible that anybody can run at that speed but they do. It would be interesting to see how they'd get on if they did it in their bare feet. Something tells me they'd still be pretty quick – just so long as they manage to steer clear of thorn branches, that is!

CHAPTER NINETEEN

ROB YOUNG

Between the 2014 and 2015 London Marathons, Richmond man Rob Young averaged more than one marathon per day after discovering a previously hidden talent for running long distances. Central to that, however, was a capacity for enduring pain, which was forged many years earlier at the hands of his abusive father.

SITTING watching the 2014 London Marathon, I turned to my fiancée Joanna. 'You know what,' I said, 'I quite fancy running that one day.' She drew me a look. 'You can't run a marathon,' she replied. It was blunt but fair. She had no reason to think I could. Until that day, the extent of my running had been the occasional five-kilometre parkrun.

Still, hearing her say I couldn't do it made me even more determined. 'I bet you 20p that I can,' I insisted. 'In fact, I reckon I could do fifty marathons.'

Initially, we both laughed. It was, after all, a little fanciful. Then it hit me: why couldn't I do it? I was only thirty-one, fit and healthy. The only thing stopping me was me.

So, that afternoon, I downloaded the route of the Richmond Park Marathon – which takes place near where we live every May – and, in the evening, laid out a T-shirt, shorts and an old pair of trainers. I put my work clothes in a backpack and set my alarm for 2.30 a.m.

When it went off, I got up, got dressed and cycled to the park. It was dark, cold and eerily quiet but I wasn't bothered; I was here for a reason – to run a marathon.

I had to walk part of the way but I did it, completing 26.2 miles in just over four hours. I subsequently got changed, rode to the train station, did a full day's work and then returned to the park in the evening where I ran another full marathon distance. I was forty minutes faster than I'd been just twelve hours earlier. I was absolutely done in but, at the same time, delighted. The previous day, I'd been sitting on the settee and musing over one day running a marathon; now, here I was, having done not one but two with absolutely zero training.

The next morning, I was out of bed at 2.30 a.m. once more to do it all again. Within seven days, I had completed ten marathon distances. At that point, a new idea started to form in my mind.

Why stop at fifty marathons? Why not attempt to run at least one a day for the next year? I found out that the world record for most marathons run in a year was 366 and was held by a Spaniard called Ricardo Abad. Breaking that record became my number one goal.

It would require commitment but I didn't see that as an issue. I'd never quit on anything in my life. It would require a patient and understanding partner but, fortunately, Joanna has those qualities in abundance. More than anything else, it would require an ability to block out pain but I had learned long ago how to do that.

My father, you see, was an abusive man. An extremely abusive man. To describe him as cruel would be a disservice to the word. Sadistic – that's much closer to the truth.

He tortured my mother; he raped my sister; he killed our family dog; and he subjected me to regular physical and psychological attacks. To be in his company was to be in the presence of somebody truly wicked.

For example, he seemed to get a twisted kick out of locking me in a suitcase and pushing it down the stairs. That happened often. Then there was his other favourite game: grabbing me by one foot and dangling me over the banister. If I made a noise, he let go. I soon trained myself to suppress my fear. I'd block it all out and wait for temporary respite from his fits of savagery.

On one occasion, he found a church leaflet in my bedroom. It had been put through our letterbox and I had picked it up and taken it there. This sent him into a violent rage and he dragged me to the top of the staircase where he drove a nail straight through my foot using a hammer. Another time, he ordered my sister to stab me in the leg with a fork for taking one of her sweets, which she did. Well, what alternative did she have? Disobey him and have even worse violence inflicted upon her?

Then came the time that I truly thought he was going to kill me. He tied one end of a rope around my neck and let me hang from a metal coat hook on a door, the breath literally being squeezed out of my lungs. He had killed our dog the same way and so I felt destined to meet the same fate; I felt sure that I was going to die here at the hands of my own father. I was eight years old. To my surprise, he loosened the rope and let me down. Maybe he couldn't bring himself to kill his own son. Maybe he realised he couldn't continue to hurt me if I was dead.

Shortly thereafter, my mother, my sister and I escaped to a safe house following the intervention of social services. From there, we travelled to Hampshire – sleeping overnight in a ditch – to be closer to my mother's family. It soon became clear, however, that she was in no position to look after us and I was put into a care home.

If I thought that was the end of my torment, I was wrong. I was bullied relentlessly by the other kids until, one day, I snapped and became the bully myself. It was a terrible and confusing time.

At the age of twelve, my life changed when I met a man named Peter Wells. He was a deputy school headmaster and a coach at the sports club I attended. He successfully applied to foster me and, over the next few years, became the father I never had. He instilled in me the importance of respect, good manners, hard work and compassion. It's ironic, the only thing my biological father ever instilled in me was fear.

When I left school, I joined the army for a few years, where I served in the Royal Corps of Signals, before leaving at the age of twenty-three, whereupon I cycled with the Milram professional team in Italy for a brief spell. That ended when my then girlfriend fell pregnant with my daughter, Olivia. That relationship ended a few years later and that's when I met Joanna on a dating website. It's fair to say I fell head over heels for her pretty quickly. Our romance blossomed and we had a little boy, Alex, in 2012. Soon after that, we got engaged. Life just seemed to be bobbing along nicely. I was running a small auto parts business and, for the first time in a long time – maybe even ever – I felt happy.

There was, though, something nagging away at me; a responsibility I couldn't ignore, a sense of duty I couldn't shake. I felt a restless urge to do something but what that was and why I had to do it I couldn't say for sure – until I watched the London Marathon in 2014 and made that little bet with Joanna.

Right then, in that instant, everything changed. It was as though I had unlocked a hitherto secret passageway to my future. People have called it an epiphany. A 'light bulb' moment. I don't know if it was or not. All I know is that in laying out the terms of the bet with Joanna, and subsequently expanding on it to make it even more challenging, I felt what I can only describe as relief. I had found something I had been searching for for most of my life: an opportunity to empower and give hope to others whilst, at the same time, pushing myself to my absolute physical limit. For perhaps the first time ever, I felt a sense of purpose. I could run, so I *would* run.

I won't lie, the first three weeks were tough. Really tough. I sacrificed a few toenails, suffered from nipple bleeding and lost around three stone in weight. But after that, it genuinely got easier. The best way I can describe it is to compare it to a pair of running shoes. At first, they feel a little uncomfortable; then you break them in and, suddenly, it's as though you've been wearing them your entire life. That's what it was like. I guess my body just got accustomed to running those sorts of distances every day. It was as though it tried to resist it at first but soon realised that, actually, it's not all that bad. That's why I truly believe anybody could run a marathon a day if they truly wanted to. You just need to train your body and your mind.

I was helped by the fact that I've got a high pain threshold. An extremely high pain threshold. I don't know why that's the case. Perhaps it has something to do with my father. Perhaps I've got a higher tolerance for it because I've experienced more of it. Who can say for sure? All I know is that many of the top ultramarathon runners have had to deal with some pretty significant things in their lives. It might just be coincidence – or maybe it's not.

The thing is, there's nothing about me from a biological point of view that should make me a good runner. Dr Courtney Kipps, an assistant medical director for the London Marathon, has run tests on me and discovered that my VO2 max, which measures how much oxygen a person's body is capable of using during exercise, is about average for a three-and-a-half-hour marathon runner. Meanwhile, my anaerobic threshold – the point where lactic acid starts to build in the muscles – is average, nothing more.

Daniel Lieberman, a professor of human evolutionary biology at Harvard

University in Massachusetts, has found one thing that works to my advantage: my running form. In contrast to many other runners, who slam their feet into the ground when they run, Lieberman – who has done a lot of research into barefoot running, in particular – found that I make very little impact on the ground. Still, good form doesn't mean zero pain.

Over the course of my challenge, I learned to use some mind tricks to get me through longer, tougher runs. For example, if my legs were feeling particularly sore, I'd bite down on my lip to redirect the pain. Likewise, if I was several hours into a long run, I'd tell myself that I'd only gone a few miles and so be able to push on further and harder. Little things like that helped enormously.

As time went on, I found myself actively seeking out more challenges. Bigger challenges. Tougher challenges. Running a marathon distance every day became too routine so I started looking for other things I could do. I signed up for official marathons, trail runs, ultramarathons . . . basically, anywhere I could run, I ran. I also left my job to become a full-time runner. Joanna and I had some savings that we figured would tide us over, and we also moved out of our rented flat and into a friend's house to save money. I think most people thought I was crazy at first but, when they realised how important this was to me, they soon came around. They recognised that this was more than just a flight of fancy; it was something I simply had to do.

One evening in the summer of 2014, I caught a train to Watford and ran through the night to the start line of a marathon in Northampton, some fifty-six miles away. I then completed the marathon.

Not long afterwards, I took part in the North Downs Way 100. It is widely regarded to be one of the toughest races in the UK. As you might have gathered from the name, it's 100 miles from start to finish. On top of that, there's an elevation change of 10,000 feet and you have to finish within twenty-four hours. Of the 180 who started that year, only thirty-six completed it. Fortunately, I was one of the thirty-six. From there, it was straight to Salisbury to complete a trail marathon. I was getting by on next to no sleep and very little food. It was difficult but I never felt like stopping.

The only time I did stop was in the November, when my left shin and ankle swelled so much that it became almost impossible to run. A scan showed bruising in the bone, which could have led to a stress fracture and, in turn, a full fracture. I had no option but to rest. For twenty-three long days, I didn't run a yard. I can't explain how frustrating that was, not least because it meant I couldn't break the record for the most marathons run on consecutive days over a year. However, because I had sometimes run two marathons on one day, I was still on to break Ricardo Abad's record.

To make up for lost time, I signed up for the Trans-American Footrace. It's basically just as it sounds: a coast-to-coast race across the United States from west to east. It started in January 2015 in Huntington Beach, California, and took a southern route over both roads and trails to Chesapeake Bay in Virginia, some 3,131 miles away.

I was one of only twelve people who took part – nine men and three women – and it was an incredible experience. That's not to say it was easy. It was as demanding as it gets, in particular because you have to navigate your own way. It's not like it's a way-marked or lined route. The other eleven runners did it the sensible way. They studied the maps we were given each day and downloaded the routes onto their GPS watches. I didn't bother with any of that. I just 'winged' it and, as a result, got lost more than a few times!

What made it even more difficult was being away from Joanna and Alexander for such a long period of time. I had used up what was left of our savings on taking part in the race and there wasn't a great deal of money coming in, which stressed us both out. Eventually, Joanna moved back to Poland with Alex to be nearer to her family whilst I tried to finish the race. It brought a great strain on our relationship and, any time we spoke on the phone, we ended up arguing. At one point, we were on the brink of splitting up but we talked it through. We both knew that quitting the race would have destroyed me as a person. I can't thank her enough for being so supportive during that time. I know how hard it was for her and people looking in would probably think I was being extremely selfish. However, I was doing what I was doing for Joanna and Alex as much as I was doing it for myself.

It was somewhere in Mississippi, on 10 April 2015, that I broke Abad's record. In 362 days, I had run 367 marathons. Naturally, I was delighted but I couldn't celebrate too much. I still had two other goals to attend to: firstly, finish (and hopefully win) the Trans-American race and, secondly, bring my journey full circle by running the London Marathon.

With the marathon taking place on 26 April and lots of America still to cover, it was logistically difficult. I had to fly home from the States, run the marathon, hop back on a plane, and get back to the US in time to rejoin the race. Under the terms of the Trans-American Footrace rules, you are allowed to leave for a maximum of twenty-four hours. So, after completing my miles for the day on 25 April, I got on an overnight flight from Atlanta to Heathrow in time to take my place in the London Marathon. My intention was to run it as fast as I possibly could before dashing straight to the airport and onto a plane back to Atlanta. The way the time difference worked, I knew it was possible.

To be completely honest, I felt quite emotional on that flight back to London. I couldn't help but think back to twelve months earlier when I was just another guy sitting on the sofa dreaming of running a marathon one day. It had been the quickest year but the longest year at the same time. I found it hard to believe how much my life had changed in that time. There had been highs, lows, injuries, arguments, blisters, opportunities, more pairs of trainers than the average person probably goes through in a lifetime but, above all, satisfaction. I had set out to do something extraordinary and to inspire others, and I feel as though I achieved that.

None of it would have happened, however, without the London Marathon. I couldn't help but smile at the realisation that I had run over 370 marathons by that point – almost half the way around the world in terms of total miles covered – but I still hadn't won that bet with Joanna; I still hadn't run in London.

To be completely honest, my memories of the race itself are a little hazy. I was tired from the flight and was more focused on the fact that I needed to run it as quickly as I could to catch my plane back to the States. The race started at 10 a.m. but my return flight was at 3 p.m. from Heathrow on the outskirts of the city. So, I really got my head down and just went for it.

It was nice to have so many people cheering me on for a change. Most of my running up to that point had either been done during the dead of night whilst the rest of the country was asleep, through hills or across America, where, apart from the occasional dog chasing you, you were mostly on your own.

The crowds in London were just superb. I suspect it was partly because of them and the adrenaline generated by them that I finished in a time of 3:07:40. It was by no means my fastest marathon time but, under the circumstances, wasn't too bad.

As soon as I crossed the line, I jumped straight onto the back of a friend's motorbike and sped off to the airport. There was no time to enjoy what I'd just done, see friends and family or anything like that. I needed to get back to the USA. Fortunately, my flight was on time and I arrived in Atlanta as scheduled.

A few weeks later, on 13 June, I won the Trans-American race. I finished thirty hours ahead of my nearest challenger, Bryce Carlson, and completed the final leg of it before the organisers arrived to set up the finish line. My official time was 482 hours and ten minutes, which is the equivalent of more than twenty consecutive days of running non-stop.

Since then, I've kept on running. Fortunately, I now make an income from it through prize money and endorsements. I also do some motivational speaking, which is something I never thought that I'd enjoy but, as it turns out, I absolutely love. I guess what I like most about it is giving people belief that anything is possible. The human body is complex but can be trained to do some incredible things. The mind, meanwhile, is strong. Even when it feels weakened and broken, it is resilient and resourceful. With the right application and determination, there's very little that you cannot do. I firmly believe that.

The London Marathon is responsible for changing my life. I'm a different person now compared to the guy who watched it on TV in 2014. I feel stronger, more energised and, above all, happier than ever. I've also made peace with my past and learned to forgive my father for everything he did to me, my mother and my sister. Forgiveness is an important part of moving on. When it boils down to it, running is about putting one foot in front of the other – but how can you do that when you're burdened by your past? I'll never forget what he did to us, nor do I ever want to see or hear from him again, but I've forgiven him. The past is the past and the future is the future.

Speaking of which, I intend to keep on running and finding new, more extreme challenges. I feel as though I've only scratched the surface of my potential. I know I can do more and I'm excited to find out what that is. I understand the risks involved with what I'm doing and that there's a chance that I might one day push myself too far but, the way I see it, I'll never know until I try.

And to think all this started with one silly 20p bet.

That reminds me – Joanna still hasn't paid up!

CHAPTER TWENTY

MICHAEL LYNAGH

A winner of the 1991 Rugby World Cup with Australia – for whom he remains the record points-scorer – Michael Lynagh has run the London Marathon twice. He did so most recently in 2013, almost a year to the day after suffering a stroke that very nearly cost him his life.

STROKES are very misunderstood. I should know. I never used to understand them. Like most people, I thought of them as something that happened to old people, or overweight people, or smokers. I never thought that somebody like me – forty-eight years of age, and a young, fit and healthy forty-eight at that – could ever have one. But I did. And it nearly killed me.

It was April 2012. I had arrived in Brisbane early one morning on an overnight flight from Singapore. I'd flown there from London three or four days earlier on business. To be honest, they hadn't been the most enjoyable few days. They were pretty intense and it had been really hot and humid, so I was glad to get to Brisbane.

I went pretty much straight from the airport to play golf with my dad and a couple of friends. Looking back, it probably wasn't the best thing to do. I was tired, dehydrated and my neck was sore from sleeping funny on the plane.

Anyway, after golf, I went to catch up with some old mates. It wasn't a wild night by any means. It was just some friends catching up. It got to 8.30 p.m. – so not particularly late – and I was starting to think about going home. That's when it happened.

I took a sip of beer at the same time as one of my mates told a joke that made me laugh. The drink went down the wrong way and I started to choke. Now, everybody knows what that's like. We've all done it. This time, though, was particularly violent and when I'd recovered I couldn't see a thing. My sight was gone.

I figured it was nothing more than a combination of being tired and oxygen-starved from the coughing fit, so I sat at the end of the table with my head in my hands trying to shake my vision back. That's when the headache started. It wasn't a normal headache. It genuinely felt as if I'd just been smashed with a baseball bat. I didn't know it at the time but my back right artery had split.

One of my friends saw I was in a bit of bother and asked if I was okay. I said, 'I'm not sure, just give me a moment.' Now, usually, in a situation like that, the guys would probably have roughed me up a bit and said something like, 'Toughen up, Lynagh. Have another beer and we'll drop you home.' On this occasion, though, they asked the right question, which was to see if I needed an ambulance, and I gave the right answer, which was 'yes'. I really didn't know what was happening – but I knew something was wrong.

Within an hour, I was in the hospital. I was still fully conscious and able to talk, so I was aware of everything that was going on. I wasn't in a good way but I could communicate and had full movement of my arms and legs, thank goodness.

The doctors checked me over and quickly came to the conclusion that I'd had a stroke. That then started about an eight-day spell of some pretty rough stuff, where I really had to fight to pull through. And by 'fight', I mean *fight*.

The surgeons had planned to operate to relieve the swelling that was pressing against my skull and spinal cord but they decided not to. They said that because I was functioning so well they wouldn't have been able to forgive themselves had something gone wrong during that procedure, which was highly possible. So, they decided on a non-invasive form of treatment instead. It basically involved dehydrating me for three days to try to reduce the swelling that way. Again, though, it's a risky approach. Unbeknownst to me, my father asked the doctors if many people come through this particular form of treatment. Their response was clear and unambiguous: no, not many.

Those three days were pretty harrowing. I was – well, it was close, put it that way. Things got so bad that I had my father come to visit me in the hospital and take a note of all the things that I thought my wife, Isabella, would need in the event that I didn't pull through. Bank account passwords and things like that. She and our three boys were back home in London and I can remember trying to prepare myself for not seeing them again. I guess, in my own way, I was trying to say goodbye. It was awful. I was lucid but in a lot of pain. At times, it felt too hard to keep fighting – but I did.

It was around the sixth day that I started to improve, both physically and psychologically, and I can remember thinking, 'Right, I'm going to beat this.' That's when I think my age, health and fitness really came into its own and, in the end, I came out the other side relatively unscathed. I've lost fifty per cent of my vision but when medical experts can't explain why you haven't been more severely affected, you know you're a lucky guy. One of my doctors told me that it wasn't a bullet I'd dodged but a great big cannonball. I was just extraordinarily fortunate the stroke didn't hit the wires it should have hit and which would have majorly impaired my movement, speech and so on. I don't know what else to call it other than a miracle.

Where does the London Marathon fit in to all this? Well, it was about six months after the stroke and I was recovering well. One particular day, I was doing some work for Sky Sports with James Gemmell and Sean Fitzpatrick when James asked me for a word. He said he was thinking about running the London Marathon to raise money for a charity that had a special meaning for him, which just so happened to be The Stroke Foundation. He asked me what I thought of the idea and I said, 'Sounds great – in fact, if you like, I'll run it with you!'

I had run the London Marathon once before, back in 2000. I'd retired from rugby only a few years earlier and I needed something to focus on, something to work towards. When you've spent years and years watching what you eat and getting up early to go to training every day, it's a bit of a shock to the system to suddenly not have that in your life any more. In that respect, the London Marathon was the right challenge at exactly the right time.

Thing is, I was never a particularly good runner. I wasn't built to run long distances; I was built to run ten yards as quickly as possible, then look for somebody to pass the ball to. The running I was used to was 'short, sharp, recover, repeat' and, because of that, a marathon meant retraining my body. It was a long process but I got there in the end and, fortunately, I managed to complete the race. More to the point, I ran it with two friends and, combined, we raised a lot of money – around £300,000–£400,000 pounds – to build an athletics track at Stoke Mandeville Hospital in Buckinghamshire. That's something I'm really proud of.

I had always intended to run the marathon again but never got round to it. I could say life got in the way – which is true – but I also never really had a reason to do it. When James mentioned it that day, though, that was all the motivation I needed. I knew pretty much immediately that I wanted to do it. I just had two concerns. One, it had only been six months since my stroke – was it too soon to be contemplating taking on a marathon? Two, I've got bad knees. Terrible knees, really. They've always been bad, going right back to when I was a kid. I kept getting tears in my meniscus and I think I've had seven or eight ops on each one to the point that there's nothing left. I'll inevitably need to get them both replaced in the next few years and, when I do, I know my orthopaedic surgeon will be thrilled. He told me back in 1998 that he had no idea how I'd managed to play professional rugby because, in his words, I had the knees of a sixty-year-old; I was only in my mid-thirties at the time! I actually saw him again in 2015 for a check-up and he said, 'Michael, there's good news and there's bad news. The bad news is that your knees are shot. The good news is you're getting closer to the day when you'll be as old as them!'

So, I wasn't really proposing to run the London Marathon with James. I was more proposing to jog, walk and just really get round as best I could. Finish the marathon on the same day as I started – that was the aim.

My training consisted of a lot of walking, albeit quickly, around Richmond Park. Nothing much more than that. In fact, I'd be lying if I said I ran at all before the morning of the race.

James, meanwhile, trained really well. He was in top condition and was looking to do it in a really good time when, with just a week until race day, he had a calf blowout which left him unable to run. As you can imagine, he was gutted but I said to him, 'Mate, don't worry about it. Forget about your time. Come with me and we'll walk it instead. If it takes six hours, it takes six hours. The important thing is doing it.' He nodded his head and on we went.

As it happened, the race was almost a year to the day after I had my stroke so it felt great to be standing there on the start line. It was kind of impossible not to reflect on everything that had happened in the previous twelve months.

My recovery had been good but not easy. Not easy by any means. It helped that, like most professional athletes, I knew my body pretty well but there were still days when it was really difficult.

I would set myself little goals to try and move it along. To give you an idea, the first of those was just to get out of bed and walk to the bathroom unaided. It was really that modest a goal and, believe me, I was thrilled when I managed it. It was slow progress at first and I was careful not to overdo things. When I was tired, I slept. When I was hungry, I ate. I took good care of myself because I knew how fortunate I'd been. I'd had a stroke and come out on the other side relatively unscathed. Most people aren't so lucky.

So, yeah, standing at the start line for the London Marathon was quite a special feeling and whether it was just thinking of that stuff or being full of adrenaline, James and I ended up jogging most of the first half of the race to Tower Bridge before walking the rest. Don't get me wrong, we walked as quickly as we could – so quickly that we even passed a lot of people – and we finally made it to the finish line, raising around £70,000–£80,000 in the act. There were actually about four or five others from Sky Sports who did it, too, and afterwards we all went back to my house for a barbecue. It was a great day. A brilliant day, really.

One part of it particularly stands out. I remember us getting to the Canary Wharf area about lunchtime. It was a beautiful, sunny day and we were walking by this point. Suddenly, a guy shouted to us from the beer garden of a pub adjacent to the route. 'Hey, Lynagh,' he called over between swigs of his beer. 'It's called *running* the London Marathon, not *walking* it!' That gave us a real laugh. I shouted back to him, 'Do you want to swap places?' He just grinned and said, 'No way, mate,' and went back to his pint.

For me, that kind of sums it up. Everyone is good-humoured and supportive. I mean, right from the very start, the people are amazing. It's quite something to run past all of these parties and pubs and barbecues and musicians performing – there's really nothing else like it.

Looking back now, completing that second London Marathon was a big thing for me. It was the icing on the cake of my intention to make my recovery not just good but really good. The thing about people who have strokes is that, when they leave hospital, most folk assume that they're cured, fixed, ready to get back to normal life. Fact is, that's when they need support the most. Having a stroke can be a lonely, isolating experience. It can shatter your confidence and make a hell of a dent in your self-worth.

A lot of people don't understand that. In my case, I don't look like a 'typical' stroke victim. By and large, I'm pretty healthy. My appearance isn't really any different after it, I don't speak any differently and you obviously can't see that I've lost half of my vision. Still, seeing is believing, isn't it? If you see someone walking around with a cast on their arm, you know they've probably broken it. It's clear-cut, simple. A stroke isn't always that obvious – and it certainly wasn't for me – so I can see why some people may think that it's a bit of a fuss about nothing. I don't blame them if they think that but it's frustrating. Sometimes it frustrates me to the point that I wish I could wear something around my neck that says, 'Hey, this happened. I beat it but it happened.' Every now and again, for example, I'll bump into someone on a train platform and they'll swear at me. Your first instinct is to go after them, tell them you didn't do it deliberately and that it only happened because you've got fifty per cent vision – but what good would that do?

Instead, the London Marathon was a much better focus for my energy. Everybody who runs it does so to satisfy a personal motivation. The first time I took part, for example, I just wanted to get to the finish line without stopping. I made that my goal because I didn't think it would be possible. The furthest I'd run during my training had been about ten miles, simply because of the state of my knees. But I turned up, did it and went round in about four-and-a-quarter hours, not stopping once. I was passed by a palm tree and a wedding cake and that sort of thing but it didn't matter. I accomplished my goal. For me, that's what the London Marathon is all about. It's exhilarating, fulfilling and intoxicating. It's just amazing.

CHAPTER TWENTY-ONE

CLAIRE LOMAS

At the age of twenty-seven, Leicestershire eventer Claire Lomas had her life turned upside down in May 2007 when a freak horse-riding accident left her paralysed from the chest down. Less than five years later, with a little help from a pioneering piece of technology, she completed the 2012 London Marathon to raise money for the Spinal Research charity.

I COULDN'T have been much more than two years old when I first got on a horse and, from that day on, equestrianism became a massive part of my life. Any opportunity I got, I'd saddle up and go for a ride.

Consequently, I don't think anybody who knew me was surprised when I got into competitive eventing. I loved everything about it: the training, the dedication and commitment it demanded of you – everything.

Of course, unlike other sports, as an event rider, you're not only responsible for yourself; you're also responsible for your horses. They need to be properly looked after, well fed, well groomed and well trained to enable them to perform to the very best of their capabilities. It's a 365-days-a-year job. Even on Christmas Day, I'd be out seeing to them. But I didn't begrudge it. Being a chiropractor was my job, but eventing was my life.

It was on 6 May 2007 that my life changed forever. I was competing at the Osberton Horse Trials in Nottinghamshire on a horse that I knew pretty well. He was very experienced and I had ridden him in competition loads of times, so we had a really good partnership.

On this particular day, the track we were riding on split in two and the horse got confused thinking that he was meant to go one way, when he was supposed to go the other. He clipped his shoulder on a tree, which unseated me and threw me straight into the same tree. I hit it quite high up, knocking the bark off, and as soon as I hit the ground I knew what had happened – I was paralysed.

I wasn't knocked out. I was able to talk and communicate with the first responders who attended to me. I just couldn't move. It was really scary. I thought to myself, 'I can't get up – I always get up.'

The doctors later confirmed what I suspected. I'd broken my back quite high up and suffered a spinal cord injury on my T4 thoracic vertebra. In other words, I was paralysed from the chest down. I had also fractured my neck, broken some ribs and punctured a lung but all this was nothing compared to finding out that I was paralysed.

It was devastating. Imagine your worst nightmare coming true and you're probably still not even close. I had always been a really independent and active person, so to suddenly find out that I couldn't get up and walk around was extremely tough to take.

What made it worse was the realisation that I'd no longer be able to ride horses. Like I said at the outset, equestrianism and eventing had been all I'd known as long as I could remember. I knew the risks, of course. It's a dangerous sport but, to be honest, I thrived on that. The higher the risk, the greater the adrenaline. I just never thought anything would ever happen to me.

In the immediate aftermath of the accident, I spent ten days in intensive care, after which I was moved to the Princess Royal Spinal Injuries Unit in Sheffield. I discharged myself after eight weeks and went over to the USA for more intensive rehabilitation. That basically involved trying to work the bits that didn't work. You know, just to see if there was any hope that I might be able to regain some movement. If I'd never tried, I would always have been left wondering 'what if' and I didn't want to be haunted by that. I needed to at least try. Of course, nothing changed. I persevered with the rehab to keep fit and healthy – I still do it, as it happens – but, in terms of regaining any feeling below the chest, there has been no improvement.

For all that, I was always acutely aware that I was in a better position than a lot of the other people who had been in the hospital at the same time. I, for example, was able to move my arms and hands. However, some of the people

I saw could not and that meant they were unable to feed themselves, dress themselves and, to all intents and purposes, look after themselves. I found it quite sad to think that, for the rest of their lives (or at least until they find a way to reverse paralysis), they're going to be dependent on other people to help them do all of the things that the majority of us take for granted.

That made me determined to try to do something to help, particularly as my own circumstances started to improve. I met my husband, Dan, about a year after my accident and, in 2011, we had a little girl called Maisie, which was wonderful. The scales had tipped and the good days now greatly outweighed the bad. But I still harboured a need to give something back.

The thing about me is that I've always liked personal challenges. When I was eventing, for instance, I was always focused on the next big competition and, as a result, I reached a pretty high level in the sport.

The accident changed what I was capable of physically but it didn't change who I am as a person. I still had the same level of determination and the same desire to test myself at every opportunity. So, I wanted a challenge, something to fill the void left by eventing, and the London Marathon seemed like a great idea.

I had always fancied doing it. I watched it on television and often thought how amazing it looked but I had never got around to doing it. Horses and eventing took up most of my time, so I could never commit to doing all of the training it required. My accident changed all of that, though, and so, in 2011, I signed up to take part in 2012.

There was just one problem: how was I going to get round if I couldn't stand up?

The ReWalk suit seemed like my best bet. It was invented by an Israeli electrical engineer called Dr Amit Goffer, who has himself been a quadriplegic since an accident in 1997. It is a quite brilliant creation. It is basically a bionic exoskeleton that consists of a lightweight suit that you wear around your legs, chest and back. It uses highly sensitive sensors to measure your upper body movements and shifts in gravity. The information gathered by these sensors is then processed by a computer system that you wear in a backpack, which initiates the walking motion that you complete by stabilising yourself against a pair of crutches. So, it doesn't walk for you, as such. You have to move the parts of your body that you are able to move in order to give the sensors information for the computer to process. In my case, that means tilting my pelvis in the direction I want to go.

However, when you can't even feel the ground you're standing on, never mind your legs, it's very hard to shift your weight at the right time because, well, how can you trust that your legs are there if you can't feel them?

So, when I got the suit (I was actually the first person in the country to get one), it took a lot of getting used to. To begin with, I just tried to learn how to keep my balance and stand upright. Once I'd mastered that, it became a matter of seeing how far across the room I could go. Only when I'd got comfortable with it indoors was I able to take it outside, which was even tougher still. I really had to focus on each step and concentrate on where I was going. Every little bump or camber on the road became a huge obstacle that had to be very carefully navigated. At times, I wasn't sure if I was ever going to get totally comfortable with it, far less cover a marathon distance in it. After all, I only got the suit in January 2012 – just three months before the race. But, like I said, I'm a very determined person. I knew I would give it everything I had. I just had to hope that would be enough to see me through.

Ultimately, the day of the race came around and I took my place in the 'Green' start area with my support team. Unlike everybody else there that morning, I knew I wouldn't be crossing the finish line in four or five hours' time. The furthest I'd been able to walk by that point was one mile, one time, so I was prepared for it to take me more than a fortnight to complete. We didn't really discuss how far we were going to go each day. We knew that would depend on how hilly some sections were or how many roads I'd have to cross because all those things really slow you down. The plan wasn't any more detailed than to put one foot in front of the other as quickly as I could for as long as it took me.

I also had to be vigilant about things like sores, blisters and abrasion. Obviously, I couldn't feel if the suit was pinching me or not, so that involved regular checks to make sure I was okay, which, again, slowed us down. Still, we were determined and excited as we lined up along with everybody else.

The atmosphere as the race got underway was truly incredible. The biggest thrill of my eventing career had been competing at the Burghley Horse Trials – one of the three events that makes up the Grand Slam of Eventing – and I never thought anything would ever match that. However, the start line of the London Marathon was actually even more of a buzz.

Spurred on by that, I walked just over two miles on the first day. The roads were closed, so I wanted to capitalise on that as much as I possibly could. It meant I was able to walk without having to worry too much about the camber or anything like that. Plus, Sir Matthew Pinsent – the four-time Olympic rowing gold medallist – turned up to support me, which was fantastic, so I ended up going further than I'd expected.

At the end of day one, I went back to where I was staying to recuperate and get ready to go through the whole thing again the next day. I was fortunate that a friend invited me to stay in her flat, whilst the Chancery Court Hotel in Holborn also offered to put me up, so I had options for where to stay. People were just so generous. I even had the same taxi driver throughout, a lovely guy called Dom, who picked me up and dropped me off every day free of charge. We would have racked up hundreds of pounds' worth of fares over the course of the challenge but he refused to accept a penny from us, which was so unbelievably kind. We're still in touch to this day.

To begin with, it was quite tough. I'd look at the map at the end of each day and it looked as though we had barely moved. On top of that, it felt like the centre of the city was really far away, so I had to dig deep to stay motivated. My supporters, led by Dan, were brilliant at keeping my spirits up, too. They were really positive and encouraging every step of the way, no matter how tough it got or how bad the weather became. It rained nearly every day – sometimes torrentially – but we persevered and just kept on moving. Nothing was going to stop us.

The support we got along the way from people we encountered was really quite humbling. The more that word got out through the media, the more people took an interest in what we were doing. Random strangers would roll down their car windows to give us a donation, so too would people walking past us on their way to work or sitting in bus shelters. Others would even come out of their houses to chip in with some money. It was incredible.

Getting to Tower Bridge was a particularly special moment. I got there eight days into the challenge and it felt significant because, for one thing, it was the halfway point. On top of that, I was met there by Kenny and Gabby Logan, as well as some of my old eventing friends. The Badminton Horse Trials should have been taking place that weekend but got cancelled because it was so wet so, instead, a lot of them came along to cheer me on. That was an amazing experience and now, whenever I see that bridge, it always brings a smile to my face.

Other well-known faces who came out to support me included Dave Vitty, Dan Lobb, Clare Balding, Bob Wilson and Matt Holland, as well as Ben Fogle, Tim Henman, Patrick Monahan, Natalie Pinkham, Tom James and David Weir. I will forever be grateful to them for braving the conditions to help me get to the finish line, which I reached exactly seventeen days after my challenge started.

I never thought that I wouldn't finish, unless, of course, forced to by an injury or sores. To be honest, I would have been more surprised if I hadn't finished. What did come as a surprise was that I felt a little bit sad about getting to the end. I mean, yes, I was ready to stop walking. I was tired, sore and very much looking forward to not having to come back and do it all again the next day. At the same time, though, I'd had a lot of fun doing it. It had been an unforgettable experience and I'd made a lot of new friends along the way, so, from that point of view, it was sad it had to end.

Once I turned the corner at Buckingham Palace, I saw a whole line of people waiting for me to complete those last few hundred metres. There were TV crews filming, photographers jostling for position and, of course, loads and loads of well-wishers cheering me on towards a finish line that had been specially erected. There was also a guard of honour comprising mounted members of the Household Cavalry – one of the most senior regiments in the British Army – waiting there for me.

I could feel myself getting quite emotional when I saw all that, so I tried to just concentrate on my feet and watch where they were going. In the end, I crossed the line with my family, Maisie included, following behind me. It's hard to put into words just how good that moment felt.

I later found out that, through all the sponsorship and donations, we'd raised more than £210,000 for Spinal Research, which was just mind-blowing.

Since that day, I've hardly stopped. I raised £85,000 in May 2013 by hand-cycling around England and, in 2015, my fundraising total smashed through half a million pounds.

On top of that, I've been able to ski (another one of my great passions) and discovered a new love of motorcycling. In fact, as I write, I'm working towards getting my racing licence. I suppose in that respect I've swapped one saddle for another! I've also started a new career as a motivational speaker, which is something I had never previously dreamt I could do.

So, my life is very different to what it was before my accident but the most important things are that I'm busy again and very, very happy. It has taken a while to get to this point and I've had some really challenging moments. There were times early on when I'd think to myself that it might have been better if I'd hit the tree a bit harder but, as the old cliché goes, what doesn't kill you makes you stronger. I'm stronger and happier now than I've ever been. I've got a wonderful husband, a beautiful little girl, a fantastic family, great friends and I've got a number of hobbies that I absolutely love. I've had doors close on me but even better ones open.

When all is said and done, that's all any of us can ask for, isn't it?

CHAPTER TWENTY-TWO

DAVE HEELEY

Diagnosed with a rare eye condition, which led to him losing his sight in his early twenties, Dave Heeley was determined never to let being blind stand in his way. Along with two friends, he ran the London Marathon in 2002, which proved to be not only the first of many feats of endurance he would undertake, but also the beginning of a whole new life for the West Bromwich man.

I WAS ten years old when I was told I had an eye condition called retinitis pigmentosa. It's a hereditary condition – my grandfather had it, too – but it wasn't until I was older that it was diagnosed by a consultant at the Birmingham Eye Hospital, who told me that it would ultimately leave me blind.

At the time, I didn't think much of it. I could still see, I could still kick a ball, I could still read a book. I wasn't able to see very well at night but it's not like there's a gauge to tell you how good or bad your sight is, so I just thought I was the same as any other kid. I would run into things and fall over things but people just thought I was a bit clumsy.

It was when I was eighteen and I went to join the Armed Forces that the full extent of what was happening first started to dawn on me. My sight had got progressively worse throughout my teenage years and now, here I was, being told I couldn't join the army because of it. I was angry, bitter and felt sorry for myself. I thought that blindness was robbing me of my life. Little did I know that it would be the start of an incredible journey.

It was when I was in my early twenties that I gave myself an ultimatum: either live my own life as much as I could or let blindness become my life. It was as simple as that. It was like a switch flicked and I started to worry less about what I couldn't do and focus more on what I could. The way I saw it, it was either sit there and do nothing or take it on the chin and adapt to my circumstances. I've managed to come to terms with it now to such an extent that I'm able to treat my blindness as a gift. I genuinely believe I was born to be blind. I'm not ashamed of it. It doesn't embarrass me. It's what I am. It's funny, I think other people are more embarrassed of it than I am. They seem frightened to use the 'B' word and will describe me as 'visually impaired' or something like that. I'm not, though. I'm blind and I'm okay with that. It's not something that anybody aspires to be, obviously, but I've got used to it and, more to the point, got a lot out of it, too.

One of those things is the London Marathon. It's a long story but starts with a dog. It was back in the mid-nineties that, after much persuasion, I got my first guide dog. It was one of the best decisions I ever made and one of the few regrets I have is not getting one sooner. I'm on my fourth dog now and it's just been a wonderful experience. They've given me back so much of my independence and been fabulous companions into the bargain.

Anyway, fast-forward to 2001. I was out for a few drinks in the local pub one night. A guy I knew, a chap called Roy, came up and asked me for a word. He said that he had seen me out and about in the town with the dog and he was so impressed by it that he wanted to do something to raise money for Guide Dogs for the Blind. I asked him what he had in mind and he said he wanted to do the London Marathon the following year, 2002. I said to him, 'You know what? That sounds like a cracking idea. I think I'll run it with you.'

Now, like I say, I'd had a few drinks, so the next morning my wife Deb said to me, 'Do you realise what you said last night? Have you any idea what you're getting yourself into?' Still, I just thought it seemed like a great idea. Before I lost my sight, back when I was still at school, I was quite a good runner. I enjoyed cross country and was the 1,500-metre champion for five years on the trot. But that was thirty years earlier. How was I going to run a marathon now that I was in my forties and blind? I didn't even own a pair of trainers! Still, I've always been a bit of a risk-taker and not one to shirk a challenge so I thought, 'I'm going to do this.'

Over the years, I'd tried to keep myself relatively fit. I used to do a bit of weight training, as well as sit-ups, push-ups, that kind of thing. I also liked swimming and, obviously, pretty much everywhere that I go, I have to walk, which is good for you. However, running a marathon is a whole other kettle of fish.

Just to be clear, I should point out that I am completely blind. I have zero vision whatsoever. I'm asked that quite regularly. Another question I get asked is, 'Can you still dream even though you're blind?' Yes, to a point. For instance, I can't distinguish people's faces in my dreams any more. I can still make out certain details but, to use my late father as an example, I still see him from time to time when I dream but I can only make out part of his nose, or part of his eyes, or part of his ear. It's as if my memory banks are diminishing because I haven't been able to top them up with 'photos', so to speak.

As another example, when my daughters were little, I'd pop my head into their room to say goodnight. Now, I knew that the lights were off, that the curtains were drawn and that the room was dark. Even so, it seemed very bright to me. The next night, it'd be black.

I can still imagine colours, too. Red, blue, pink, yellow, green, you name it. I can't see them but I can imagine them, if that makes sense. I'm lucky enough to know, for example, what a red jumper looks like. I can still construct a visual of most of the things I saw before I lost my sight completely. However, if you were to ask me to describe an iPod or an iPhone, I couldn't tell you – not without feeling it, anyway – because I've never seen one.

In the main, I'm quite good around the house. It's a normal household for the most part. I can make my own cup of tea, do the washing-up, do the hoovering, make stuff in my own workshop, so I like to feel that I'm as independent as I can be but I also understand and accept the fact that I need help. There are obviously some things that I can't do and that's just the way it is. There's no point pretending otherwise.

The other thing people want to know is if your remaining senses are heightened when you go blind. For example, they'll say, 'Your hearing must be a lot better than mine.' Believe me, it's not. I just use it in a different way. Whilst most people cross the road using their eyes, I cross the road using my ears. I listen to more of what's around me than most other people do. Ninety-five per cent of the typical person's day consists of sight. Ninety-five per cent of mine is sound. So, you don't gain a 'sixth sense'; you just get conditioned to using the senses at your disposal differently.

Running is a good example of that. Obviously, I can't just go out for a run.

I need to have a guide that I know and trust and, on top of that, I have to pay attention to what my senses are telling me. I don't have my eyes to rely on like most other people.

Luckily, in Roy and another friend, Joe, I had two fantastic guys to train with for the 2002 London Marathon. I still remember the very first training session we did. I'd borrowed a pair of trainers, a pair of shorts, a running top and off we went down to a local running track. Each holding on to opposite ends of a towel, Joe and I ran round it twice and I don't mind admitting that it really took it out of me. I remember thinking, 'Bloody hell, I'm knackered after two laps of a 400m track – how am I going to manage a marathon!'

Still, I was undeterred. All I wanted to do was find a way to run better and more efficiently. First things first, that meant finding something more suitable than a towel for me and my guides. At the time, I was doing some carpentry and weaving, so I adapted some canvas strapping and had loops sewn onto both ends of it to slip our hands through. That worked pretty well.

After a few sessions on the track, we figured we needed to take our training to the next level. We decided to stay away from grass and off-road surfaces as much as possible because, besides anything else, Joe and Roy had trouble seeing ditches and potholes in them. We decided instead that tarmac roads or gravel paths would be a better option for us.

We started off running small laps at first, just a mile and a half at a time. It wasn't a particularly great distance but it was a good place to start. This is where walking with a guide dog for a number of years really came into its own. I was used to listening, sudden movements and that kind of thing. So, when we started running, Joe or Roy would tell me when there was a kerb coming up. What happened at first was that we'd stop, I'd step off, run across the road, stop, step back up onto the pavement and go again. It was quite stop-start at first. However, as the confidence started to grow, it became much more fluent. They'd say, 'Kerb coming up, off now, on now.' For the most part, it worked really well. Occasionally, I'd have a little stumble but that can happen to any runner whether they've got their vision or not.

In the first few weeks of our training, we probably only got up to about two or three miles at a time but, gradually, we started cranking up the distance and, within two months, we were up to ten miles. We trained in the local streets of West Brom and Sandwell. Sometimes we ran into Birmingham and back. Other times we ran through Walsall or to Wolverhampton. We had a nice variety of routes to keep things interesting and to really build up our confidence. We worked really well together and gelled in no time at all.

Anyway, our training went really well. We did all of our long runs – eighteen miles, twenty miles and twenty-two miles – so we felt nice and prepared going into the race itself. We hadn't managed to get in through the ballot but, luckily, we were given places by Guide Dogs for the Blind, which was fantastic.

The weekend of the race arrived and we took the train down to London on the Friday. The first thing on our agenda was going to the Expo to get our race numbers and packs so that we were ready to go on Sunday morning. On the Saturday, we just tried to chill out and go for a little walk around London with our families but, before we knew it, it was Sunday morning and time to get going.

We were up bright and early, pinned our numbers to our tops, got into our tracksuits, I popped my white stick under my arm and, together, we caught the train to Blackheath. I remember walking from the station to the park, hearing thousands of other people milling about and the burr of a helicopter hovering above us. Immediately, I had a sense of how big an event it was and how incredible a day lay in store.

The camaraderie was extraordinary. People came up to us and asked us where we had come from, who we were running for, whether we had run before. It was such a warm, friendly environment.

We had arrived about an hour-and-a-half before the race was due to get underway but it all went by in a flash and, next thing I knew, we were gathering in our 'pen' ready to get going. We went in the four-and-a-half-hour pen – that was our target time – and I remember just standing in amongst thousands and thousands of people thinking, 'Blooming heck!' I'd always imagined it would be quite a big deal but I had absolutely no inkling as to the scale of it all. It was mind-blowing.

Once the first runners set off, it took us about five minutes to reach the official start line – that ought to give you an idea of how busy it was – but, finally, it was time to get going. It was slow going at first. We were trotting more than running. It was just wall to wall bodies. I knew that the race was big and that thousands ran it but until you're actually there and standing shoulder to shoulder, chest to back and back to chest with everyone else, like you're in some kind of sardine tin, you don't really understand what it's like. I was a little worried to begin with. I thought that I would be falling or accidentally tripping other people up pretty much constantly but Joe and Roy were great. They steered me to perfection, telling me when to move left or right, when to speed up, when to slow down, what to watch out for. But it wasn't just that. They also described everything magnificently. They told me when we went past a major landmark, like the *Cutty Sark* or Big Ben. They told me about the crowds. They told me everything I needed to know and more. They were exceptional, as were the other runners taking part. If they got a bit too close, Joe or Roy politely pointed out to them that I was blind and they all respected it and gave me space.

All the way round, all I could hear was people chanting and shouting and singing. There were bands playing, barbecues sizzling, people yelling 'Oggy! Oggy! Oggy!' and so on. It was unreal. It seemed like the further round you went, the more intense the spectators became. Coming down the Embankment, for example, they were screaming at you to keep pushing, keep digging deep, keep on moving. It was something else. Just thinking back to it makes the hairs on the back of my neck stand on end.

I had actually been given a tip to put my name on the front of my shirt and it was one of the best things I did. I lost track of the amount of people I heard shouting, 'Come on Dave,' 'You can do this Dave,' and so on. Knowing that stranger's voice was, at that moment in time, aimed specifically at me made it so personal and so special. It really kept me going.

My favourite moment was when we went underneath the river for the last time to rejoin the Embankment. Just as we exited the underpass, I shouted 'Oggy! Oggy! Oggy!' as loud as I could. I must have timed it to perfection because the 'Oi! Oi! Oi!' that came back at me was deafening. It sounded as though there were 20,000 people shouting it to me. It was deafening, an absolute cacophony of noise.

The last couple of miles were quite brilliant. We turned right at Big Ben, came down through St James's Park, passed Buckingham Palace and – wow – the noise. People were screaming and cheering and clapping, and that propelled us forward for those final few hundred metres.

Crossing the finishing line (in a time of 4:16, for what it's worth) was possibly the most amazing feeling I've ever had in my entire life. You are absolutely consumed by this intense euphoria but, almost immediately, your body starts to let you know what you've just done and you are hit by all of these aches and pains. I remember crying, laughing, shouting – there were just so many emotions rolled into one.

The three of us stood just past the finish line for about five minutes to gather ourselves when this young lady approached us. She said, 'Excuse me but I'm with Sky TV and we're looking for three English guys who've just run the marathon. Would you mind us interviewing you?' Roy pointed at me and said, 'Sure, we're three English lads but he's blind.' Next thing we knew, we were getting interviewed live on telly. I remember them asking me, 'What was it like running the marathon blind, Dave?' I said, 'I started out in Blackheath as a blind guy. Now I've finished, I'm blind and knackered!'

For a lot of people, running the marathon just once would have been quite enough but, for me, it was only the beginning. From that moment on, I've been constantly on the look-out for the next big race, the next big challenge. Since then, I've run on every single continent but, believe me, there's nothing like London. You go to New York, for example, and shout, 'Oggy! Oggy! Oggy!' and nobody has a clue what you're on about! But Londoners get it.

The London Marathon in 2008, incidentally, was the seventh of my seven marathons in seven days on seven continents. The challenge took me to the Falkland Islands (Antarctica), Rio de Janeiro in Brazil (South America), Los Angeles (North America) and Sydney (Australasia), followed by Dubai (Asia), Tunisia (Africa) and finally London. Because of the scale of the challenge and, of course, my blindness, there was a lot of media interest in the subsequent days and weeks.

During all of that, an idea formed in my mind. I figured I had become pretty good at speaking in public. Perhaps I could become a motivational speaker? I gave it a go and, lo and behold, I've done it ever since. I absolutely love it but it would never have happened without the London Marathon and the buzz I got from finishing that first one in 2002. It made me hungry for more challenges; those challenges made me accustomed to speaking about overcoming adversity; and that led me to become a motivational speaker.

It's funny how life turns out, isn't it? I had my own ceiling business that I lost during the recession in the early nineties. I then planned on setting up my own carpentry and woodturning business only for the political and economic landscape to change again and leave those plans on the scrapheap. But now, through the London Marathon, I've been able to become something I never thought I would be. It has taken me all around the world. Ireland, France, Spain, Dubai – you name it. And you know what? I absolutely love it.

It's funny. Even now, people make excuses for me because of my blindness. They'll say, 'You can't do that, Dave.' Well, that's nonsense. I know my capabilities and, believe me, they are so much more than most people would think. Why? Because I don't let fear get in the way. If I can do something, why would I be scared of it?

Life is a series of opportunities and challenges. The more you put in, the more you get out. It took going blind for me to realise that, and it took running the London Marathon for me to use that to my advantage.

It's no exaggeration to say that it has changed my life, and changed it for the better.

CHAPTER TWENTY-THREE

LAURA ELLIOTT

When they got engaged, Paul Elliott and Laura Harvey quickly decided they didn't want a traditional wedding. Instead, they wanted something that would better represent their sporty personalities. The 2015 London Marathon proved to be that 'something' . . .

WHEN people ask me to describe my experience of running the London Marathon, it's pretty easy really. I started it with a fiancé; I finished it with a husband.

To explain how this happened, we need to go back to December 2007. That's when Paul and I met in a nightclub in Clapham. We were on a night out with mutual friends from a sports club and we just clicked straight away. We were both living in London at the time. I was working for Merton Council doing sports development, whilst Paul was in HR at Imperial College London.

We started dating, things went great and, like any couple, as our relationship developed, we started planning for the future. The subject of getting engaged had come up a few times but Paul being Paul, he still managed to completely surprise me when it happened.

I had run a 10km race in Hyde Park early one morning and, afterwards, we went into the city. We were walking through Leicester Square when he suddenly decided he wanted a caricaturist to draw our picture. I thought nothing of it and sat and posed with him for it, completely oblivious to the fact that Paul had pre-arranged it all. This wasn't some random caricaturist. It was, in fact, someone he had hand-picked and given instructions to draw us as normal but with a speech bubble coming from him which said, 'Will you marry me?' It was only when the guy turned the picture around for us to see it that I realised what was happening. Naturally, I said yes straight away. It was very romantic, very inventive.

Of course, getting engaged is just the first step. You've then got to actually organise the wedding.

We had talked previously about the possibility of getting married during the marathon. Neither of us is particularly into the whole 'traditional' wedding thing but we're both quite sporty. Plus, Paul had always fancied running the London Marathon – I'd already done it once before in 2009 – so it seemed like a good way to combine those two things. So, after we got engaged, we decided to look into it a little more seriously.

To be completely honest, I'm not sure that either of us really expected it to work because it had the potential to be a real logistical nightmare. Still, we were keen to see how far we could go with it.

The first item on our agenda was finding a venue. We started to research places along the route and, by chance, we found The Dickens Inn in St Katharine Docks. It's just 100 yards or so off the marathon route and is located shortly after Tower Bridge. We wanted something around the halfway mark, so it was absolutely perfect. We went to check it out and we loved it straight away. It's a really pretty building with a nice, chilled atmosphere. We first looked at it around the May or June of 2014 and, by chance, the manager there had run the marathon just a few weeks earlier. He raved about the experience and, when we told him what we were planning, he got really excited. In fact, he was probably even more excited than we were. I think he immediately had this vision of what it would be like, which was a real boost to our plans.

He also said that he'd be able to give us a discount on the price to help us out, which was superb. In the end, he actually donated the whole of the hire charge to our nominated charity – Cancer Research UK – which was an incredible gesture.

Running for Cancer Research UK was very important to us. Paul's father died from bowel cancer in 1995, so it was close to our hearts and running the marathon for that particular cause was something Paul wanted to do to honour his dad. It was his way, I guess, of having him be a part of our day.

We contacted Cancer Research UK, explained to them what we were planning to do and, fortunately, they kindly gave us two of their charity places.

So, that was another box ticked as, until then, we didn't even know if we'd get to run or not.

Next, we had to get permission from the race organisers to leave the route for the ceremony and, more to the point, return to it afterwards. I phoned up the London Marathon offices and, after initially being told there was no way we could possibly do that, they agreed. I don't know if they decided it would be good publicity for them but I'm glad that they got on board with the idea otherwise, again, that could have been the whole thing ruined.

So, we had our venue, our places in the marathon and permission to leave the route. Suddenly, the realisation hit us that we were doing this. It's funny, when you find out that you've got a place in a marathon, your first instinct is to draw up a training plan. To be honest, though, training was the furthest thing from our minds at that point. We still had a lot to organise, not least what we were going to wear.

For obvious reasons, wearing traditional wedding outfits was out of the question. Even so, we still wanted something that resembled them. The trick was finding a way to make them practical for running twenty-six miles. In the end, I decided to make them.

For Paul, I chose a black running top that had a zip you could almost open up and add bits to, to give him the appearance of wearing a tuxedo, shirt and a tie. I then took another top and turned it upside down to make tails. My mum was a great help with her sewing machine. My outfit, meanwhile, was a kind of tennis dress customised with pieces of basic lace dresses and other details. I actually got a lot of fantastic ideas from a really nice guy in a dressmaker's in Balham, in south London, which was brilliant. I explained what we were doing and he was incredibly helpful. He gave me some great suggestions to make it look like a proper wedding dress but still be practical for running in. I was so pleased with how it turned out. It even had a strip of buttons sewn down the back of it, as suggested by a friend's mum, which made it look really authentic.

By the Christmas of 2014, we had done the vast majority of our planning, which was really important because we knew that we'd have to really step up our training in the New Year. We also sent out our invites and it was then that people finally started to believe that it was really happening. I think most people thought we were crazy and, right back at the start, when I told my parents our plans, it's fair to say they were a little sceptical. However, as it all started to come together, everybody supported us and I think that having a bit of coverage in newspapers and on TV in the lead-up really helped build the excitement. We even got to go on *Blue Peter* and get a Blue Peter badge, fulfilling one of Paul's childhood dreams! Put it this way: I doubt any of our guests had ever been to a wedding like it before.

Before we knew it, the big day arrived. I didn't really have much in the way of pre-wedding nerves, weirdly enough. Sure, when I woke up in the morning, I remember thinking, 'I'm getting married today,' but I knew that there was still a big thing to overcome first, so I was too busy trying to prepare myself psychologically for running those first thirteen or so miles to dwell on any jitters. It was actually a nice distraction to have.

Logistically, there were a few things we had to get right to make everything go to plan and, fortunately, the race organisers were really accommodating. They gave us places in the media's 'Green' start, which goes off close to the front of the race. Had we been deep in the pack, we could have been caught up in bottlenecks and the like, which, when you're working within reasonably tight time parameters like we were, you want to avoid if you can. So, being further up was a great help. While we were at the start, we were also interviewed separately, by Colin Jackson and Gabby Logan, which certainly added to the adrenaline!

We gave ourselves about three hours to get to The Dickens Inn, which, in the end, was more than enough. But, again, we were erring on the side of caution in case there were any issues with the registrar. Like anyone who has ever been married by a registrar knows, they run to strict timeframes. The problem with that, of course, was that we couldn't book one of them until much nearer the actual wedding day, so that was a little bit of a worry, not knowing if they would be okay with us arriving ten minutes later than planned or whatever it might be. But, as it turned out, it wasn't an issue.

The other main thing we had to get right was ensuring that we didn't see each other. That's where I guess we probably are a little bit traditional. Although we stayed in the same place the night before – albeit in separate rooms – we left separately to avoid seeing each other and, again, the organisers were fantastic in making sure that we were kept apart at the start line. We knew that I would probably run faster than Paul, so I was put close to the front in the 'celeb tent' at the 'Green' start, with Paul starting nearer the back of it. If it had been the other way around, there's a good chance I'd have caught up with him, which would have ruined it, but we didn't think there was really any chance of him catching me, so doing it that way worked really well.

After an amazing first half, encouraged by lots of good wishes from other runners, I arrived at the venue first, as we'd expected. This gave me a chance to see my bridesmaids and compose myself a little. My dad actually met me at the edge of the course and walked me over, which was lovely. Paul's best men met him, too, and when he walked into the room for the ceremony, everybody gave him a huge round of applause.

Of course, we couldn't really afford to stop for long as we knew the longer we weren't running, the harder it would be to get going again. So, the ceremony lasted about twenty minutes, including a lovely reading by my sister which drew comparisons between marathons and marriage. All in all, I reckon I stopped running for around an hour. Getting there first, I obviously had a little bit of a wait for Paul to arrive. Then there was the ceremony, followed by some pictures and another BBC TV interview with Colin Jackson. By the time we got going again – with confetti being thrown over us as we jogged off – we had started to tighten up a little bit. It wasn't really any surprise when Paul's knees started to hurt quite soon after we re-started. If anything, we probably went off a little too quickly on account of the adrenaline of having just got married, plus I think I would naturally have run it a little bit quicker than him anyway. I remember him saying that we had to just drop the pace a little, which was fine.

Of course, because we'd stopped for quite a while, we had fallen a long way back down the 'pack', so to speak. I think we were running close to a six-hour pace, so, by the time we reached the area around Docklands, the crowd was starting to thin out. There were even some big stretches where you felt as though nothing was going on, which was a bit weird. Even so, the people that had stayed out were absolutely superb and cheered us all the way. A lot of them seemed to have seen our story and were shouting out congratulations and support in pretty much equal measure, which was lovely. We even had other runners congratulating us.

Around mile twenty-one, our wedding guests appeared to give us another cheer and that definitely gave us a massive boost that helped get us to the finish.

One of the nicest bits, though, was coming up The Mall. They were filming us on the big screen and announced us as we made our way towards the finish line. I can remember turning to Paul and saying, 'I can't believe we've done this.' It really was an incredibly ambitious thing to do and there were a million things that could have gone wrong along the way, so to reach the finish and have it all go so well was such a brilliant feeling. Plus, just before we crossed the finish, Paul scooped me up and carried me over the threshold, which was great fun. Everyone in the crowd cheered at that. I think they really appreciated the effort, although I did have to run back over the finishing line to activate the chip on my trainers and get an official time!

Afterwards, we dropped in past the Cancer Research UK post-run party to say our thanks to everyone for all of their support before getting a taxi back to the hotel we were staying in close to The Dickens Inn. We grabbed a quick shower, changed into more normal wedding attire and, complete with our marathon medals, went back to rejoin our friends and family for the reception. People often ask us how our first dance went after running the marathon. It was slow – very, very slow! Neither of us had much to drink, either. I don't think Paul touched a drop and I only had a glass of Champagne. Anything more than that could have tipped me over the edge! Still, we had a great time and a lovely evening to cap a fabulous, unforgettable day.

Our first morning as a married couple started with an unexpected 8 a.m. phone call from BBC London for a radio interview. We then allowed ourselves a couple of days in a really nice place in Brighton, where there was a huge hot tub that we were able to soak our weary legs in and watch our toenails fall off! After that, it was off to the Bahamas for our honeymoon. It was quite funny, really: one week, we were trying to put the finishing touches to organising our wedding, whilst also preparing ourselves, mentally and physically, for running the London Marathon; the next week, we were sunning ourselves on a beautiful, paradise island. I think we earned it, though!

The London Marathon is an enormously special event for everybody who runs it but it's nice that, for us, it's extra-significant as it will always be a reminder of our wedding day. It will be fantastic to watch it in the years to come and remember all those amazing experiences we had on 26 April 2015. I should add that the support for us from Cancer Research UK was exceptional, too. We were so happy with our fundraising total of £9,000 and so grateful to everyone who donated in our name.

To us, the London Marathon is so much more than a race. It's a key part of what makes us Mr and Mrs Elliott.

CHAPTER TWENTY-FOUR

MICHAEL WATSON

Nicknamed 'The Force', Michael Watson was one of Britain's top boxers in the late 1980s and early 1990s. However, he almost lost his life in the ring after a brutal, bruising fight with Chris Eubank that left him with lasting brain damage. Incredibly, and against all the odds, he fought back from the brink of death and, in 2003, demonstrated his strength of character by defiantly completing the London Marathon.

ON SATURDAY, 21 September 1991, I walked into the ring in the middle of the pitch at White Hart Lane – the home of Tottenham Hotspur Football Club – ready for the biggest fight of my life. Sure enough, I got it. It just wasn't the fight I'd anticipated.

My opponent that night was Chris Eubank, the prize was the WBO Super-Middleweight title, and the stakes were high. Very high. We had fought each other for the same title just a few months earlier at Earl's Court in Kensington, which resulted in one of the most controversial results in British boxing history.

Never mind what the result says – I beat Chris Eubank that night. I knew it, the thousands watching it live knew it, everybody watching at home on TV knew it, even Chris himself must have known it. The only people who seemingly didn't know it were the only people whose opinions mattered – the judges. They awarded the title to Chris by majority decision, much to my disbelief. It was crazy. Absolutely crazy.

A rematch was quickly arranged, this time at White Hart Lane. All the talk in the build-up was about this being one of the biggest fights ever seen in Britain. Me, 'The Force', the 'People's Champion', against the flamboyant, eccentric Eubank, the man the public loved to hate. For me, though, it was never about any of that. It was about fulfilling my destiny, completing a journey that started at the age of fourteen in the Crown and Manor club where I first started to box.

I prepared for that fight like never before. All day, every day, I thought about Chris. I thought about the injustice of the decision earlier in the year and of beating him the second time around. I trained hard to make sure that I was in the best condition I'd ever been in. I never wanted to beat anybody more than I wanted to beat Chris that night.

I *was* beating him, too. I was ahead on points in the penultimate round – with thirteen million people watching on television and 22,000 people squeezed into the ground – when I knocked him to the floor with a right hook. In that moment, I thought I'd done it. Eubank was on his hands and knees on the canvas. He was on the brink of being stopped, no question about it. Next thing, he was back up. That's when it happened. I don't remember much about it. All I know is that he hit me with an uppercut, knocked me to the ground and I hit my neck off the bottom rope on the way down.

I got back up just as the bell rang for the end of the round. I was hurt but I knew I was still ahead. All I had to do was get through the next three minutes and I was going to be the world champion. There would be no doubt this time, no bad decisions. It later turned out I was ahead on all three judges' scorecards. It was a done deal. I went back to my corner and told myself I just needed to keep my hands up, get through the final round and that would be that.

Chris came out fast and furious in that final round. He had no other choice. He had to finish me off. I just had to endure it. Twenty-nine seconds after the bell rang to start that last round, the referee, Roy Francis, stepped in. Just like that, it was over. I had lost.

As Chris turned away with his gloves in the air, I went back to my corner. I was devastated. I felt my spirit floating away. And that's when I collapsed.

I only know what happened next because of what other people have told me. I lost consciousness around 10.55 p.m. I had been sitting on my stool when I slumped forward onto my trainer, Jimmy Tibbs. I woke up in hospital forty days later.

I lay unconscious in the ring for several minutes before help arrived. There was no ambulance on site that night and no emergency resuscitation equipment at the side of the ring. It wasn't until around 11.10 p.m. that doctors wearing dinner jackets climbed into the ring to help. I was then carried out of the ring on a stretcher to an ambulance, which took me to North Middlesex Hospital. However, it didn't have any of the right equipment or even the proper medical professionals needed to treat me.

By this point, my pupils were fixed and dilated and I had extensive bleeding on my brain which was forming a blood clot the size of a saucer. I was dying.

Shortly before midnight, I was transferred to a different hospital, St Bartholomew's, in Smithfield. I was prepared for surgery and in theatre by 1 a.m. It was to be the first of six operations on my brain – each and every one of them life-saving.

I wasn't expected to survive. Too much time had passed between me collapsing and receiving medical attention, and the bleeding on my brain was extensive. But I'm a fighter; not just by profession but by nature. That's one of the reasons I pulled through.

I was also in great physical condition. My neurosurgeon, Peter Hamlyn, later said that I was one of the best physical specimens he had ever seen. Peter, too, was a major factor in my survival. He had been at a family party that night when he got called in to operate on me. I will always be grateful to him for everything he did and he has become a true friend. However, perhaps more than anything else, I believe that I survived because of my fighting spirit and because I kept the faith. It is only by the grace of God that I'm still here.

Even when it looked as though I might survive, the prognosis still wasn't very good. The doctors warned that I might remain in a persistent vegetative state for the rest of my life. I can actually remember lying there in the hospital bed hearing the doctors say to my mother, 'Mrs Watson, I don't think your son is going to live.' I could hear them but I couldn't do anything to respond. It was as though I was already dead.

For days and days, I lay there, not moving. I wanted to but I couldn't. Nothing responded. I pleaded silently with God to help me. It was all I could do. Pray and pray and pray. Finally, he answered and I was able to move my hand.

It was slow progress and, for someone who had always been so active and so healthy, that was like torture. But I never gave up. I never quit on anything in my life and I wasn't about to start then.

I can still remember when my recovery really kicked into gear. I was lying in bed when a nurse came to my bedside. 'Michael,' she said, 'you've got a visitor.' She didn't say who it was. The next thing I know, this big, imposing figure enters the room. 'Hey, it's the great Michael Watson,' he says, leaning over me, getting real close. 'You're a fine-looking young man. But you ain't as good-looking as me!'

There was no mistaking that drawl. It was the man himself.

'The Greatest'.

Muhammad Ali.

Hearing Ali say that made me laugh for the first time in months and, suddenly, I felt energised. I had gone from being almost unable to make a sound to, right there, in that moment, laughing. It was as though he turned up and smashed his fists through whatever had been holding me prisoner. After that, I felt unstoppable. There was no holding me back. Just ask my nurses. They got chatted up every day from then on!

I started to improve considerably after that, although I had to learn to do everything again. Move, talk, stand, walk, write – everything. I spent six years in a wheelchair, which, after everything I had been through, might have been enough for some people. But not me. I needed to walk again, so I made it my mission. I remember the first time I stood after the accident. I held onto the frame and I felt in control again. It was a great feeling.

How does the London Marathon fit into all of this? Well, it was Peter who gave me the idea. My recovery was going great and one day he said to me, 'Do you know what, Michael? You're doing so well I reckon you could do the marathon.' I thought about it and realised that, actually, it wasn't so crazy an idea. Instead, it was just the kind of challenge that I needed. I was getting better but I missed the discipline of training for a fight. It demanded focus, hard work and sacrifice – and I loved it. In a way, signing up for the London Marathon would help to fill that void. I knew it wouldn't be easy. At that time, I could still hardly walk across my living room without assistance. But remember: I'm a fighter. Fighting is what I do.

Plus, all I've ever wanted is to inspire people and make a difference. Spending so much time in hospital made me really appreciate how lucky I am to have lived the life that I have. I've climbed to the top of my sport and conquered great athletes along the way. I've also been at the very bottom and fought my way back to health. I know I'm in a position to make a difference. Seeing teenagers with cancer and other people suffering from ill heath, it just makes me so sad. It's not right. I can't help them medically but I can give them hope. I can show them where I've been, what I've come through and what I've done since my accident and make them realise that it's important to never give up. You must never, ever give up.

So, I registered for the 2003 London Marathon and chose to raise money for the Brain and Spine Foundation, which Peter himself established many years earlier. I knew I couldn't complete the whole distance in one day. Instead, I thought I could manage maybe four or five miles at a time. The organisers were okay with that and, once I was signed up, it was then a matter of getting down to training.

Before all of my big fights, I liked to be isolated away from the world so I could train somewhere quiet and peaceful to really prepare properly. I needed seclusion. I needed to keep the 'Eye of the Tiger'. So, that's how I decided I would train for the marathon. I took a small group of my very closest friends to Cornwall where we basically set up a training camp at the Hustyns Resort. It is a fantastic facility that has everything you could ever need. Most important of all, there are no distractions. It's a huge estate where we could train every day – morning and afternoon – with nothing and nobody bothering us.

We returned to London, ready to start the race on 13 April 2003, along with everybody else. The days that followed were tiring and challenging but I had an incredible army of supporters, led by my friends Len and Patrick, who helped keep me going. Because of them and my faith in Jesus Christ, I grew stronger and more determined with every mile that passed.

In the morning, I walked two miles, averaging an hour per mile, and I did the same again in the afternoon. At night, I slept in a support bus that followed me along the way. I heard it was once used by the rock band Oasis on one of their tours.

A lot of great people came out to walk some of the way with me. People from the boxing world – like Audley Harrison and Frank Warren – joined me, as did the former Southampton footballer Jason Euell, and the comedian Ricky Gervais. Many other people shouted support or honked their car horns to cheer me on. That really lifted me. I felt overwhelmed by it. I had always felt like a champion when I boxed. The marathon helped me reclaim some of that.

Finally, six days and two hours after I started, I got to The Mall where the London Marathon organisers had erected my own special finishing line. By this point there must have been about 2,000 people either walking with me or cheering me on. They sang, 'There's only one Michael Watson,' and 'We love you Michael, we do!' It was amazing. Just amazing.

I was joined for that last mile by Chris Eubank and another fellow boxer, Spencer Oliver, as well as my support team, including Peter, Len and Patrick who had been by my side every step of the way.

People often ask me how I feel about Chris given that it was his punch that led to me ending up in hospital. The truth is that I've never felt any ill-feeling towards him. I mean that. He didn't intend for what happened to me. Every time a boxer gets into the ring, they do so knowing the risks. It was the same that night at White Hart Lane. Sure, we both wanted to beat each other – but we never wanted to hurt one another. That's not what boxing is. I know Chris felt guilty for a long time afterwards and I suspect he still does, to an extent. He was never the same boxer after that night and I can understand why. But in terms of feeling anger or resentment towards him? No, not at all, so it was nice to be joined by him at the end of my marathon. He held one end of the tape at the finish line for me as I walked across it and straight into a hug with my mum. The clock above me showed six days, two hours, twenty-seven minutes and seventeen seconds. I was finished. The London Marathon became the latest opponent defeated by 'The Force'.

I had no doubts I would complete it. None. The way I felt about it was the way I felt before my fight with Nigel Benn. We fought each other in May 1989 – almost exactly two years before my first fight with Eubank – in Finsbury Park in London for the British Commonwealth Middleweight title.

Nigel was a great boxer, whose biggest attribute was his power. He was one of the hardest punchers I ever came up against. Maybe even the hardest. He had won all twenty-two of his previous fights by knockouts and even insured his hands for ten million pounds. They were his weapons, his tools, and he used them well.

I think a lot of people expected him to beat me. He was the more powerful man and had an impressive track record. But I didn't see it like that. I knew I was going to beat him from the time I saw him at a function not long before we faced each other in the ring. We caught each other's eye and he was the first to look away. From that very moment, I knew I would win our fight. I knew it in my heart and I knew it in my head. The outcome was already decided. I just had to turn up and fight the fight. That's how I felt about the London Marathon. It lit something inside me that had been missing since I had to give up boxing and so, as soon as I decided I was going to do it, I knew I was going to finish it. (*By the way, I did end up beating Nigel. I floored him with a left jab in the sixth round after he had worn himself out.*)

Completing the London Marathon was important to me for many reasons but, most of all, it gave me an opportunity to thank everybody who had supported me since that night in September 1991. We ended up raising over £200,000 for the Brain and Spine Foundation, which is something I'm very proud of. I also really hope that it lifted other people's spirits and showed them that anything is possible. I should have died in the ring that night. I know that. But I didn't because I never lost my faith and my belief that I would pull through. When you've got that, anything is possible.

Looking back, I don't feel bitter about what happened to me. It was my fate. It was all part of God's plan for me. The injuries I sustained and the lack of medical assistance on-site prompted many changes in boxing regulations, which has probably saved the lives of many boxers since then. That's something I'm proud of. What happened to me happened for a reason. Everything does. I thought my destiny was to become a world champion boxer. Instead, it was something much more important than that.

The London Marathon was a big piece in the jigsaw of my recovery. It was an incredible, electrifying experience and an important part of me winning my biggest ever fight: my fight for my life.

CHAPTER TWENTY-FIVE

CHARLIE SPEDDING

Prior to 1984, Charlie Spedding had never run a marathon. By the time dawn broke on New Year's Day, 1985, he'd won two and earned an Olympic medal over the distance. To date, he remains the last Brit – male or female – to win an Olympic marathon medal. Here's how he did it . . .

FOR me, the London Marathon is much more than just a race. It's the reason I got to realise my lifetime ambition of being an Olympian and complete my journey from 'zero' to 'hero'.

I grew up in a small County Durham mining town called Ferryhill and attended the local junior school. I was what I guess you'd call a bit of a slow developer. I was near the bottom of my class for pretty much every subject. In those days, there was a chart on the wall of the classroom which showed where you ranked after every test and, of the thirty-two boys in my class, I was consistently either thirtieth or thirty-first. I was never thirty-second but I was always right down near the bottom.

Part of my issue was that I never had good eyesight. I was born with a squint in my left eye, which made it particularly hard to read. I was also never that good at ball games, again partly on account of my vision. I was always active, though. I was always doing something. Even if I was by myself, I'd be outside running around.

It was as I got older that I was introduced to longer distance running. It was only a couple of miles to begin with but I tried really hard and, in the first race I entered, I ended up finishing second. That was a big moment for me. It was the closest I'd ever come to being successful at anything, so I made it a goal from then on to try really hard any time I had the opportunity to run.

By the time I was sixteen, I was on the school team for a variety of different sports but it was clear that I was best at running. Around the same time, I joined a running club – Gateshead Harriers – and I started to take it more seriously. Gradually, I got better and better to the point that, by my mid-twenties, I was entering some minor international track events.

Things just snowballed from there, really. I qualified to represent Great Britain in the 10,000 metres in both the 1982 Commonwealth Games in Brisbane and the 1983 European Championships in Athens, finishing fourth and eighth respectively. It was around that time that I first thought to myself, 'Okay, Charlie. You can call yourself a runner now.' It had taken a while but I'd finally made myself proud.

Still, as good as I was, I knew that I couldn't get much better on the track. I figured that I had peaked. I just wasn't fast enough to make the improvements necessary to contend for medals and so, in that sense, I'd fulfilled my potential. Also, the Olympic Games were coming up in Los Angeles in 1984 and I desperately wanted to be a part of them. I just couldn't see any way that I could qualify for the Games on the track. That's when I first started to consider the marathon.

I always thought it would suit me but I needed to know for sure, so I went over to Texas in January 1984 to run in the Houston Marathon. It was the first marathon I'd ever taken part in – and, unbelievably, I won. I needed a sprint finish to do it, too. Honestly, there couldn't have been anything more than the thickness of a vest between myself and an Italian runner called Massimo Magnani.

He was ahead of me with fifty yards to go but I found a little something extra in reserve and caught him just short of the line before I dipped into the tape. That was an old habit from my track days. Shorter distance runners typically dip into the finish to get whatever part of their body they possibly can across the line first. You tend not to associate that with marathon runners. Still, it was just an instinctive reaction and proved to be just enough to grant me the win. Magnani wasn't at all happy. He was convinced he'd won and didn't take kindly to the four judges ruling in my favour but there you go. I had a feeling the race was mine, so I was delighted. I had gone over there with no real expectations. All I wanted was to see whether the distance was going to suit me or not; winning was just an added bonus.

From there, I returned home and immediately switched my focus to preparing for London. I won't lie, the prospect of qualifying from it for the Olympic Games was uppermost in my mind. That's what it was all about. I just wanted to punch my ticket for Los Angeles. Nothing more, nothing less. In my mind, this was my best and possibly last chance to be an Olympian, so I had to give it my all.

Of course, it wasn't that straightforward. Nothing ever is. There were a maximum of three places up for grabs for the British team but two of those looked highly likely to be going to two runners who had decided not to run in London that year. The first was Hugh Jones, who had won London two years earlier in a time of 2:09:24, one of four marathons he won between 1981 and 1983. The other was Geoff Smith, who was a senior at Providence College in the USA at the time, and had finished a very close second in the New York Marathon in 1983. He had come home in 2:09:08, which, under most circumstances back then, would have been enough to win. As it was, he had to settle for second, just nine seconds behind the winner, Rod Dixon.

It was widely accepted that Hugh and Geoff were already on the plane to Los Angeles, which left a whole bunch of us to battle it out on the streets of London for the one remaining place. That was a particularly good era for British distance runners. The standard in the early-to-mid-eighties was extremely high. There was a much deeper pool of talent than there is now.

One of the favourites for the remaining place was a Scotsman called John Graham. He was a very experienced marathon runner. In addition to winning the Rotterdam Marathon in 1981 and finishing third in the New York Marathon in 1980, he had been fourth in the Commonwealth Games marathon in 1982. Then there was Mike Gratton, who had won the London Marathon a year earlier in an exceptionally fast time of 2:09:43.

Of course, what all of these guys had over me was experience. Sure, I had raced plenty of times and been successful on the track, plus winning in Houston just a few months earlier had been great for my confidence. But these guys had run way more marathons than I had and I didn't need anybody to tell me they were all more than capable of running exceptionally good times. I knew I was going to have to run the race of my life to stand any kind of a chance. The way I saw it, the 1984 London Marathon was going to be the race that defined my career. I'd either qualify from it for the Olympics and take myself to a whole new level, or I would miss out and have to accept that I was good but just not good enough. The stakes were that high. There was absolutely no margin for error.

Needless to say, I was extremely nervous for the whole week leading up to the race. The butterflies kicked in early and multiplied as it got closer to the start time.

I'd booked myself into a hotel on Blackheath Common near the start line, so I didn't have to travel any distance on the morning of the race. Of course, that's of no such concern to the top runners these days, who are put up in a nice hotel and chauffeured to the start line!

I woke up nervous and, if I remember rightly, my breakfast that morning consisted of a cup of tea and one slice of toast. That was totally by design. I didn't want to risk having something sitting in my stomach that might cause it to cramp up later in the day.

After finishing my modest breakfast, I got ready and made my way to the start line where I just walked around and tried to avoid people as much as I could. A lot of people like to have a chat before a race. Personally, I always preferred to be in my own space and try to mentally prepare myself for what was to come. I didn't want to hear anybody else's stories of having had a cold that week, or having not slept well the night before, because that was often just a bit of gamesmanship to lull you into a false sense of security. You'd hear their complaints and immediately assume that you had them in your pocket, only to be unpleasantly surprised when they performed near-enough flawlessly. Runners trying to get into other runners' heads was quite common. I'm sure it still is. The margins in these races being as fine as they are, you've got to try to claim whatever advantage you can. However, I wanted nothing to do with any of that, didn't want any negative thoughts creeping in, so I tried to keep to myself as much as I possibly could.

The moment we started running, my nerves disappeared. It was as though somebody flicked a switch and they were gone. In an instant, my focus fixed on the task in hand and, in a marathon in particular, that's very important because you have a lot of time to think. It's not like the 100m, 200m or 400m where it's all over in the blink of an eye. With a marathon, you're out there for hours on end, the action is very steady and repetitive and, as a consequence, your mind can easily wander. But you can't let that happen. As soon as you open that door even just a tiny fraction, you're inviting in all sorts of unwanted and unhelpful thoughts. *Can I sustain this pace? Should I be trying to keep up with them? Am I sure I'm not going too fast? Is there something that they're doing that I should be doing?* Any time spent on those doubts and worries is a waste of energy – and you need every last bit of energy you've got, particularly in my case and particularly that year where the competition was so fierce. It was absolutely crucial that I settled quickly and focused intently. I had come with a game plan. Now, it was up to me to execute it.

There were two Tanzanian runners in the field – one of whom was strongly tipped to win an Olympic medal that year – and they set off really fast. That wasn't much of a surprise. I'd expected them to set a pretty quick pace. What did surprise me was that so many of the British guys went with them. I just ignored it and concentrated on my own race.

That also meant trying to block out the crowd as much as possible. It was a bright, sunny day and loads of people came out to watch. The streets were lined for the vast majority of the route with people applauding as you went past.

At times, around the busiest parts of the route where there were people on both sides of the road, it was like running through a tunnel of noise. It really was that loud but, again, I tried not to let myself get too excited by it. Of course, there's a part of you that wants to respond to the support and really just soak it all in, but you have to try to shut it out as much as you can, not get carried away and just do your job.

By the halfway point, I was in the third group but was still bang on track to run 2:10, so I wasn't worried. For me, it wasn't so much a case of trying to catch the guys in front. Instead, I knew that if I sustained my pace, they'd have to go seriously fast to avoid falling back towards me.

At that point, my focus still wasn't on winning the race. All I was concentrating on was being the first Brit across the finishing line. It didn't matter if I was second, third, fourth, fifth – being the first Brit was my one and only goal.

It was around mile fifteen that I started to overtake some of the guys who were ahead of me because, just as I'd expected, they'd overcooked it and were starting to struggle. That's a notoriously difficult part of the course in any case but even more so when the grim realisation hits you that you've gone off much too quickly and still have ten miles to go. As their shoulders slumped, my chest was puffing out.

It wasn't until I saw the leaders around seventeen miles in that it occurred to me that I had a chance of actually winning the race and, when I caught up with them at mile eighteen, it was very much 'game on'. As soon as I drew level, I had the sense it was my race to lose. I was the only one who hadn't gone out particularly fast by that point. I knew it and they knew it. Plus, I had the psychological advantage of knowing that I had chased them down and not the other way about. I was the cat, they were the mice – and I had them by the tail. That was a massive boost to my confidence. Don't get me wrong, I was tired – I defy anyone to run eighteen miles at that pace and not feel it – but I felt in complete control.

Still, one of the Tanzanians, a fantastic runner called Juma Ikangaa, was not going down without a fight and he kept making these surges to try and separate himself from the pack. It was a futile effort, though. Every time he did, he soon came drifting back. Again, that just made me more confident. I knew that every break he made tired him a little more each time, so it was just a matter of biding my time and waiting to make a move of my own. I knew that, if I judged it right, neither he nor anybody else would have enough left in them to respond, which would leave me very much in the box seat.

It was just short of the twenty-mile mark that Ikangaa made yet another of his surges and, as he drifted back towards us, I made a surge of my own. Just as I expected, he couldn't keep up. Next thing I knew, I had put some good daylight between myself and the chasing pack. I was well aware that I was six miles from the finish but it felt instinctively like the time to pounce.

As soon as I pulled away, that's when I started to believe that I was going to win. It was hard to see any other outcome. I just had to hold myself together and not get too excited or do anything stupid.

Once I got ahead, I tried to resist the urge to look round to see if anyone was coming at me or to see how big a lead I had. There were a couple of right-angled turns that enabled me to cast a quick glance, but I avoided looking around other than that. It's too risky. You might trip yourself up and, besides anything else, it can suggest to your opponents that you don't feel completely in control, that you're worried or maybe even struggling physically. No matter how tired you feel physically, you can't afford any mental lapses like that.

It was around twenty-four-and-a-half miles in that I started to really feel the effects of running at a 'personal best' pace. I could sense the exhaustion taking hold and so the last couple of miles were a case of gritting the teeth and just kicking. It would have been really nice to come down towards the finish line and feel fantastic but, in reality, I was absolutely spent and had to focus, with every fibre of my body, on just holding myself together.

Fortunately, I did. I won in a time of 2:09:57 and the feeling as I crossed the line was just brilliant. There's actually a really nice picture that one of the finish line photographers took which shows me with a huge grin on my face just as I'm taking the tape but, believe me, there's not a chance in hell that I was smiling fifty yards earlier! I was hurting and working hard right up until the line but, as soon as I crossed it, I just felt a rush of emotions: delight, pride, satisfaction and, most of all, relief. I knew that I hadn't just won the race; I'd achieved my goal of qualifying for the Olympics. More than a decade's worth of work, effort, commitment and sacrifice had just paid off in that very instant. It was an immensely exhilarating moment. I can't compare it to anything else I've experienced before or since.

The immediate aftermath involved a lot of routine things: interviews, a press conference, the prize-giving ceremony and a drugs test (which, on account of my dehydration was actually anything but 'routine'!) Once all that was over, I had a chance to let the enormity of what I'd just done sink in.

I was in a bit of a daze for the rest of the day. When something significant happens, people's first reaction tends to be, 'I can't believe that's happened.' I certainly felt a bit of that, even though I had carefully planned for it and worked hard for it for a very long time. I still had to pinch myself to believe that it was really happening.

The next day, I got a call from the selectors to confirm my place in the Olympics and, well, coming home from LA with a bronze medal was just the icing on the cake. Going into the race, I felt quite strongly that I had it in me to get a medal. I wouldn't have put a bet on it but neither did I think it was beyond the realms of possibility. I told myself that if I ran to the very best of my ability, then I'd have a chance. You can't underestimate the importance of having that belief. You've got to trust that you have the capability to surprise even yourself. If you just turn up hoping for the best, you won't get a medal. Instead, you need to believe – not hope or think – that you can do it. That's exactly what happened that day. I ran an excellent race and finished just two seconds behind the silver medallist from Ireland, John Treacy. It didn't particularly matter to me that I hadn't won gold or even silver. I won an Olympic medal and that's something that nobody can ever take away from me. To think that I'm the last Briton – either male or female – to have won an Olympic marathon medal is really quite incredible.

I've come a long way from being that kid who was near the bottom of the class in school and hopefully I've demonstrated that, with will and application, you can achieve all of your goals. I was just a kid from a small village in County Durham and I made it all the way, via London, onto an Olympic podium in Los Angeles. That was my dream and the way I see it, if I can make mine come true, then there's no reason why anybody else can't.

CHAPTER TWENTY-SIX

JILL TYRRELL

On 7 July 2005, four suicide bombers carried out coordinated attacks on London's transport network, killing fifty-two civilians and injuring over 700 more. The deadliest of the attacks took place on a six-car London Underground train travelling between King's Cross St Pancras and Russell Square on the Piccadilly line. Twenty-six people were killed in that particular explosion. Miraculously, Jill Tyrrell survived the attack, despite having been in the same carriage as the bomber. She subsequently spent two-and-a-half months in hospital as a result of the injuries she sustained but, incredibly, recovered well enough to take part in the 2006 London Marathon.

THURSDAY, 7 July 2005 started out the same as any other working day.

It was a grey morning but the mood in London was buoyant with the city having been awarded the right to host the 2012 Olympic Games the day before. The then Prime Minister, Tony Blair, had hailed that news as 'a momentous day' for Britain. Little did he know that the following day would prove to be even more significant – and in a completely different way.

I work as a secretary for a luxury watch retailer in Mayfair but I live in Enfield, so I commute each day. I got dressed that morning as normal. Black skirt, cream blouse and black shoes. I had my hair pinned up and was wearing earrings.

I took the bus to Oakwood Tube station – the second most northerly stop on the Piccadilly line – and got on the next train that arrived. It was approximately 7.45 a.m.

I picked up a copy of the *Metro* newspaper and sat in my usual seat in the front carriage of the train, close to the driver's cabin and next to one of the door wells. That's one of the advantages of getting on the train so early into its journey from the depot. Not only can you get a seat but you can, by and large, get the same one every day.

We had only gone two stops when an announcement came over the tannoy that there were some problems further down the line at King's Cross. I think they said there was a fire alert and that they may need to terminate the train where we were sitting, at Arnos Grove. 'Great,' I thought to myself. There's nowhere to go from Arnos Grove. It would mean taking a bus to Finsbury Park and starting again from there where there is a busy interchange. Other passengers clearly had the same idea. Mobile phones were pulled out of pockets all along the carriage and I sat tight amongst them trying to plan a new route in my head.

However, the train continued to chug on through the stations, stopping regularly. People impatiently checked their watches and frantically examined their phones. We were running about half an hour late by this point but, eventually, seemed to pick up some speed. Before we knew it, we arrived into Finsbury Park. I remember turning round to look at the station name behind me and, as I studied the letters on the wall, I wondered whether or not to get off. 'The Victoria Line goes through here,' I thought. 'Maybe that would be quicker?' In the end, I stayed where I was. The doors closed and the train moved on. They say life hinges on the little decisions we make, the minutiae amongst the minutes. I could have got off the train at Finsbury Park. But I didn't. It was a 'nothing' decision that changed everything.

The train pulled into King's Cross station and, as usual, the carriage suddenly filled as commuters piled in, jostling for position. The familiar announcement rang through the speakers: 'Stand clear of the doors.' They slid shut and the train began to move on again towards the next stop, Russell Square. It was 8.50 a.m.

It only took a split second, the briefest instant where reality seemed to be suspended. The newspaper was torn from my hands. The clip was blown from my hair. My earrings were ripped from my ears. Everything went black and I felt as though I was the only person in the whole of existence. It was lonely, frightening and it happened so violently and without warning. A terrifying thought appeared in the front of my mind: *Is this what it's like to die?*

From out of the blackness came a harsh metallic light and a rushing sensation, almost a 'whooshing' sound and yet there was no noise. Then, as quickly as it happened, the explosion subsided, leaving in its trail an instant of silence. Almost immediately, it was broken by the sound of people screaming. I sat there in silence, not knowing if I was dead or alive.

Because the train had braked suddenly, people had fallen on top of me, crushing me under their weight. I tried my best to heave them off me and I started to hear some isolated voices amidst the commotion. I could hear a man's voice saying, 'Calm down.' Elsewhere, a woman repeated over and over, 'Thank God, I'm not dead; thank God, I'm not dead.' Instinctively, I tried to wiggle my feet and was relieved that I could. However, I had no shoes. They were gone. *Where had my shoes gone?* I felt bewildered. I still had no idea that, not only had a suicide bomber detonated a device, but that he had been in the same carriage as me, just a few metres away.

I reached a hand down to the lower part of my leg. It was wet and slimy. I seemed to be covered in blood. A man's face looked up at me from the ground. He looked ashen and panicked. 'My legs are shot,' he told me. 'Dear God, my legs are gone!' I took his hand in mine and felt his blood with mine. 'It will be all right,' I told him, trying my best to sound reassuring. 'You will be okay.' I have no idea whether I was right or not. I can only hope I was.

I felt around me and was relieved that I still had my handbag. It's hard to explain but discovering it was there was like finding a long lost friend amidst the chaos. I'd had another bag on my lap but it was gone. Vanished amongst the bedlam.

It was only then that I looked around at the rest of the carriage for the first time. Everything was black and covered in soot and dust. I was suddenly aware that the doors to the driver's cab and from the cab down onto the track were open and that there was nobody to the left of me. 'They must have already got out,' I thought. I got to my feet, walked to the cab door and looked out. For some reason, I then turned back, my feet crunching on the broken glass, and I sat down again in an empty seat, not knowing whether to go or stay and wait for help. The tunnel looked black and foreboding, almost menacing. In the end, I came to the conclusion that I couldn't realistically do anything to help anyone else and that the best thing to do would be to get myself out.

I returned to the cab and climbed down onto the track. A man appeared beside me and identified himself as the train driver. I asked him if he was okay. He said he was but that he would probably never drive again. I asked him if he would walk along the tracks with me and enquired as to whether or not the rails were live. He thought they probably were but that we would be okay if we kept to the tracks between them.

Another man had now climbed down onto the track but he was very unsteady on his feet. The driver and I tried to hold him up, one of us on either side of him, but he fell forward almost at once and hit one of the rails. For a moment, my heart stood still. Fortunately, he was okay. The tracks had clearly been deactivated so we moved on. I was in front, with the driver holding onto my hand behind me and pulling the other man with him. This seemed to work quite well. I steered a path along the track, barefoot, my clothes in shreds. Suddenly, a thought flashed through my mind: 'I'm going to be very late for work.' Two-and-a-half months late, as it turned out!

Eventually, the lights of Russell Square station appeared up ahead and we emerged from the tunnel. A man came down from the platform and ran towards us. He grabbed me under one arm and the driver climbed up onto the platform, took me under the other arm and hoisted me up next to him.

I was ushered over to the wall where I was sat upright. I could hear the noise of vending machines being smashed around me and somebody brought over some water. To my shame, I don't know what happened to the 'unsteady' man after that point. I didn't see him again. I hope he was okay.

The driver of the train said he was going back to the carriage to get other survivors. Paramedics were, by this point, arriving on the scene and one of them went to go with him. 'It's not pretty back there,' I warned, feeling the need to prepare the medic for what he was running into. It was, as it turned out, the understatement of the year.

Somebody quickly appeared, surveyed my leg and tied a bandage around my calf. I was covered in blood and soot and my stockings were hanging off me. I just sat there, blankly looking around, taking it all in. After a while, two people came up to me and said they were taking me up to the concourse. They hauled me up by the underarms and we headed for the lifts. I looked back where I had been sitting and saw a smear of blood.

We emerged onto the small concourse where others were already sitting, some wrapped in blankets. Everybody looked dazed.

It was around 9.15 a.m. It occurred to me that, if I had my bag, I had my phone. I was struggling to find it when a lady appeared and asked me if I wanted some help. Her name was Jackie. She had been passing by the station when it all happened and, bless her, she was just doing what she could to help people in those first, confusing minutes. She helped me find my phone and dial my office. They asked me if I was okay. I replied, 'I'm at Russell Square, I'm covered in blood and I've got no shoes.' For the first time, emotion slammed into me and I felt my face begin to crumple. I saw Jackie try her best to keep it together as she watched me. I told the people in my office where to find my husband's number and they called him on my behalf. Eventually, he was able to get through to me from a friend's phone. It felt safe and reassuring to hear his voice.

After a while, I was suddenly helped to my feet again and quickly led through the ticket turnstiles. I asked what was happening and was told that a suspicious vehicle had been found outside and so they had to evacuate the station. I felt my stomach tighten in anticipation of another explosion and yet, at the same time, there was a part of me that didn't really care any more. I was exhausted and, in a strange way, at peace with the world. If this was it, this was it.

Word quickly filtered through that the threat from the vehicle in question had been taken care of and so I was sat down again in another part of the concourse near the street. I noticed a man lying near me. The lower half of one of his legs was missing and his trousers were a mangled, blood-stained mess. He was on the edge of consciousness. Stretchers and wheelchairs came and went. People asked if I would be all right for a little while and I said I would. A vicar appeared and offered me his blessing.

Sometime later, I was told that a room had been made available in a nearby hotel if I wanted to wait there until an ambulance arrived. It would, I was informed, be more comfortable and so, with some help, I tottered out into the street. A blanket of curious, scared onlookers stared back at me. Before I knew it, I was in the narrow foyer of the hotel and being ushered towards a small room. There were already half a dozen other people in there, in a variety of conditions. As I was lowered onto a nearby settee, I remember thinking what a mess all of this would make of the furnishings!

A man identifying himself as a neurosurgeon appeared and put himself in charge of assessing us all. He listened to our chests, looked at our hands, assessed our wounds as best he could, and offered us reassurance.

Soon, it was my turn for an ambulance. As I was helped from the room, I caught a glimpse of my face in a mirror. I barely recognised my own reflection. My forehead and right cheek were covered in blood. The eyelids on my right eye felt heavy. I assumed it was the weight of dried blood.

I was helped into the ambulance. It was 12.15 p.m. and I was told I was being taken to Great Ormond Street Children's Hospital. I later discovered that those of us who were taken there were the first adults to be treated in the hospital since the Blitz.

There followed the start of my recovery. Doctors examined me and quizzed me.

'Does this hurt?'

'Does that hurt?'

'Where does it hurt?'

'Just going to check your blood pressure.'

'Just going to shine this light in your eye.'

'Just going to check your legs.'

'When did you last eat? What did you have?'

Thankfully, there were some answers in there, too. 'Good news, your organs are okay,' and 'Good news, nothing's broken.' They were, though, very concerned about my face and, in particular, my eye.

Soon, I was being prepared for theatre. I had suffered various injuries to my legs, the worst being the damage to my right ankle. The skin had been blown clean off it all the way down to the bone. That required a reconstructive procedure called a 'free flap', where tissue is transferred from one part of the body – in this case, my inner forearm – to another.

It's funny, I can remember the doctors getting me ready for surgery and cutting my clothes from my body. I watched them snip away my underwear and I thought, 'Please, no, that was really expensive!' It's strange the things you think about, particularly in times of crisis and trauma.

Sometime later, I came around after surgery. I don't remember a great deal about the rest of that night, only that the whole of my right leg was thickly bandaged. I was attached to drains, had a vacuum dressing on my ankle and was wired up to a morphine dispenser and a drip.

The next morning, I was told that I would be transferred to St Thomas's where they had a better ophthalmology department to treat whatever was wrong with my eye. At the same time, I became aware that I was in a small ward of three. All of us had been in the first carriage of the train. There was a girl with blast and shrapnel injuries to her leg, similar to me, and a young man with a broken shoulder and burst eardrums. We were all in standard-issue hospital gowns. Our clothes had been turned over to forensic investigators.

At St Thomas's, I was admitted to the eleventh floor where there was a lovely view of the Thames. When I arrived, I had to go over everything again with a nurse, which was very upsetting. For the first time since it all happened, I cried.

I was taken to theatre again for further debridement – a medical term for getting rid of debris and, generally, cleaning you up – whilst the mobile ophthalmic team assessed my eye. There was extensive damage and a bleed into the vitreous chamber, so they could not see much. The pressure was very low, so all they could do was monitor it and give me eye drops.

Visitors started to appear and flowers arrived thick and fast. The windowsill looked like a florist's. I was so touched by everybody's concern for me. Still, I was pleased to be in the hospital. The prospect of being outside scared me a little. News of the full extent of the attacks was emerging and it was incredibly scary to think that I had been so close to them. I had been within a few feet of unspeakable evil and that was an incredibly disconcerting thought. Being in hospital made me feel safe.

Just as things were looking up, I was given some devastating news.

A nurse came to see me. 'Jill, I've got something to tell you,' she began. 'Do you remember when you came in you were swabbed for MRSA?'

I had heard of MRSA before then. I knew it was a notoriously hard-to-treat 'superbug' that, in many cases, could have fatal consequences.

I nodded to the nurse.

'I'm afraid you've tested positive,' she said. 'I'm so sorry.'

I stared at her in disbelief. I could almost feel my already-fragile world collapsing around me. In that moment, I was absolutely convinced that I was going to die. I had survived a suicide bomber's attack but this was going to kill me.

The only good news was that the MRSA bacteria had formed on the surface of my skin. Had it infected my wounds, it would have been much more difficult to treat. Still, I was scarcely comforted.

Within minutes of receiving the news, preparations were made to quarantine me. About 1 a.m. the next morning, I was taken into a room, the door of which was marked with the words: 'ISOLATION PRECAUTIONS'. I felt completely ashamed.

Over the days and weeks that followed, I was treated from a relative distance. I always knew when the doctors or nurses were coming because I could hear them pulling on their protective aprons and gloves outside the door to my room. The crackle of the plastic as they smoothed down their aprons soon became unmistakable.

The treatment, particularly the latter stages of it, was quite traumatic. I had to have intravenous antibiotics twice a day, which stung my veins. The cannulas bruised my hands. All I wanted was a hug but, of course, nobody could risk getting that close to me. It was physically and emotionally tiring. However, it was worth it: my wounds stayed clean and, finally, I managed to produce the three clear swabs required to rejoin humanity.

After two-and-a-half months and eight operations, I was finally discharged from hospital. The damage to my legs was healing, whilst an artificial lens had been fitted in my eye to counteract the cataract-style defects they ultimately were able to determine had been caused by the explosion.

I didn't go straight back to work – I took a few days to get used to being home – but, when I did, my bosses very kindly let me have a minicab for the first week or so to avoid having to use the Tube. Inevitably, though, I had to get back on it eventually and I was actually okay when I did. Obviously, I felt a little apprehensive at first but I had to tell myself that the bombers weren't targeting me specifically. They were making their point against London as a city. Plus, I took a little comfort from the fact that they were suicide bombers. Had they still been alive and at large, I think I'd have felt a little different getting back on the Tube. But they weren't. They were gone.

The atmosphere in the city certainly felt different for a while after it all happened. On the Underground, in particular, people seemed quite subdued and I think everybody paid more attention to who was in the carriage with them. Any time I felt uneasy, for example, I got off at the next available station. I still do that today, as it happens. It doesn't happen as often as it used to but I think it's a natural reaction when you've gone through something like that.

It was shortly after Christmas that I decided to run the 2006 London Marathon. I had already run it twice before, in 2004 and 2005. I had always enjoyed running and keeping fit, so when the opportunity to run it for the first time came along, I decided to give it a go. The first time, I did it in 4:42:16, which I improved by almost a quarter of an hour in 2005 (4:29:14). Running in 2006 never really occurred to me until one of the directors at work helped to get me a place running for a multiple sclerosis charity. It seemed like a good goal to work towards. Plus, I had the motivation of wanting to prove to the bombers that they didn't, couldn't and never would win. They did what they did for whatever reasons they believed in but, in the end, they lost. They'll never win. The treadmill of life keeps moving, no matter how many twisted people try and interfere with it. London, in particular, is very resilient. It has a tremendous capacity for bouncing back in the face of adversity and so completing the first marathon after the attacks became my personal mission.

Training went well and the morning of the race was upon me before I knew it. It was Sunday, 23 April 2006 – just 290 days since the bombings. I remember that the weather wasn't especially great. It was cold, wet and generally quite grotty. As I walked around Greenwich Park before it got underway, I felt as though everybody was looking at me. My arms and, in particular, my legs bore the fresh scars of the attack and that made me feel quite self-conscious. I tried to block it out and just convinced myself that nobody knew why I was there or what had happened to me.

It was when I heard a voice on the loudspeaker saying, 'This is the Flora London Marathon and this is the Red Start,' that I started to relax. I felt proud to be part of something important for London, something bigger than me, something that demanded a personal challenge but did not mind how you achieved it – only that you tried. The marathon was my personal 'Everest', the biggest physical challenge I will probably ever undertake, and particularly that year.

It was certainly more of a struggle to get round than it had been in either of the two previous years, for obvious reasons, but my legs held up remarkably well. I was very stiff at the end but, under the circumstances, I felt okay and only stopped once because I was tired and a bit emotional.

There was a very poignant moment as I came around the Embankment, about the twenty-second or twenty-third miles. As you take that bend, you can see St Thomas's opposite Big Ben and the Houses of Parliament and that made me well up a little bit. The enormity of everything that I had been through came flooding back. I had almost been killed below the streets of the capital just months earlier and yet here I was, running through them in one of the country's greatest and most defiant sporting events.

Still, it was a relief to finish. It was one of the hardest things I've ever done – but the fact remains that I did do it and I'm so proud of that.

What happened on 7/7 has changed me. For one thing, I carry the physical scars. I see them every day and, as a result, I think about what happened on a daily basis. It's never going to leave me. I wouldn't say that it haunts me but it's there and it's a part of my life. For a long time, I was angry about the injuries I sustained and, because of them, I don't like to show my legs any more. Equally, though, sometimes I see them and I think of them as my 'badge of honour'. I can look at them and tell myself that, as awful as the bombings were, I survived. I'm still here. I'm lucky. Things could have ended so differently. Twenty-six people died on the train I was on. In that sense, I'm one of the fortunate ones. What happened to me could have been so much worse. That's why I will be forever grateful to the surgeons at Great Ormond Street who got me through those first twenty-four hours, and to the plastic surgery and ophthalmology teams at St Thomas's who put me back together in the weeks that followed. I also owe a great deal to my friends and family who kept me going when the going got tough.

Everything I've experienced has made me much more appreciative of what I have. It's changed my outlook on life. I now don't delay in doing the things I want to do because you never know what is just around the corner.

So, as difficult as it can sometimes be, I try to focus on life's positives. Things come to you in unexpected ways and from loss can come gain. Some people have said I am more 'happy go lucky' than I was before. I hope that's true.

As far as running goes, it's still a part of my life and I've run the London Marathon again since 2006. These days, however, I don't run to chase a 'personal best'; I run because I can.

I can and I will.

26 TIPS FOR RUNNING
THE LONDON MARATHON

DURING TRAINING

1. Find a training plan and stick to it. There are lots of fantastic, customisable plans on the internet, so create your own and commit to it.

2. Be realistic. Every marathon runner wants to believe they can run under three hours but it is reckoned that only two per cent ever will. It's okay to be in that other ninety-eight per cent, you know!

3. Buy a GPS watch to track your training sessions. There are plenty out there to choose from and they're worth their weight in gold.

4. Eat healthily – but allow yourself some treats. A lot of amateur runners cut down on carbohydrates, sugar and alcohol during marathon training but allow themselves a 'Cheat Day' (every Saturday, for example) where they can eat what they like. This helps make the sacrifices on the other six days much more bearable!

5. Practise eating and drinking on the run, particularly drinking. It's a tricky skill to master but get it right in advance and you'll be able to take full advantage of the water stations.

6. Don't ignore injuries. Listen to your body. Many little niggles can be easily cured but, if left untreated, may turn into something much worse.

7. If you can, train on parts of the course. It's amazing how a little bit of local knowledge and familiarity can inspire confidence on race day.

8. Tell people what you're doing. It will help you to stay committed and you'll thrive on their support and good wishes.

9. Assign a friend or family member to each mile. Thinking of them for that particular mile will help to occupy your mind.

10. Speaking of friends and family, plan where to meet them after the race. The finish line and surrounding area is typically very busy so make sure you know where you will rejoin them.

11. Write or print your name on your T-shirt. Hearing the crowds shout it will really spur you on.

12. Set yourself mini-goals. Twenty-six miles seems like a long way to run once – but running just over ten kilometres four times, or just over five miles five times, sounds much more manageable, right?

13. Plan how you're going to get to the start line in advance and allow plenty of time to get there. You don't want to be stressed on the morning of the race.

14. Take an old jumper and/or jogging trousers to the start line. Your body can get cold standing around waiting to get going so keep yourself warm in something that you don't mind throwing away just before you start.

15. Embrace your nerves. No matter how well your training has gone, you are going to have butterflies in your stomach. Don't let them cripple you; instead, enjoy them.

DURING THE RACE

16. Don't wear anything you haven't trained in. That goes for trainers as well as clothes. You need to feel completely comfortable in what you're wearing in order to run your best.

17. Start slowly. There will be a lot of adrenaline flowing in the first two or three miles but try not to give in to it; you'll only burn out quicker.

18. Run your own race. Don't try and keep up with other people. Go at a pace you are comfortable with.

19. Don't wear headphones. Most race organisers advise against this anyway on safety grounds but, on a purely psychological level, the noise of the crowd cheering you on will do wonders for your spirits.

20. Avoid running along the camber of the road. Try to stay close to the middle where it is typically more level.

21. If you're really struggling, try counting to 300 in your head. That works out at approximately five minutes, which, depending on your ability, could be the best part of anything from a kilometre to a mile.

22. Most importantly – enjoy! This is what you've trained for, so smile, laugh, wave to the crowds and savour every second – even the painful ones!

AFTER THE RACE

23. Try to keep moving. Your muscles will quickly stiffen when you stop, so get where you need to go before resting for too long.

24. Refuel. It is estimated that the average runner will lose approximately 2,600 calories during a marathon. That's around 100 per mile. It's important, therefore, that you get a good meal in you as soon as you can after you finish.

25. Don't overdo the celebratory drinks. Alcohol is a diuretic. That means it encourages the body to lose more water than it takes on which, in turn, dehydrates you. Given that you're already going to be very dehydrated, it would be bad to have too much.

26. Enjoy the pain! There's no doubt you will hurt the next day and perhaps even for a few days after that, so take things slowly. Clear your diary of any non-essential business and take pride in knowing that the aches you're enduring have been achieved from doing one of the most special things you will ever do.

26 LONDON MARATHON FUNDRAISING TIPS

1. Take your fundraising online. Create a fundraising page (JustGiving and Virgin Money Giving are two good places to do this) so that people can easily sponsor you.

2. Set a fundraising target. According to Virgin Money Giving, 81% of fundraisers set a target and those who do raise an average of £1,495, compared to an average of £914 raised by those who don't reveal their target amount.

3. Start as early as you can. Much like training for a marathon, charity fundraising can be a slow process. If you try and cram it all into a few weeks, you won't get far.

4. Share a link to your fundraising page through social media, i.e. Facebook, Twitter, LinkedIn and so on. Don't be afraid to keep sharing it regularly, too.

5. If you can, set up a way for people to donate via text message. It's quick, convenient and doesn't require fishing around for credit or debit cards as the amount will, in most cases, be added to the user's next mobile phone bill.

6. Don't be shy. Asking people to part with money can feel awkward but remember: you're not asking for you – you're asking for the charity you have chosen to support.

7. Get friends and family to help out. Encourage your loved ones to ask their own friends and colleagues to support you. The wider you cast your net, the more chance you have of landing something.

8. Start a blog. Not only is this good for keeping you motivated, it's the most efficient way to keep your supporters up-to-date with your progress. One of them may even see something in one of your entries that persuades them to dig deep (if not deeper) to support you.

9. Ask your employers if they are open to the idea of matching your fundraising efforts. In other words, for every £1 you raise, try to convince them to pledge £1 of their own.

10. Change your signature . . . your email signature, that is. Update it to include a link to your fundraising page.

11. Show people where their money will go. It's all well and good telling them the name of the charity you're fundraising for but if you can actually show them examples of what that charity does – for example, via YouTube video links or email newsletters sent by the charity itself – it will have a far more profound impact.

12. Personalise your fundraising. Explain to people why you are supporting your particular charity. Doing so will make your efforts more relatable and appreciable.

13. Lead by example. Give up a personal vice for the duration of your training – for example, wine, chocolate, crisps or something similar – and put the money you would otherwise have spent on that habit in a jar. By the end of your training, you will have saved an impressive amount of money that you will be able to donate to your cause.

14. Stage a fundraising event. This is a quick and simple way to raise a lot of cash. For instance, ask your local pub if you can host a quiz one evening, charging every team a minimum of £20 to take part. If you manage to get ten teams involved, that's £200 straight away. Many pubs will allow you to do this free of charge, too.

15. Turn your fundraising into a giant raffle. See if you can get local

businesses or sports teams to donate a valuable prize which you can then use to tempt people to sponsor you. For example, everyone who donates £20 goes into a draw to win one of the prizes you collect. People are much more likely to donate if they think they might get something out of it – sad but true!

16. Cash in on payday. Email your friends to tell them what you are doing and why, but aim to do this either at the end or the beginning of the month when they will most likely just have been paid and are, therefore, more likely to donate.

17. Alert the media! Write to your local newspaper and radio station to tell them what you're doing and, if they pick up your story, politely ask that they include details of how people can sponsor you in any coverage they give you.

18. Create business cards with your fundraising details on them. These are very cheap to produce and don't just give them to your friends; leave them wherever you can (coffee shops, libraries, restaurants and so on).

19. Consider running in fancy dress. Completing a marathon is impressive – but doing so in a wacky costume is doubly so!

20. Have a spring clean! Use those weeks when you're tapering down towards race day to empty the house of all the things you've been meaning to get rid of by selling the contents of your cupboards or attic at a car boot sale. [*Author's Note: I did this three weeks before race day in 2014 and raised over £500!*]

21. Get baking! Office bake sales are extremely effective ways to raise money, not to mention a fun and easy way to boost morale. Make it competitive, too, and negotiate with your employer to see if they'll put up an extra hour or half-day off work for the person who is judged to be the event's 'Star Baker'.

22. Call off Christmas – the card-giving part of it at least! Ask your friends and family if they would be willing to forgo Christmas cards for one year and, in return, donate £5 (a reasonable amount for a card plus postage) to your cause. If 20 of them agree to this, you'll bank another £100 for your charity.

23. Wear your fundraising info. Get a baseball cap or T-shirt made up with details of how people can sponsor you emblazoned on it nice and clearly. Even if only one random passer-by sees it and donates a few pounds, it has been a worthwhile exercise.

24. Get friends and family to push your fundraising on the day of the marathon. [*Author's Note: I gave my wife the log-in details to my Facebook account on the day I ran the 2014 London Marathon. She was able to post updates of my progress, including some pics, to all of my friends. No doubt realising that I was coming good on my promise to run the race, more of them contributed on race day than any other day in the build-up.*]

25. Become a designated taxi driver! Are you giving up alcohol for the marathon? If so, offer to be the designated driver for friends and family on nights out in the weeks and months leading up to it in return for a minimum fare of, say, £10. Make ten such journeys and, just like that, you'll earn another £100 for your charity.

26. Remember to say 'thank you' to everyone who supports you. Personalise the message, too. Don't just send a group email or post a generic update on social media. Show people you appreciate their support and they'll be more likely to sponsor you should you decide to run again in the future.

ACKNOWLEDGEMENTS

BRINGING THIS book to life has been an extraordinary honour and pleasure but, suffice to say, it would not have been possible without the support of a number of people, who are undeniably due a note of thanks.

Firstly, to the twenty-six remarkable individuals featured within this book. To Dick, Lloyd, Sir Steve, Sadie and Claude; to Steve, Dave, Nell, Kannan and Jamie; to Jo-ann, John, Guy, Andy and Dale; to Liz, Phil, Luke, Rob and Michael; and to Claire, Dave, Laura, Michael, Charlie and Jill. Without each of you, this book wouldn't have happened. Simple as that. I can't thank all of you enough for indulging the intrusions of a total stranger into your lives and allowing me to tell your stories.

To Len Ballack, Geraldine Davies, Don McRae and Katie Leggate; and to Jill Beardsley, Trudy Baxter, Alex Eagle and Lucy Waterlow. Thank you for all of your help.

To Tom English, one of the finest sports writers I've ever met, whose advice about how best to transform *Running the Smoke* from an idea to a reality was invaluable.

To Mark Eglinton, a true gentleman and an exceptional writer/biographer, who was always there to offer the benefit of his experience and well-timed words of motivation.

To Penny Dain and the team at the London Marathon, and to David Drozdziak, Charlie Williams and the team at Great Ormond Street Hospital. My thanks to you all.

To my colleagues at PSP Media Group, in particular Paul Grant, Tom Lovering and Bryce Ritchie. Bryce, especially. He's been my editor for several years and likes to think of himself as my 'mentor'. You know what? He's not wrong. Thanks to you all for your interest in, support of and good humour about this project. I promise I'll find new things to talk about in the canteen from now on . . .

To Peter Burns and the team at Arena Sport. I cannot even begin to explain how thankful I am to you for taking a punt on a rookie book writer and giving me the opportunity to do this. You have been a joy to work with and have made this such a fun and rewarding experience. I sincerely hope it's not the last project we work on together.

To Ian Greensill. Thank you for your eagle-eyed and assiduous editing of this book. It is very much appreciated.

To all of my friends, particularly my two closest confidants about this project, Michael Hoare and Kris Gilmartin. Mike, we've been pals for longer than I care to remember; Kris, you have become a deeply valued and trusted friend. You've both played a bigger part in this book than you even realise. I'll explain how over a beer sometime soon.

To my Mum and Dad, Madeline and George, who have given me and the other three absolutely everything. You supported me completely when, probably around the age of six or seven, I decided that I wanted to be a sports writer. That support has never once wavered. I'll never be able to thank you enough.

Likewise, thanks to my in-laws, Christine and Michael, for taking such a keen and genuine interest in this book and, again, for all of your support. It's much appreciated.

Most importantly of all, to my wife, Juliet. Where do I even begin? For all of the coffee (there was a *lot* of coffee), for all of your patience, for all of your encouragement, for all of your diligent proofreading and for all of your love, support and kindness, thank you a million times over. I'm a lucky, lucky man. The luckiest, actually.

ABOUT GREAT ORMOND STREET HOSPITAL

FOUNDED with only ten beds on Valentine's Day, 1852, Great Ormond Street Hospital is now an international leader in paediatrics, caring for more than 255,000 sick children every year.

It has also become a global leader in developing new and better ways to treat childhood diseases. Some of its breakthroughs include appointing the UK's first consultant paediatric surgeon, Denis Browne, in 1928; pioneering the first heart and lung bypass machine for children in 1962, to help repair heart problems; becoming Europe's first children's hospital to offer a portable haemodialysis service in 2010; and opening Europe's first research centre to tackle birth defects, the Newlife Birth Defects Research Centre, in 2012.

Throughout its long history, Great Ormond Street Hospital has relied on public support, even after the founding of the NHS in 1948. At present, it needs to raise over £90 million every year to help give hope to very sick children and their families.

You can find out more about the hospital at www.gosh.nhs.uk and its charity at www.gosh.org.

ABOUT THE AUTHOR

MICHAEL McEWAN is a sports writer based in Glasgow, Scotland.

He is currently the assistant editor of *bunkered*, one of the UK's leading golf publications. In his spare time, he is a keen amateur runner, and has, to date, completed three marathons: the 2011 Loch Ness Marathon, the 2012 Berlin Marathon and the 2014 London Marathon.

Running the Smoke is his first published book. He is donating all of his proceeds from its sales to Great Ormond Street Hospital Children's Charity.